T0366312

FAMILIES ARE *Forever*

FAMILIES
ARE
Forever

Bentz and Kalk Families.
A History of Two Families Joined through Stories and Pictures

JOYCE BENTZ ROESCH

iUniverse

FAMILIES ARE FOREVER
Bentz and Kalk Families. A History of Two Families Joined through Stories and Pictures

iUniverse books may be ordered through booksellers or by contacting:

iUniverse
1663 Liberty Drive
Bloomington, IN 47403
www.iuniverse.com
1-800-Authors (1-800-288-4677)

Because of the dynamic nature of the Internet, any web addresses or links contained in this book may have changed since publication and may no longer be valid. The views expressed in this work are solely those of the author and do not necessarily reflect the views of the publisher, and the publisher hereby disclaims any responsibility for them.

Any people depicted in stock imagery provided by Thinkstock are models, and such images are being used for illustrative purposes only.
Certain stock imagery © Thinkstock.

ISBN: 978-1-4917-6490-9 (sc)
ISBN: 978-1-4917-6491-6 (e)

Print information available on the last page.

iUniverse rev. date: 05/22/2015

CONTENTS

Dedication

This family history is dedicated to all the past, present and future descendants of the Bentz and Kalk families.

I want to especially thank my brother Robert Bentz and his family for their efforts in compiling much of the information contained in this book. Thank you to all the other family members who contributed their stories and pictures. This book would not exist had it not been for their participation.

I regret if there are any errors or omissions.

Joyce (Bentz) Roesch 2015

What It Means To Be Family

Being family means sharing celebrations when good times abound and having arms to hold you when tears fall.

Being family means you belong somewhere special where you are known and loved just as you are, and where you are encouraged to become the person you still hope to be.

Being family means that every season of the year you have a place to call home, a place of your own, where they hold you forever close to their hearts.

HISTORY OF JOHANN JAKOB BENZ

According to the census records of Neudorf, S. Russia, in the year 1816, Johannes Benz, (born in 1787) emigrated to Neudorf, near Odessa, from Mettenzimmern, Ludwigsburg, Wurttemberg, Germany in the year 1808. He was 21 years of age and had married a widow lady with two children. Her name was Christina Wetzler. They had two children together, Johann Jakob 1st, born in 1810, and Anna Maria born in 1816. Christina's two children were Dorothea, born in 1803, and Anna, born in 1807.

Long before the Benz family decided to emigrate, the Empress Catherine II, in 1763, invited all foreigners to settle in the Russian Empire. They were offered many incentives to come and develop the uninhabited regions of Russia. The Russian Government offered to pay their travel expenses, they were free to choose the area where they wished to live, they could build their own churches and follow their own religion. They could live in colonies, they were granted exemption from military duty, and were granted exemption from taxes for 30 years.

During these early years, there were many hardships in the German homeland - political suppression, military duty, crop failures, years of hunger, and burdens of taxation. At that time these were sufficient reasons to turn one's back upon the homeland and to seek a new and better home in a distant country.

Johann and Christina's son, Johann Jakob 1st, married Juliane Henne and together they had several children - George Friedrich, Johann 2nd, Michael, Peter, Juliane, Philip, Friedrich, Jacob, Christian and Margareta.

Of the Johann Jakob 1st family only two of their sons, George and Philip, came to America. The date of their immigration is not known. George who was born September 23, 1832, died March 18, 1921, and is buried at Bethlehem Cemetery near Fairfax, South Dakota. Philip who was born April 16, 1844, died December 12, 1928. He is buried at Dallas Cemetery in Dallas, South Dakota.

Son Johann 2nd, who was born in 1834, married Magdalena Stroh and they had ten children together; Christine, born in 1858, Johann 3rd, born in 1859, Margaretha, born in 1860, Julianna, born in 1862, Georg, born in 1865, George, born in 1867, Jacob, born in l869, Katherine, born in 1871, Frederick, born in 1873, and Julianne, born in 1876. Many of their children must have died in infancy, or when very young. It is not know which ones survived to adulthood, with the exception of Johann 3rd, whose descendents are included in this history.

Later some of Johann Jakob's grandchildren came to America. One of which was Johann 3rd, who came to America with his wife Magdalena (Raile) in the year 1899 along with seven children. It is presumed that about this time the family name was changed to Bentz instead of Benz. It is not known why or exactly when this change took place.

It was a time when living in Russia became more difficult. In1875 the Czar of Russia sent out a decree that the German colonists had lost their100 years of special privileges and must fulfill the same duties and military obligations as all other Russian citizens. For 100 years they had kept their Germanic customs and traditions, and were clannish from their Eastern Orthodox Russian Neighbours. To continue their life in Russia they would have to adapt to Russian traditions.

Johann and Magdalena began their family in Neudorf, Russia. The known children who went to America with their parents were:

John Adam - Born March 15, 1883
Jakob - Born July 23, 1885
Magdelina - Born February 6, 1890
George - Born December 10, 1892
Ottilie - Born April 10, 1894
Adolph - Born April 27, 1897
Edward - Born 1898 (exact date unknown)

They left the Ukraine in 1899 when the eldest son John Adam was fifteen years old. They travelled by train from Odessa to Bremen, Germany, and sailed to America on a ship named The "Lahn", leaving Bremen on or about April 4, 1899. The ship was owned by Norddeutscher Lloyd, Bremen, Steamship Company. On the way across the ocean the whole family contacted small pox. One infant son, Edward, succumbed to the pox at four months of age and was buried at sea. They arrived at the port of New York on April 21, 1899. The whole family spent some time in quarantine on Ellis Island, New York, all except for Magdelina and her father, Johann Sr. The family then travelled to Martin, North Dakota by train, and eventually settled on a homestead there. Two more children were born after their arrival in North Dakota:

Edward - Born October 8, 1901
Benjamin - Born December 17, 1903

Johann and Magdalena had a total of sixteen children, eight of whom died in infancy. They may have had other children born in Russia but they must have died in infancy. There are no names available.

Johann Bentz and family Ship Manifest April 4, 1899

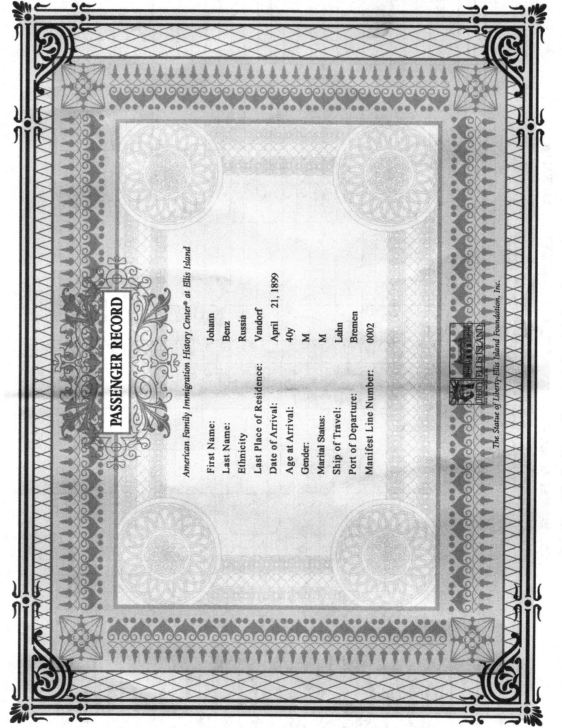

PASSENGER RECORD

American Family Immigration History Center® at Ellis Island

First Name: Johann
Last Name: Benz
Ethnicity   Russia
Last Place of Residence: Vandorf
Date of Arrival: April 21, 1899
Age at Arrival: 40y
Gender: M
Marital Status: M
Ship of Travel: Lahn
Port of Departure: Bremen
Manifest Line Number: 0002

The Statue of Liberty-Ellis Island Foundation, Inc.

Johann Bentz Passenger Record Certificate 1899

4

Johann & Magdalena Bentz 1920's

Johann & Magdalena Bentz 1925

Johann & Magdalena & Family on their 50th wedding anniversary in 1931.
Back L-R: George, Edward, Ottilia, Magdalena, Adolph and Ben.
Front L-R: John Jr., Father Johann, Sr.,, Mother Magdalena and Jacob.

Johann & Magdalena Bentz 50th Anniversary 1931

John & Magdalena Bentz (far right) and their neighbors
and friends, taken in the 1930's.

Magdalena Bentz – 80th Birthday 1938

HISTORY OF JOHN BENTZ AND MATILDA (KALK) BENTZ

John was born on March 15, 1883 and Matilda was born on September 22, 1888. They were united in marriage on November 7, 1907 in Martin, North Dakota.

Matilda was born at Edenwaldt, (now Edenwold), Saskatchewan, near Regina but at the time that country was still known as North West Territories. Her parents were immigrants from Romania. When she was about six years old she moved with her mother, sisters and brothers by train to Martin, North Dakota. Her father came by covered wagon. Matilda's mother died when Matilda was nine years old.

John Bentz was born in a village called Neudorf which was located somewhere on the route between Odessa and Kiev in the Ukraine, Russia. John was about fifteen years old when he left the Ukraine for America with his parents in 1899. On the way across the ocean some of the family contacted small pox. One infant brother, Edward, succumbed to the pox at four months and was buried at sea. The family spent some time in quarantine on Ellis Island, New York. They then travelled by train to Martin, North Dakota.

John left home in 1905 and homesteaded near Hardisty, Alberta for a short time. He soon returned to Martin, North Dakota where he met Matilda Kalk and they married in 1907. They had a double wedding with Matilda's brother Adolf and John's sister Magdalena.

John Bentz was a very talented man. He attended a Russian school for a very short period of time to complete his academic education. The school of experience helped him to become a carpenter, welder, Ferrier, mechanic, machinist, steam engineer, a violin player (which he played by notes), plus a religious instructor.

After their wedding in 1907, and before moving to Saskatchewan in 1915, John and Matilda had farmed at Martin, North Dakota and also at Dogden, North Dakota. John and Matilda moved to Ravenscrag, Saskatchewan in May, 1915 and homesteaded nine miles north and one mile east of Ravenscrag, on the east half section 9, township 8, west of the range 23, 3rd Meridian. By this time they had a young family of four children, two sons and two daughters:

> Edna - Born January 26, 1908
> Elaine - Born December 16, 1909
> Lewis - Born November 13, 1911
> Robert - Born October 22, 1914

John had made a trip to Canada earlier in 1914 to file on their homestead. His brother, George, and his sister, Magdelina (with her husband Adolf Kalk), had arrived in Saskatchewan in 1914. Another brother, Jacob, also shared box car facilities with John when they moved. Jake and his wife, the former Anna Pepple, their daughter Elizabeth, and son Walter, homesteaded kitty-corner to the southwest corner of John Bentz's homestead.

Jake's wife Annie, and their two children along with Matilda and the above mentioned four Bentz children arrived by train in Shaunavon, Saskatchewan, on a Friday with no train west until the following Monday. The party hired a livery team to take them as far as Eastend, 26 miles away. From Eastend, they caught a ride with a farmer (Mr. Martin) from the area. He had two horses and two mules hitched up to a wagon-load of oats and so they continued the westward trek to the so called "Bench". Matilda said it was a very desolate ride through hills, coulees with lush grass but no sign of any people. The first night was spent with Matilda's sister, Mary Heth. Mary and her husband, Fred, had obtained a homestead in 1913 on the next quarter of land north of John Bentz.

In the following years they added seven more children to their family:

Alice - Born March 31, 1917
Calvin - Born April 10, 1919
Harvey - Born January 30, 1021
Magdalena - Born December 22, 1922
Irene - Born January 3, 1926
Joyce - Born January 16, 1932
Raymond - Born January 19, 1933

They lived out the hungry thirties at this location, facing many hardships. When the great depression of the 1930's finally ended, and after many years of farming the homestead and facing year after year of crop failures, John and Matilda finally loaded some of their belongings in a "box car" and moved to Barrhead, Alberta, in the fall of 1937. This "new country" offered them a whole new life where they could make a fair living on a good farm. Their new farm was in the Mellowdale district, near Barrhead, where they resided until they retired and moved into the town of Barrhead.

John Bentz and Matilda Kalk in1904

John & Matilda Bentz 1926

John Bentz and Family in 1926.
Back L-R: Lewis, Edna, Elaine, Robert, Matilda and John.
Front L-R: Harvey, Calvin, Alice and Madge.

Bentz-Kalk Reunion held at Summerdale

Descendants of the Bentz and Kalk families held a reunion at Summerdale, July 24 and 25, 1982 with about 202 attending.

Relatives came from Colorado, Illinois, North Dakota, California, Oregon, Washington, B.C. and Saskatchewan.

Mr. John Bentz married Mr. Adolph Kalk's sister "Matilda" and Mr. Adolph Kalk married Mr. John Bentz's sister Magdelina. It was a double wedding on the 7 of November, 1907 at Martin N. Dakota, U.S.A.

Eleven children were born to each couple. The Bentz's had 6 daughters and 5 sons, and the Kalks had 5 daughters and 6 sons.

All attended the reunion, except 2 boys of the Kalk which were deceased.

There were two 5th generation uncles and 5th generation aunts by generation marriage.

Some cousins hadn't met for 51 years and for younger cousins, aunts and uncles it was a first meeting.

The 2 days started out with pancake breakfasts. The food and refreshment were great both days. The afternoons were spent by playing ball, horse shoes etc. and a lot of visiting, followed by music and dancing in the evening.

Ending Sunday evening with a lot of fond memories.

Bentz and Kalk Family Reunion 1982

Bentz and Kalk Family Reunion 1982.
Back L-R: Hayden Pepple, Bennie Pepple, Adeline Pepple,
Dan Bentz, Ella Pepple, Lee and Sonny Pepple.
Front L-R: Theresa Bentz, Elizabeth Unrath, Novella and Ed Bentz, and Ben Bentz.

Lewis Bentz and his wife Katie (Heberling) Bentz, and son Herb, taken in 1960.

Herb & Jackie Bentz on their wedding in1986.

Madge Bentz and Violet Bentz in 1936, with other
students attending Crossfell School, in Sask.

John and Matilda's Daughter Madge, in 1960's

13

Harvey & Alvina (Radke) Bentz on their wedding day in 1948.

Harvey & Alvina Bentz on their 40th Anniversary in 1988. with their family.
Back L-R: Lorne, Dale and his wife Laurie, Janice and her husband, Robert (Max) Maxwell.
Front L-R: Michael, Harvey, Alvina, Bradley and Melanie. (Michael and
Bradly are Lorne's sons, Melanie is Janice and Robert's daughter)

Harvey and Alvina's Daughter Janice, on right,
and her husband, Robert (Max) Maxwell, taken in 1960's.

Harvey and Alvina's son, Lorne, on right,
and his wife Judy, taken in 2002.

Harvey and Alvina's Son Dale, on right, and
his wife Laurie, taken in 1990.

John and Matilda Bentz & Family taken in 1963.
Back L-R: Joyce, Raymond, Madge, Harvey, Irene, Calvin and Alice.
Front L-R: Elaine, Edna, John, Matilda, Lewis and Robert.

John & Matilda Bentz on their 50th Anniversary in1957.

John & Matilda Bentz, on their 50th Anniversary in1957.

Matilda Bentz, 89th Birthday - 1977

Matilda Bentz, and family on her 90th Birthday in 1978
Back L-R:Madge, Raymond, Irene, Calvin, Alice, Harvey and
Joyce. Front L-R: Lewis, Elaine, Matilda, Edna and Robert.

Raymond & Sheila (Dick) Bentz & Family in 1981, at wedding of Brian and Lorraine.
Back L-R: David, Marty, Barry, Neville and Donald.
Front L-R: Sheila, Lorraine, Brian and Raymond.

THE EARLY YEARS - A STORY OF BYGONE DAYS FROM 1888

Written by Matilda (Kalk) Bentz, February 27, 1973

I was born near Regina, Saskatchewan, on September 22, 1888. I started school when I was six years old. I don't remember too much about those years. We moved to North Dakota when I was about six years old. My Dad started out with a covered wagon. My Mother and the children went by train. That was a lot of fun for me. When we arrived in a little town called Martin, we had just a little shack to live in, but I was very happy. I started school but didn't go for too many years. My Mother died when I was only nine years old. I was sad. It was heart breaking to lose my Mother. Mother left a little baby, my youngest sister, Susan. Then I had quit school and started working on the farm, herding cattle for a few years.

My father got married again in less than a year after my mother died, so I had a step mother. At first I was happy to have another Mother, but she was not my own mother. She was good to me, and the years went by. My youth was a happy one, but with some disappointments here and there. My brother, Adolf, who was older, took me out to many places in and around our home. My older sister Annie was very good to me. She was always more like a Mother to me. I had five sisters in all and one brother, but my Father, and his second wife, had seven more children so I had five half-brothers and two half-sisters; also two step-sisters and one step-brother. We all grew up together. That was a lot of children to feed and take care of.

In 1907 I met and married John Bentz, and then my own troubles started. In the years that followed, I had eleven children of my own. We went through hard times and sickness. I had to have a big operation for gall stones. I was very sick. After that, I felt better than I had for years. Joyce and Raymond were born after that, so I felt really young.

When we moved from North Dakota to Saskatchewan, my sisters-in-law and I got as far as Eastend. The trains didn't go to Ravenscrag every day, so we got a ride with one of our neighbors. He had four horses and a wagon with a load of oats. We and the children sat on top of the oats. We thought we would never get there; a twenty-mile drive, with nothing but hills and a very rough road. We were very happy to get to our new homes, although our home wasn't much of a home, only a small shack. We finally got settled, and put in 24 years of what we called hard times, but very happy days as we were young and healthy. Our homestead life was really lots of fun, too, as everyone, of course, was in the same situation -- poor.

Then in October of 1918, my Father was killed in an accident. They drove into a train. He was hurt very badly, and after three days, he died. We lived a long distance away in Saskatchewan, but we all went to the funeral, which took place in Martin, North Dakota. Calvin was six months old at the time.

I was nineteen years old when we got married, and we lived together almost 60 years where there were hard times and good days, too, in all our married life. Our oldest daughter, Edna, was already married when we had two more children, Joyce and Raymond.

I never did like living in Saskatchewan. We had very poor land - so many gophers. They ate all our crops. Then the grasshoppers came and finished the crops, and we had no rain all summer.

Matilda Kalk 89th Birthday - 1977

HISTORY OF ALEX AND EDNA (BENTZ) ERNST

(Source: Between and Beyond the Benches - Ravenscrag, Vol. 1 (1981).

Edna came to the Bench in Saskatchewan with her parents, John and Matilda Bentz, in the spring of 1915. Alex came to the United States with his parents from Russia in 1903 and then moved to the Bench in 1915. Both Alex and Edna attended Crossfell School.

In 1931 they were married and lived in the Kealey Springs area for one year. They then moved to the Kalk's place in East Fairwell District for the next three years. They then moved back to their place in the Kealey Springs area. Their four sons were born here and attended school in the Kealey Springs School. The eldest son, Edwin, was born in 1931, Ernest was born in 1932, Albert was born in 1934, and the youngest, Clarence, was born in 1937.

Alex had taken a homestead but like most people of the prairies, the family had difficult times during the "depression" and what became known as "the dirty thirties". Alex and Edna worked very hard on their land to make ends meet and raise their children. Alex was a rodeo contestant and a fan and he followed up all the rodeos around the countryside for many of his younger days.

Finally In 1948, they sold their property in Saskatchewan and bought a place near Barrhead, Alberta where they lived for many years, until they decided to retire in a new home in the town of Barrhead. Alex passed away in 1979.

After that, Edna started a new life with her second husband, Alfred Dodgson. They were able to enjoy many years together, until Alfred's death in 1994. Edna passed away in 1995.

Edna (Bentz) & Alexander Ernst and Family – 1941
Back L-R Edna, Clarence, and Alexander
Front L-R Edwin, Albert, and Ernest

Alexander and Edna Ernst - 1941

Alexander and Edna Ernst & Family – 1949
L-R Edwin, Ernest, Alexander, Edna (Bentz), Albert, and Clarence

Edwin Ernst & his wife Audry (Airlie)

My Grandfather's Desk by Riley Ernst*

Isn't it strange how sometimes you think you know people without ever meeting them? That's the way I feel about my grandfather. He passed away a decade before I was born. I never had the opportunity to meet him. As I write this essay, I am sitting at the desk he built, more than 60 years ago, for my mother. I ask myself, is it possible to know my grandfather through his workmanship?

Well, the quaint desk is modest, compared to most wooden desks. It's not enormous, but it is the proper size for a younger and a smaller person. If a person cut the desk down the middle it would make two fine end tables, but that would be sacrilegious. Every piece of the desk has a bit of my grandfather in it. It is my understanding that he collected and saved scraps of wood from wherever he could scrounge them. Each piece was sawed, shaved, and sanded. My grandfather's treasured gift to my mother was lovingly thought out, composed, and assembled. When I closely examined this family heirloom, I found unique pieces of wood throughout its design. This distinction gives the desk character and a life of its own.

While I sit in front of this precious souvenir, I notice how well built it is. My grandfather set the desktop on top of eight sturdy legs. The two by two oak legs have no sharp edges; the outside corners are diligently sanded. Narrow grooves were painstakingly cut into the posts for the sides and back to rest in. Even after 60 years, the eight legs make the desk solid, similar to how my grandfather must have been. Not only is the desk steadfast, it is also level and balanced. A person would be hard pressed to find this type of quality today.

I also discovered that the desktop appears to be made out of three planks. Each piece is a different size. A sheet of old-fashioned particle board is tightly glued to the planks and every corner is fastened down with tiny finishing nails. Around the edge of the desk is a two-inch piece of wood that was skillfully cut by hand. It looks like a fancy modern day moulding; this detail exquisitely finishes off the desk top. With clever expertise, my grandfather must have cut the edging close to the shape he wanted and then meticulously sanded the edge smooth and round. Only a master craftsman could make each joint fit together so perfectly.

One day, before I moved the desk into a back bedroom, I had to take each one of the squeaky drawers out. The sound was soft and sweet. As I did this, something caught my eye. At the back and top of each drawer was my grandfather's wobbly printing: left top, right top, middle left, and bottom right. He personally marked each drawer because, although they all look like exact copies, no two drawers are interchangeable. One drawer will not fit in the other's space.

Under even closer inspection, I realized the drawer fronts were made of four different pieces of wood. Each drawer includes one solid plank for the inside front; then, like a skin, a thin outside face is glued to the first piece to cover the full exterior. For an inch all the way around the face there is a smooth, tenderly sanded bevel that gently thins towards the edges. This surface is complemented with a third piece of wood, which gives the drawer front a layered and textured appearance that sets off the sculptured door handles. The door handles are tediously sanded to the same angle, the same bevel. All four pieces seem to melt together into one. Everything was done patiently by hand. The desk proudly shows off its craftsmanship; a completed work of art.

Standing back, I can see the deep walnut stain that not only gives the desk colour but also gives it depth. This appearance gives my grandfather's desk its demeanor and captivating good looks. The simple desk becomes something more than just practical; it has a life of its own, life my grandfather lovingly worked into it. I can imagine him brushing in the colour from outside in with some ripped up old rags and a jar of pungent smelling stain which he probably conjured up from some work site more than 60 years ago.

Not only wood, glue, and nails went into its construction, there was also dedication, devotion, and determination. The family jewel has a spirit and a soul of its own. It's an even-tempered and well-adjusted desk. This showpiece not only shows the blood and sweat that went into its creation, but it also shows its age. The cuts, the scrapes, the scratches, and the scars agree with the bruises time has given it.

Like a monument to my grandfather, the cherished keepsake stands in its own little room, still proud to be used to read on, write on, and learn on. Hopefully, my own grandchildren, and maybe even their grandchildren, might, some day, read, write, and learn on it. By then though, it will be very old, but maybe, if it remembers, it can open up its heart and tell the stories it has heard and the thoughts it has been told.

Can I know my grandfather through his desk? I think so. I can see he was an even-tempered and patient man. I'm sure he was devoted and dedicated. I know he was an artist and a masterful craftsman. I can tell he had little in the way of money, but he managed just fine, so he had to be frugal, which made him wise. I am sure my grandfather was meticulous, pragmatic, and determined. There is also no doubt he was sober, sound, and strong. And of course, he had to be a tender loving man to bring such a gift as this treasure into the world for his 15-year-old daughter. Yes, I am sure I can know my grandfather through his workmanship. I have no doubts about that at all. His name was Patrick Airlie, and he build on incredible desk.

Written about Grandfather Patrick Airlie, his mother Audrey (Airlie) Ernst's father.

HISTORY OF ELAINE (BENTZ) LARKINS

by Elaine (Bentz) Larkins
Written: January 2000

I was the second born of a family of eleven. I had five sisters: Edna, Alice, Magdalina, Irene and Joyce. Five brothers: Lewis, Robert, Calvin, Harvey and Raymond.

Ma and Pa lived near Harvey, North Dakota from 1907 to 1913. I was born on December 16, 1909 on a farm near Harvey, Section 3, Twnshp 150, Range 73 in Wells County. Sister Edna and brother Lewis were also born there.

I remember my first car ride, before Robert was born, when I was four years old. Pa was looking after baby Lewis and I while Ma and Edna were going with a horse and buggy to Uncle Jake's place to do the chores. Well, when I saw them start out, I ran after them crying that I wanted to come along. But, no way! Ma just made the horse go faster and yelled: "go home". I had run quite a stretch down the road when I saw a strange noisy machine coming at me, so I went off the road as far as possible. The car had two men in the front seat and two women in the back seat. The women wore big hats tied with long scarves, since the car's top was down. The car stopped, and one man got out and came over to me. If he spoke to me, I didn't understand him, since I understood only German at the time, and the man didn't. Anyway, he buttoned up the "endgate" of my underwear, picked me up and carried me to the car and held me on his lap. It seemed so high up and felt great as we chugged along. Then the driver stopped at the farm gate and the same man carried me to the gate. When he saw me run to the house, he knew that's where I came from. Then I had to answer some questions to Pa. When Ma came home and was told this story, she told me that those strangers could have taken me far away to some place and dumped me into a big tub of boiling water! That scared me so much and is why I never forgot this episode. I did hear Pa say that it was a Ford. Now I'm not sure when Fords were first made, probably in 1913.

Most of the children called our parents Pa and Ma. Later on it became Dad and Mom, and if to be more proper, it was Father and Mother.

Then we moved to a a different farm near Martin, North Dakota. In 1914, Pa and Uncle Jake Bentz filed on homesteads in the Cypress Hills, Saskatchewan, called the "Bench". They shipped some machinery by rail and hired some neighbors to do some haying, etc. Pa did some building. He built a house for his family, a two-story hip-roofed house, 14 x 20 feet. Some relatives and friends had arrived in the same area a year or so earlier. Mom's uncle Bill Kalk was a carpenter by trade, and he built his own house, a two-story hip-roofed house, which was later owned by Uncle George. Then he built houses for Uncle Adolph Kalk and Uncle Sam Miley. They all seemed to like that house plan of a hip-roof.

In the spring of 1915, Dad and Uncle Jake left North Dakota for their homesteads in Saskatchewan. Their wives and children followed by train as far as Shaunavon, Saskatchewan, then taxied by a dray-man to Eastend, where they met John Martin, a brother-in-law of the Tantows. Martin's lived a few miles east of our place. We had another long wagon ride, about twenty miles, to our destination. Robert was only six months old, being born on October 22, 1914. Lewis was three years, Edna was seven and I was five. Aunt Annie, who travelled with us, had Lizzie, age six, and Walter, about one year old.

Our town, named Ravenscrag, was ten miles south, down in the White Mud river valley, which was rather pretty. Our close neighbors were Uncle Jake and his family, whose two-room shack was a block southwest of us. Uncle Sam's place was about a mile west. To the north, a quarter of a mile, lived Uncle Fred Heth and Aunt Mary, and further north, the John Heth's. To the east, lived the Ernst's, who lived in a sod house which I thought was the most beautiful house in the inside. To the south, on the hill (the "Big Hill", or so we thought it was), Harry and Bill Thompson, bachelors, built a beautiful house. Bill rented it out to people by the name of Proctor for a time, until he found himself a bride, "Maggie Beaton", a sister of Dave Beaton. Dave later bought the Sam Miley place. The Bill Thompson's lived on the hill for some years. They were lovely people. I used to spend a lot time with Maggie whenever her husband had to be away. Uncle Jake and Aunt Annie later bought the Thompson place. We still call it the Jake Bentz place, and most all of us have gone back to have a look at it from time to time over the years.

SCHOOL DAYS: 1917 - 1925. Crossfell School District No. 3764.

School started in August, officially the first of September, with 32 students registered from grade one to four. Miss Ivy Carpenter was our first teacher. Students were: four Bentz's, eight Heth's, seven Weber's, two Kopitoski's, two Navratil's, four Ernst's, one Roberts, one Hodgson, one Miley and two Willan's. School closed just before Christmas, after a concert, which was always a great event. Then we had almost a three-month vacation. School started again about the middle of March. The school house was used as a community center, such as for dances, a church with Sunday school, and for socials of sorts.

My schooling finished at grade eight in 1925. My last teacher was Miss Madra Hall. Grades one through eight were taught in the Crossfell School at that time. Later, grade nine and ten were added.

When I turned sixteen, I was able to do housework. My first job was for a lawyer and his wife in Eastend for a short time, while her parents visited them. I was happy to have earned enough money to send for a coat and hat from Eaton's catalogue. My next job was working for the Bacon family, west of Ravenscrag, then at the Agars, who were very hard up, but had babies one after another. Mrs Agar was expecting her fifth child when I was there. When she was ready to go to the hospital in Eastend, she asked me if she could borrow my hat and coat and I agreed. She was a lovely person. They ended up with ten children. I also worked in Medicine Hat, Ravenscrag and Piapot. In the summer of 1935, I got a job offer from the Wagner's at Olds, Alberta. I worked there until October, when I got a job in the town with the Murray's. It was a much easier job.

Then in 1937, I was offered a ride to Vancouver, British Columbia, so I jumped at the chance. I knew wages were much better there, even though it was the start of my unemployment. When I heard that my folks were planning to move to the Barrhead, Alberta area in the fall of 1937, I decided to go and see them in the summer of 1938. I got a job in the hotel cafe in Barrhead right away. Then I met Ed Larkins, who came to Barrhead from Lamont, Alberta in the spring of 1939. We became acquainted the latter part of that year. In 1940 we got engaged and were married in 1941. Before Ed came into my life, my sister, Madge, and I rented a little house with three rooms, right behind the Red and White Store in Barrhead. By then, Madge worked in the Post Office. Soon after Ed and I were married, Madge left Barrhead and got a job in the Post Office in Edmonton.

Joyce Bentz Roesch

OUR MARRIAGE: February 24, 1941.

Ed was twenty nine years old, and I was thirty one. We were married in the United Church in Barrhead, by Captain Graham. The bridesmaids were Ed's sister, Velda Larkins, and my sister, Alice Bentz. The best men were Ed's brother, Lawrence (Buster) Larkins, and my brother, Calvin Bentz. The reception had to be kept to a Minimum on account of a shortage of cash! The afternoon was spent at the Larkins home with a keg of beer, which was Ed's treat. Mom Larkins served a nice lunch. The wedding supper was put on by my parents, and it was a very nice meal. My Dad supplied the wine. Only the immediate families were in attendance. We didn't have a dance.

OUR FAMILY:

We were blessed with three great children. Arlene, born January 22, 1941, Stuart, born May 31, 1943 and Carol, born December 11, 1944. In 1944, we bought a house in Barrhead, with two lots, for $850.00, and we lived there until we managed to have a bigger house built in 1956.

On the 19th of May, 1958, we were terribly shocked and saddened by the death of our son, and brother Stuart. He saved Carolyn Bassani's life when she accidently fell into the Paddle River and could not swim. Stuart, being a good swimmer, took off his boots and jacket and swam in and brought her to shore so friends there could help her out of the icy water. No one else there could swim to help Stuart and he was unable to climb ashore and was drowned. We were presented with a gold medal, posthumously awarded to Stuart, by the Royal Canadian Humane Association. We also received the Silver Cadet Award for Bravery, presented to Stuart posthumously, by Air Commodore H. H. Rutledge. Stuart was an active leading aircraft man, sponsored by 526 Elds RCAC Sqn. Barrhead, Alberta.

Elaine Bentz – 1925

Elaine Bentz & her husband Edward Larkins on their wedding day – 1941

Edward and Elaine Larkins & Family – 1947 Edward and Elaine Standing
Front L-R Carol, Arlene, and Stuart

Elaine & Edward Larkins on their 25th Wedding Anniversary – 1966

Elaine Bentz (Larkins) & Daughters Carol & Arlene - 2007

HISTORY OF ROBERT AND GERTRUDE (DEMERS) BENTZ

By Robert Bentz

(Source: Between and Beyond the Benches - Ravenscrag, Vol 1 (1981.))

I came to the Bench in Saskatchewan to live in 1915 with my parents and family, John and Matilda Bentz.

Although there were hard times, I have happy memories of my young years. In spring time it was following the East Fairwell Creek in flood time, drowning gophers, hunting magpies' and crows' eggs. Going to friends' homes to sleep, or having a friend spend the night at my home, caused much excitement. It was always a certainty, that when I heard Dad would be going to town with the team of horses, I would suddenly have a headache, too bad to go to school, but always clearing up in time to go along with Dad to town. Drowning gophers at school was lots of fun causing the teachers a hard time to get us back into school for classes. But, boy! Did I ever hate putting out gopher poison, as it was always a Saturday chore?

I remained on the old home place, which was already lost to the Mortgage Company, when my parents left for Barrhead, Alberta in 1937. These were the relief years, so I wasn't able to plant many acres as the government didn't hand out too much seed. This first crop was hailed out one hundred percent the first week of August, 1938.

Gertrude Demers came from Dollard, Saskatchewan to Ravenscrag in late April, 1938. She kept house for me for one month and stayed with my cousin Violet and Uncle Jake Bentz. While she was working for Bob David, a real romance developed between us. We were married August 1, 1938 in Medicine Hat, Alberta, at the United Church. We were "shivareed" by the neighbors (now a thing of the past). Later on, we were married in Eastend, Saskatchewan in the Catholic Church.

In late April, 1939, after a bad blizzard and snowstorm, our first daughter, Fern, was born. I left my wife with Uncle Jake while I went to the neighbors to ask them to go to Eastend for the doctor. When I got back at 3:00 AM, our daughter had been born fifteen minutes earlier. I had already cut the cord, under instructions from Uncle Jake, and bathed and dressed the baby, under instructions from my wife, when the doctor arrived at 6:00 AM.

In the fall of 1940, we hadn't made any money, so my brother Lewis and I shipped a carload of our belongings from Ravenscrag to Barrhead, Alberta. While here, we had no extra money, but always had enough to eat and clothes to wear, and the neighbors were of the very best. Everyone partook of community life such as picnics, dances, ball games and skating. Friends in a city are not as easy to acquire.

Our family became larger: Claudette, Trevor, Allan, Dallas and Sharon were born. After thirteen years in the Barrhead area, we moved to Edmonton, where Wesley and Anthony were born. We also adopted three babies: Rhonda, Lisa and Korine. We spent many years caring for and looking after special welfare children.

The Ravenscrag and Crossfell memories are very happy ones. I love to have someone visit us from those days. I have driven around the Bench and it is hard to realize that so many people lived there at one time. Now, all the old home sites are gone. You can only guess where they once were. The Crossfell School is gone, as are the trees around it. Ravenscrag is practically wiped out too, and the river seems so much smaller now. The road from Ravenscrag north goes straight, a thing which was thought impossible in the years when we lived there.

Time erases everything. The men and women who spent their lives in this district are gone, and there is nothing to show that they were even there. But memories cannot be erased.

I thank everyone that I ever knew and associated with for the happy memories I have of Ravenscrag and district.

Robert & Gertrude Marie (Demers) Bentz & Family – 1960
Back LR: Allan, Wesley, Dallas, Anthony, & Trevor
Front LR: Robert, Gertrude, Claudette, & Sharon

Robert & Gertrude (Demers) Bentz – 1978

Robert & Gertrude Bentz - 1985

HISTORY OF ALICE GERTRUDE BENTZ

I was the fifth child born on March 31, 1917 to John and Matilda Bentz, in the old farmhouse on the Bench near Ravenscrag, Saskatchewan. I was delivered by a midwife in the kitchen of this farmhouse because the bedroom was part of the kitchen at this time.

I started school at the age of six years of age in the school at Crossfell. I started school with my brothers Robert and Lewis. We walked two miles across country to school, through pastures and fields because it was further to go by way of the road. Our school term was from March through December. After Christmas the school was closed because we always had such harsh winters. At the end of the school term we always had a Christmas Concert. It was one of the best in the country. We did skits, sang Christmas songs, did recitations, and had dance drills, which all took lots of practice. My father, John Bentz, accompanied us with his violin at the concerts. We always had a huge Christmas tree that reached to the ceiling, decorated with red and green crepe paper chains, popcorn strings and it was lit with wax candles. It was very beautiful, even if there was a danger of fire.

Occasionally at school in winter there would be a terrible blizzard and we would all be stranded at school for the duration of the blizzard. A year or so after I was through school (I went through grade ten), there was a severe blizzard and my brothers, Calvin, Harvey and my sister, Madge, were at school. The teacher tried to keep everyone in school, however, one boy, Dallas Heth, had a sister-in-law at home by herself. She was expecting a baby anytime and Dallas did not want her to be alone, so he insisted he had to go home. He always rode a horse to school. He never made it - he froze to Death on the way. His horse stayed with him. He had taken the saddle off the horse and the horse stayed right there. There was a big search by neighbors when he didn't arrive home. The next day my brother, Robert, found him and his horse. It was too late. That was very sad for his family and all who knew him. He was fifteen years old.

While I was still in school, I had to go to Ravenscrag to write my grade eight exams. I stayed with a family by the name of Whitefoot. I was happy to have passed the exams.

When I was a young girl we had a large family. On Saturdays, we had to clean house. We washed windows, washed all the 150 rungs on all the chairs, blackened the stove, scrubbed all the floors, and if we had time we had to go out in the fields to poison gophers. At this time gophers were a real menace to farmers. They ate the crops and dug holes in the fields. In the spring we took empty Rogers Golden Syrup pails (the ones we used to carry our lunches to school), filled them with water and poured the water in the gopher holes to drown them. When we had a bunch of tails gathered, they were taken to town to sell. We were paid a small bounty for the gopher tails, probably one or two cents each. I think we got the money from the Province.

We lived close to our Uncle Adolph Kalk and his wife, Aunt Maggie. I use to stay with them and my cousin, Lorraine, their daughter, or she would come over and stay with me. We were great friends and close to the same age. We often went to visit our Aunt Mary Heth and her two daughters, Lillian and Sophie. We visited back and forth quite often.

My mother was a marvellous cook. She had a large family and lots of company. She could whip up a gourmet meal out of next to nothing with limited ingredients. She was also a great gardener and we always had lots of vegetables to eat in the summer. She did a lot of canning of vegetables to eat during the winter months. A basement under the house always held a lot of potatoes, carrots, and other vegetables to keep us well fed in those cold winter months. She also canned meat from a cow or pig or chickens, and she and my dad made lots of sausage that they hung in a smokehouse to cure, as well as bacon pieces and hams. It was a lot of work for the farmers in those days, but we never went without food.

On Sundays we all went to church and then it was visiting and eating a good noon-day meal at a neighbors place or sometimes at our place. We seemed to take turns going to neighbors for Sunday dinners.

We always had a long way to go to get water from a creek about a quarter mile away. The creek was half way to our Uncle Jake's place. He lived on top of a hill. One day while Calvin, Harvey and I were playing behind the house with stones and rocks for horses and cows (we had to make our own fun and games in those days). The oval rocks were horses and the round ones were cows. We decided to dig a well for our make believe animals so we dug a small hole about one foot or so deep and we hit water! We reported this to our dad and he decided to dig a well in the basement about 12 to 14 feet deep and we had all kind of water. Dad put a pump upstairs in the kitchen with a pipe down to the well in the basement and we practically had running water.

One day my cousin, Sophie Heth, and I were baby sitting my little sister, Irene. Sister Madge was there, too. I was making pancakes for supper when an electrical storm came up and it was really thundering and lightening. The lightening hit so close to the house at one time it shocked me. I let out a yell, scared the others, and it really shook me up. That night we all four slept in mother's bed.

When we were in our late teens, we went to dances all over the countryside - Ravenscrag, Keely Springs, and Maple Creek. In the winter we went to the dances with horse and sleigh and in summer we had a car that we drove to the dances. I never had a date that I didn't have to take my younger siblings along, however, I never minded.

In the fall of 1932 after a failed harvest my parents moved to Medicine Hat with myself, Calvin, Harvey, Madge, Irene and baby Joyce. After the New Year, on January 19th, brother Raymond was born, the youngest, and the last. In the spring we moved back to the farm.

In 1937, in the late fall, dad and mom, along with Harvey, Irene, Joyce and Raymond moved to Mellowdale, Alberta, and rented a farm there. Lewis, Calvin, Robert, Madge and myself stayed behind on the farm. In the spring of 1938, Calvin, Madge and myself went to Mellowdale. Robert and Lewis stayed in Saskatchewan. We went by train from Maple Creek and our dad met us in Calgary, Alberta. Madge and I were just getting over the chicken pox and were still very itchy. On the way from Calgary to Mellowdale we had a slight car accident and had to leave the car in a garage for repairs. We spent the night in a hotel in Didsbury, Alberta. It wasn't a first class hotel and the pillows were like sand paper, and they were itchy also. The next morning we took a bus and went the rest of the way to Barrhead, which was not too far from Mellowdale, our destination.

Calvin, Madge and I formed an orchestra and we played at dances in the Barrhead area. Calvin played the violin, Madge piano, and I played the guitar. We played for usually five to six hours for $1.50 each.

Later I got a job in the Barrhead Hotel Cafe and I was paid $5.00 per week. Tips were nearly non-existent at the time. I then got a job at the Barrhead Red and White Mercantile store, where I first met my future husband, Swede (Arthur) Warehime. I was also a hair dresser for awhile after that.

Swede was born on August 5, 1919, at Mosside, Alberta. He was the eldest of four children. He had two brothers, Frank and Jack, and one sister, Margaret, who was the youngest.

In 1946 I married Swede Warehime in the United Church in Barrhead and our wedding reception was held at mom and dad Bentz's home in Mellowdale. The best man at our wedding wired the wedding ring to the box and made it very difficult to get it out. Swede was quite agitated and the minister who married us, Reverand Graham, said, "take your time laddie." Some people were amused, others were amazed!

We lived in Barrhead for six years where our two daughters, Myrna and Lynn, were born. Myrna Alice was born on November 12, 1946 and Lynn Shari was born on May 18, 1948. Swede was in the trucking business and hauled all kinds of freight from Edmonton to Barrhead.

In 1952 we moved to a very quiet remote homestead in Moose Wallow, about thirty-five miles from Barrhead, where we resided for the next forty years, farming and raising pure-bred cattle. The roads to our homestead were dirt roads in the beginning and whenever it rained we had to drive through mud and sometimes got stuck so badly we had to get the tractor to pull us out. Later on we had gravelled roads which made our trips to town much easier. It was a good living but we worked very hard on the farm.

Our girls had to stay with their Grandma Warehime to go to school in Mosside for the first few years. They stayed there all week and came home on weekends. This country school taught grades up to nine. One year they were home-schooled by correspondence. Then they had to go to school in Barrhead. A school bus came within five miles to pick them up to take them to Barrhead. We always had to drive them the five miles to catch the bus and then pick them up in the late afternoon. That went on for one year, then the county finally built a better road to our property which was gravelled. The bus came right into our yard to pick up the girls.

Myrna married Lee Chadd on November 12, 1966. They have five sons, Zene, Lonnie, Lowell, Dana and Quentin. Lynn married Lowell Cramer on May 11, 1968. They have three daughter, Rechelle, Tammy and Christina, and one son, Robin. Sadly, Lynn's husband, Lowell, died in a farming accident on August 5, 1992.

In early 1992 we sold the farm, retired, and moved to Barrhead where we bought a house. By this time we had nine grandchildren who were married and had children of their own. I had always had Christmas for the whole family, doing all the cooking and preparing. The last time was in 2003 when we had 36 family members for Christmas dinner. I was 86 years old in 2003 and didn't feel I could do it any more.

In 2004 we sold our house and moved into a Seniors' Complex in Barrhead. By this time Swede's health was deteriorating and in 2005 he had to go to a nursing home where he passed away on December 7, 2006.

I still reside in the same Seniors' Complex and keep myself busy make yo-yo type bedspreads, of which I have made 45 to date. I also like to knit and crochet. I still have very good health and I was 90 years old on March 31, 2007.

Alice (Bentz) & Arthur (Swede) Warehime on their wedding day – April 27, 1946

Lynne & Myrna Warehime, Alice and Arthur's daughters – 1952

Myrna (Warehime) & her husband Lee Chadd - 1989

Lynn (Warehime) and Lowell Cramer – Wedding 1968

Alice & Swede 50th Anniversary – 1996

HISTORY OF CALVIN BENTZ

FIRST PERSON REFLECTIVE
An Eighth Grade School Project,
Written by Amanda Saura,
For her Grandfather, Calvin Bentz

I was born into a large family, being the sixth child and having five born after me. We were farmers and when we were old enough we had to work on the farm. There were a lot of animals and the tame ones became our pets. I had little ponies that I trained to take my cap off my head. You see, they bit onto the little knob on the top of the hat, and pulled it off my head. There was one incident where a feisty little pony ripped out some of my hair as well.

Well, back to my family. My father's family is originally from Russia and my mother's from Canada. I was born in Eastend, Saskatchewan, in 1919 and lived there until 1938 when I was nineteen years old. There were eleven siblings, I am the middle child. We were children who always got along and never fought with each other.

I got my first job working for a farmer. I did a lot of things for him. Well, actually, I did everything I was asked to do, usually things like feeding the animals, milking, driving a tractor, and helping with the harvest.

It was 1940, and I was twenty-one years of age, when I met Josephine. She was a nurse, and I guess you could call it first love. But good thing it wasn't serious because then I don't know what would have happened to Katie! Let me take you back a ways and set the scene as best as I can remember. Our family were friends with Katie's family so I really met her when she was ten and I was already nineteen. We were married on December 17, 1946 and we lived in Camp Creek, Alberta, when we were first married.

Donna was our first born. She was born in 1948 and in 1964 she passed away. It was one of the worst parts of my life, that, and losing Katie in 1984. Our twins, Jerry and Jane, were born in 1951 and ten years later we got a surprise package which we named Nancy. Since we're talking about kids, I must tell you about my grandchildren. I'll start with the oldest. The oldest is Charlene. She has finished college and she is a social worker. She is twenty-five and has spent seven years in university and college. Charlene is a hard worker and a wonderful woman. Her sister, Christy, is finished college, too. She didn't have to go to school as long as Charlene. Christy is a wonderful granddaughter as well. They are the daughters of Jane, who is one of the twins. Jerry is the other twin, and he has three daughters. Sarah is the oldest. She is twenty and is not quite sure what she want to do with her life, yet. Andrea is graduating this year and already knows what she wants to do with her life. She and Lisa are in gymnastics and they are both doing very well at competitions. Lisa is the youngest of Jerry's three and, as I said, she is in gymnastics. She does very well in school and she is actually one of the top in her class. So is Andrea.

Nancy, our surprise package, has two children. Amanda is the eldest of the two and she is one of the grandchildren that is closest to me. She and I go camping every year together and she comes to visit me on her lunch breaks at school sometimes. She and her family live about a three minute drive from my place. Jessica is her little energetic sister, who calls me on the telephone almost three times a day. I love all my grandchildren very, very much.

I have two sisters who live in Kelowna. Joyce, who is the youngest girl in the family, is married and Madge is single. I usually see them once a week or so.

Well, my birthday just came last week and I turned eighty. My children and grandchildren are throwing me a party of some sort, but I'm not allowed to know more than that. So that's my life so far, and may I say, it's been "A Wonderful Life"!

Calvin & Katherine (Metzger) Bentz – Wedding 1946

Calvin Bentz & Children 1958

LR: Jerry, Donna & Jane

Calvin Bentz' son Jerry and daughers - 2004

LR: Jerry, Sarah, Andrea, & Lisa

Calvin Bentz' daughter Jane & Joe Hoffman – 2002

Calvin Bentz' daughter Nancy & Family
LR: Amanda, Mauri Saura, Nancy & Jessica

HISTORY OF IRENE BENTZ STEFANI

By Irene (Bentz) Stefani (1926-2012)

I was born in the hospital in Eastend, Saskatchewan, on January 3, 1926. My parents were Matilda and John Bentz of Ravenscrag, Saskatchewan. Since I was the first baby born in the hospital in the New Year, my parents received a card and a gift of baby products from Johnston & Johnston.

We lived on a farm, in a district called the "Bench," ten miles North of Ravenscrag, along with my 4 brothers (Lewis, Robert, Calvin and Harvey) and four sisters (Edna, Elaine, Alice and Magdalena (Maggie)).

In the spring of 1926, my Mother became very ill with gall-stones and had to have surgery. She had to go to Medicine Hat Hospital in Alberta for her surgery. Our neighbors, Mr. and Mrs. Ernst accompanied my Mother and Father to Medicine Hat. My Mother had to take me along because I was only six months old and I was still being nursed. After my Mother was admitted to the hospital, we left and started our trip back home. Mrs. Ernst took care of me on the way home. The trip home took about 6 hours driving on very rough roads. When we arrived home my two older sisters, Edna and Elaine, took care of me.

I remember when I was about five years old, sister Maggie and our cousin, Violet Bentz, who lived very nearby, always played together. They would never let me play with them saying that I was too young and too little to play their games and, no doubt, I was.

One day, my Dad went to our neighbors, the Willan's, where he was building a house for them. He was a very good carpenter and built quite a few buildings for different neighbors. I coaxed him to let me go along and I played all day with the Willan's daughter, Muriel, who was about my age. She had a little baby sister named Nancy and we played with her for hours. The Willan family raised a lot of sheep. Mrs. Willan served us mutton for dinner. Often, they paid my Dad for his labour with a sheep or two. I remember riding in the car to get to the Willan's place. It was a "touring car", early 1920's vintage. The car had button-down windows made of isinglass and black leather upholstery inside. I thought it was very elegant. Sister Elaine drove that same car to Ravenscrag one day, but didn't get there. She lost control and it rolled down an embankment and landed upside down with Mother, Edna, and Robert in it. Luckily, no one was seriously hurt, just shook up a little, and the car was repaired.

Before I started school, Mother brought home a little baby sister. She was born on January 16th, 1932. They named her Joyce. She had beautiful curly hair. Mother brought her home from the Eastend hospital.

I started school in March, 1932, when I was six years old and attended Crossfell country school. Our school year started in March through December. January and February were always such severe cold months that we had our school break at that time. We had to walk two miles across the countryside to school. My first teacher was George Harlton. Mr. Harlton was a very strict and mean teacher. It was more than my nerves could stand to hear him harshly discipline my sisters and brothers. He boarded at our home and his viciousness did not stop at school. Within a few months I suffered a nervous breakdown and could not continue going to Crossfell School. By this time, sister Edna had married Alex Ernst and they lived on a farm not far away. Also, by this time, Elaine was out on her own and working in Olds, Alberta.

In the fall of 1932, we moved into Medicine Hat, Alberta, where eight members of our family lived in a two-bedroom house on 773-11th Street. The older boys, Lewis and Robert, stayed on the farm. Alex Ernst, Edna's husband, moved our household things in his one-ton truck. We followed behind by car. In January of 1933, my brother Raymond was born. This time a midwife attended the birth. Shortly after that, my sister Alice and I had to have our tonsils removed. My health seemed to improve from then on.

In March, 1933, we moved back to the "Bench", where I again attended school at Crossfell with teacher George Harlton. The teacher was just as mean, unpleasant and unfair as before. It wasn't long before my nerves collapsed again and I suffered another nervous breakdown. It was probably in March, 1934, when Dad decided to take me to Eastend. He hitched up two horses to the sleigh (it was still winter) and we drove to Ravenscrag. At the time, a cousin, Lillian Heth, was staying with us and she decided to come along with us to Eastend. In Ravenscrag, Dad boarded the horses in the local livery barn and we took the train to Eastend. They took me to the local hospital where I stayed for ten days. Mother and Dad immediately went home after they admitted me. The Doctor could do nothing to help me and wasn't able to diagnose my condition. Dad and Mother came by car to take me home. I suffered for another two weeks and my nerves became worse than ever.

I sometimes played with another neighbour's daughter, Lillian Wildeman. Lillian's mother was a very kind lady and became very concerned about my health. She suggested to my parents that they take me to Medicine Hat Hospital to seek better medical help for my condition. Mrs. Wildeman and her son, Frank, very kindly offered to drive us to Medicine Hat, Alberta, where I entered the hospital. In those days we did not have money for medical expenses, so I was admitted under a welfare/relief plan. Mother and Dad then went back home and I was left thoroughly alone, and feeling very lost. My one joy in the hospital was receiving an Easter parcel through the mail from my sister, Elaine, who now worked in Vancouver, B. C. It contained Easter bunnies, chocolates and candies.

I seemed to get the right treatment this time and very soon improved and felt much better. It was determined that I had a disease called "St. Vitas' Dance", another name for Chorea, a nervous disorder, especially of children, marked by uncontrollable and irregular movements of the muscles of the arms, legs, and face. My parents picked me up after about two weeks and I was very glad to be home again. I continued going to school, this time with different teachers and did very well at learning.

When I was ten years old, I went to babysit Edna and Alex Ernst's children for one day. At that time they had three little boys, Eddie - five years old, Ernie - four, and baby Albert - two. This was a big responsibility for me; I felt needed and was proud that they trusted me to baby-sit. The parents had all gone to pick berries for the day. Edna gave me instructions not to play with matches or light the wood-burning stove. For our noon dinner, we had a special treat - a bowl of shredded wheat. It was a very hot day - 100 degrees in the shade. We had only warm water to drink. They had a well with a pump which was run by a motor. I asked Eddie if he could start the motor, but he couldn't until little Ernie came and pushed a button somewhere and the pump started. We then had nice cold water to drink. Of course, we couldn't tell Alex or Edna that we had started the motor or we would have been disciplined. The three of us swore to secrecy never to tell.

On November 12, 1937, when I was eleven years old, Mother and Dad packed up the youngest three children, Joyce, Raymond and myself and, along with our friends Mrs. Detert and her two daughters, Gertrude and Ella, left the farm on the Bench, and set out for Freedom, Alberta. Lewis, Robert, Calvin, Alice and Maggie were left on the farm to fend for themselves.

During those years, farming was not very good in Southern Saskatchewan because of a terrible drought that lasted several years. The Provincial Government had been paying the farmers "relief", or welfare. The government provided three rail cars for our two families to move our stock, farm equipment and household items to Alberta. Mr. Detert, his son, Henry, and my brother, Harvey, rode in the rail cars to take care of the stock.

When we arrived at Freedom, Alberta, the Detert's had already rented a farm and my family stayed with them for about two months. I should mention that this farm had a very small house with two bedrooms downstairs and an open upstairs, where eleven people lived together, seven children and four adults.

Our Dad went to Edmonton to visit the Land Titles Office to see if there was any land for rent in the district around Barrhead. Fortunately, he talked to a man who worked in the Land Titles Office by the name of Ernest Duke, and Mr. Duke said that he had a farm on the Schoal Lake north of Barrhead and he was looking for new renters. This seemed to be a very good opportunity and Dad accepted his offer. Dad and Harvey loaded up some machinery and, on the way to Schoal Lake, stopped at Burke's farm and Mr. Burke highly recommended the Duke farm for our family.

When we finally moved to Schoal Lake, we children had to sleep in a granary. We ate in a one-room house where Mother and Dad also slept. About one month later, we were able to move into the big house when the present renters moved out. This new place was always referred to as "The Duke Place". The house required extensive repairs, which Dad did because he had a lot of carpentry experience. The house was small, with two bedrooms, living room and a spacious kitchen. The house had a very large veranda extending along the entire north side overlooking Schoal Lake. It also had a large attic where some of the older children slept. Mother was very pleased because she had lots of room for a big garden and the growing season seemed to be better than it was in Saskatchewan.

After we settled in, Calvin, Alice and Maggie were able to take a train from Ravenscrag to Calgary, leaving Robert and Lewis behind to run the farm. They could only go as far as Calgary because money was limited and they could not afford the whole fare to Barrhead. As a result, Dad drove his Model A Ford car to Calgary to pick them up. It was a long trip of approximately 300 miles. The roads were not very good and not paved or gravelled in those days. On the way home, Dad had a slight accident with the car and they had to leave it and take a bus to Barrhead. Dad had to go back later on to have the car repaired and drive it home.

One drawback living at The Duke Place was that it was too far away from a local school. My sisters Madge and Joyce and I had to go to school in Barrhead. When Maggie arrived in Barrhead the family decided to call her "Madge", which she liked better than her real name of "Magdalena" or the name "Maggie". Mother and Dad had to rent a room in a rooming house for us. The rent they paid was $3.00 per month. I was in grade six and Joyce just started in grade one. Madge also went to school and started in Grade 10. She found the school work very difficult in Alberta after having attended a country school in Saskatchewan where the school systems were much different. After two weeks in school, she decided she would quit. Elaine, who had recently moved to Barrhead, told her that there was a job available in the hotel cafe where she worked, so Madge stayed in the hotel with Elaine and they both worked as waitresses. That one year in Barrhead was very bad for us. Sometimes, we didn't have much to eat. Elaine often brought us a loaf of bread, which she said cost her five cents for a loaf. The roads were sometimes so muddy and impassable that my parents could not get to town to bring us supplies or take us home for weekend visits. We sometimes had to stay in town three weeks by ourselves.

The second year, brother Raymond started school and we moved to a two-room apartment on Main Street and the rent was $5.00 per month. Alice also came to stay with us and she worked in the Red and White General Store as a clerk.

It wasn't long before Mr. Hardy of the Barrhead School Board approached our Dad and said a tuition fee would have to be paid in order to allow his children to attend school in Barrhead since we did not live in the district. Dad said he couldn't afford the tuition and said he would take his children out of school and take them home. Mr. Hardy came over to where Dad was loading up and said he had worked it out after realizing we lived too far away from a local school. The Duke Place was five and a half miles from the Mellowdale School, which would have been the closest one. I was very happy again to be able to continue going to school.

My happiness in school didn't last long because I had another nervous breakdown. The other children made fun of my poor clothing and teased me unmercifully. It was more than I could stand. Nevertheless, I finished grade seven and passed all the final tests. It was June, 1940. I was 14 years old, and after being treated for my illness, the doctor recommended that I not return to school. Our neighbor, Mrs. Burke talked Mother into taking me to Edmonton to see a special doctor. He recommended seven different medications and, after taking them, I slept for two days and two nights. My first memory after awaking was being outside walking in the yard, and brother Calvin saying to me that I was doing real well. That gave me the encouragement I needed. I never had a recurrence of this illness after that treatment. I was very sad not being able to return to school, but I stayed home and helped my Mother in the house.

Sister Elaine had married Ed Larkins and they lived in Barrhead. Elaine became very ill with diabetes and was going in and out of comas. Elaine was pregnant with her second child, Stuart. This was when I was sixteen years old and I went to Barrhead to stay with the Larkins family to take care of their first daughter, Arlene. Elaine improved somewhat after the birth of their son, Stuart.

I had a certain talent for doing hair. I had a few customers in Barrhead and did their hair weekly. When I was 21 years old, a lady by the name of Mrs. Robinson recommended me to Mrs. Catherwood, the owner of a Beauty Shop in Westlock. At that time the going price was 65 cents for a shampoo and set and haircuts were 10 cents. The only kind of permanents that were done in those days was "heat" perms for $2.50. I worked in the Beauty Shop for $1.00 a day, plus my room and board. I was finally on my own and away from my family. Mother didn't want me to go because I was a great help to her and she thought I wasn't well enough to be away from home. I proved her wrong in the long run.

It wasn't long before I met the love of my life. I fell in love with Gus Stefani and after going together for one and a half years; we got married on January 3rd, 1949. I first met Gus when he had a bet with his brother and a friend who bet him that he couldn't get a date with me. He marched right over to the Beauty Shop where I was working and asked me for a date. I hesitantly said OK. Our first date was a country dance at a local community hall named Hazel Bluff. He won the bet!

Gus had bought a farm through the Veterans' Administration, since he had been a soldier, and served in the Second World War. The farm was located in Eastburg district. It was 160 acres which at that time cost him $5,500.00. We paid it off in ten years. The farm didn't have any buildings on it at the time so Gus built us a two- bedroom house, dug a well, built a cow shed and made other improvements.

On October 25, 1949, our son Wayne was born in Westlock Immaculata Hospital. Wayne was quite sickly in his young years with eczema and asthma. We had a very hard time taking care of him. I suffered a miscarriage about a year later. With the trauma of Wayne's illness, my nerves were much frayed and that was the reason I had the miscarriage. Our son Murray was born on January 1, 1953, at the same hospital as Wayne. Murray was another New Year's baby, the same as I was, and we received many gifts from the local merchants.

In November of 1953, I became quite ill with a tumor on one of my ovaries. The tumor was filled with liquid the size of two gallons. I had surgery to remove the tumor and one ovary. Luckily, it was not cancerous.

Wayne had to wait until he was seven years old to start school. The first year he attended Springwell country school, which was two miles from where we lived. He either walked to school or rode his horse. Unfortunately, he was allergic to horses and he suffered asthma attacks quite frequently. Once we realized he was allergic to horses, he had to stop riding to school.

Gus was very unhappy with farming and decided he would like to change careers and get back into the armed forces. In the fall of 1958, we left the farm and rented a small house in Westlock where I lived with the boys and my Mother-in-law, Pauline Stefani. We rented the farm to some neighbours. Gus went to Edmonton to join the forces and was sent to Shiloh, Manitoba, for his basic training.

During the six months that Gus was in basic training, I assisted my Mother-in-law in purchasing an old house from my brother, Harvey, in Mellowdale and had it moved into Westlock on a lot that she had purchased. My Mother-in-law lived in the house while we were away and we eventually purchased the house from her.

It was not until 1959 when I was able to join Gus in Winnipeg where we rented a very nice old house. Another army family lived there also and helped to pay the rent. Murray started his first year of school in Winnipeg and Wayne continued his education there as well.

We lived in Winnipeg for the next five years. After the children were settled in school, I had time on my hands and decided to find a job. Gus suggested that, instead of finding a job, I should see if I could get into a hairdressing school, since hairdressing seemed to be my calling. In January, 1960, I got into the Scientific School of Cosmetology and worked at that training for one year. I took two months off during the summer when the boys were out of school. While I attended the school, I reported every morning at 8:30 AM to set up supplies for the day and was able to leave at 4:00 PM (a half hour before the other students) to catch my bus across town. I always got home at 5:30, after a very long bus trip.

I graduated in January, 1961. Before writing my Government examination I had to have a medical check-up. I was fortunate and passed the hairdressing exam with honors. My first job was in a Beauty Shop in Winnipeg close to home. I was able to walk there and back. This job did not last very long (about two months) because I was not happy with my boss. Wages were very low and the work was demanding. I then quit this job and started working on my own in our home.

In January, 1964, Gus, who was in the NATO Peace Keeping Forces, was sent to Westfalia, Germany, for a three year tour of duty. I and the boys were not able to join him until six weeks later. We had to go to Trenton, Ontario by train from Winnipeg and then flew to Wiesbaden, Germany. The plane was filled with army families going to the same place. An army bus picked us up and took us to the camp. From there, Gus took us to our new home which he had previously rented, near the camp in a place called Hemer.

We remained there about four months and then moved into a PMQ (Personnel Military Quarters) where we stayed for the remainder of Gus's tour. The boys went to a Canadian school on the base. Everything we needed was right on the base including grocery and department stores, theatre and many other services.

I had quite an experience in a German Hospital when I became run down and anaemic. The Doctor confined me for a week in the hospital and prescribed medication to build up my system and to get lots of rest. I recovered very quickly.

During Gus's furloughs, we made many trips touring around Europe visiting many countries like Spain, Italy, France, Switzerland, Holland, Belgium and Austria. It was a very enjoyable time of our lives.

At the end of Gus's three-year tour of duty in Germany, we were sent back to Canada in February, 1967, and were stationed in Gagetown, New Brunswick, for the next seven years, until Gus's retirement at the age of 50. The boys continued their schooling in Oromocto where we lived in a PMQ.

Wayne left home to be on his own in 1967 at the age of 17. He went to Toronto, Ontario, but soon came home again to continue going to school for another year. He left again when he was 19 to go to Vancouver, B. C. where he worked and obtained his mechanics license. He married Cheryl MacDonald and they had a son, Mark, born on March 25, 1970. They later divorced when Mark was four years old.

When Murray was 19 years old (in 1972), he also went to Vancouver to make his home there. He and a partner started a business called Castle Masonry and they did very well for several years. Wayne and Murray had many jobs and lived in many places for the next few years.

When Gus retired, we moved back to Westlock, Alberta in 1974, where we were able to move into the house with Gus's Mother. Gus did extensive repairs and updating on the old house. Our first job when we got back was working for the Elk's Lodge at Lac La Nonne Beach Resort as caretakers for one summer. Gus's Mother moved out of the house and into the Pembina Lodge at Westlock. She was at this time 80 years old and needed help caring for herself. Gus then went to work for the Provincial Highways Department in 1977. While working for the Department, Gus injured his back and had to have two surgeries six months apart (1978 and 1979). It took him a long time to recover. When his final back brace was removed, he had to go for more surgery in 1981 because this time the doctors discovered he had cancer in his bladder. He had surgery and the doctors removed a portion of his bladder. He had ten Cobalt treatments and then Chemotherapy. These treatments lasted for five months. He was very, very ill throughout these treatments and we didn't know if he would survive or not. He finally recovered and his cancer went into remission, but it was a long battle for him and me.

In 1987, we bought the house and lot next door to where we were presently living in Westlock, had the building demolished, and began the big project of building a new house, something I had been wanting for many, many years - a new house all our own. The new house was finished in September, 1987, and we moved in. Later on in 1993, we built a double car-garage at the back of the property.

Wayne and Murray had been living together on an acreage in Richmond, B. C. They had a very nice life in that they had some cattle on eight acres. Gus and I visited them many times, especially for Christmases. Wayne had a heart attack and then had to have open heart surgery and a quadruple heart bypass. He was not able to go back to work as a mechanic and had to take life easy. He finally had to go on welfare to get the care and treatments he needed.

Gus and I had a wonderful celebration for our 40th Wedding Anniversary in June, 1989, which we celebrated with sister Joyce and her husband Hugh Roesch for their 25th anniversary. This seemed to be a-once-in-a-lifetime celebration, so we wanted to make it special. We rented the Legion Hall in Westlock and we had a wonderful party with drinks, dinner and dancing. We shared the expenses with Joyce and Hugh, and we invited all our relatives and good friends.

We were very happy in our new home and our boys came home to visit quite often. Then, disaster struck again. In 1994, Gus had an aneurysm in his main heart artery which required more surgery. The doctors had to replace the artery. He came home for about six months and then it was discovered that his one kidney was blocked. When the doctors were going to repair the kidney problem, Gus had quite a severe heart attack while on the operating table. The doctors managed to sustain him while they repaired the kidney. He was in intensive care for ten days because of the heart attack. He finally recovered enough to come home, but was still very ill and he had to have a lot of medication, which didn't always agree with him. He was going downhill every day, but he did live for two more years. His final pleasure was attending the 50th Wedding Anniversary of sister Alice and her husband Swede Wareheime on April 27, 1996. Gus finally succumbed on May 5, 1996 with cardiac arrest.

I dearly missed Gus when he passed away, but I find great comfort in remembering that when you love someone and they love you, they are never lost to you. I will always have the wonderful memories of the times Gus and I shared together in our 47 years of marriage.

Murray came home to live with me in March, 1997. He helped me a great deal and I was happy to have his company. Wayne remained in Richmond, B.C. where he could continue seeing his doctors who had taken care of him for all these years. The climate in B.C. seemed to be better for his health, too. In the summer of 1999, Murray purchased a five acre parcel of land in the country near the farm that we own. The acreage contains our old house and some farm buildings. The house was a little run-down because no one had lived in it for several years, but Murray worked hard doing repairs to make it liveable once again. The house is equipped with natural gas and electricity.

On March 6, 2000, Wayne passed away very suddenly when he suffered a massive heart attack. He was 50 years old. Murray and I were both saddened and devastated at our loss of a son and brother. Murray was very supportive during this difficult time, and made several trips to Richmond, B. C. to make arrangements and to settle Wayne's estate. Wayne was cremated and his ashes were scattered on our old farm, a place that he had always loved and visited many times in the last years of his life.

Westlock, Alberta June, 2001

Irene (Bentz) & Gus Stefani – Wedding Day 1949

Irene (Bentz) & Gus Stefani's sons Murray & Wayne – 1955

Irene (Bentz) & Gus Stefani – taken in the 1960's

THE BENTZ FAMILY EXODUS

FROM SASKATCHEWAN TO ALBERTA
Written by Joyce (Bentz) Roesch and
Irene (Bentz) Stefani
January 2003

We left the "Bench" in Saskatchewan on November 11, 1937. There was snow on the ground and it was very cold. Dad was driving our 1928 Model "A" Ford car. It was tough going because there were big snow drifts along the road. We often had to drive off the road to avoid the snow drifts. Brother, Robert, came along during the first leg of the journey, with a team of horses pulling a rubber-tired wagon, which were used to pull the car through many snow drifts along the way. Robert sometimes drove ahead of the car and sometimes followed the car, for a distance of some thirty miles until we got to the main highway at Piapot, Sask. Then Robert left us and drove the horses and wagon back to the farm on the Bench.

To help keep us warm, we had heated rocks as well as lots of blankets in the car. The car, of course, had no heater. Our friend, Mrs. Detert, was with us on this trip, along with her two daughters, Ella and Gertrude. Mrs. Detert, her daughters, and Irene rode in the back seat, while Dad, Mother, Joyce and Raymond, rode in the front. It was a big job for Dad to drive and try to keep the windshield from fogging or icing up so he could see through. Mother brought along a bag of salt that they used to rub on the iced-up windshield. It would temporarily remove the ice from the glass.

At the time, Irene was eleven years old, Joyce was five, Raymond was four, Gertie was twelve and Ella was ten year old. The older children, Lewis, Robert, Calvin, Alice and Madge all remained at the farm on the Bench. Edna had married Alex Ernst in April, 1931. They had their own place and stayed on in Saskatchewan. Their first son, Eddie, was born there in 1931, and their other three sons were also born in Saskatchewan. Ernie was born in 1932, Albert in 1934, and Clarence in 1937.

By 1925, when Elaine was sixteen years old, she had already left home to go to work. She worked for various families doing housework in Eastend and Ravenscrag, Saskatchewan, and then in Medicine Hat and Olds, Alberta. In 1937, she went to Vancouver to work for about a year.

After Robert left us, there were still some snow drifts on the road and we stopped often for Dad to shovel snow so we could drive through. The first night we arrived in Suffield, Alberta. We stayed overnight in a very cheap hotel. We had two rooms, which Mrs. Detert paid for. The cost was $3.00 for the two rooms. There were bed bugs in the beds. Mrs. Detert, Joyce and Raymond slept in one room. It had one bed. There were curtains hanging on a wall, but no window. The other room had two beds. Mother and Dad slept in one bed while Irene, Ella and Gertie slept in the other. The bed bugs were so bad that the girls did not want to cover up with the hotel blanket and used coats instead to cover themselves. Mother and Dad each had fur coats, very warm, that they had ordered from the Eaton's catalogue before leaving on the trip.

The Detert family had some money, and with their help, we were able to leave the Bench. There was a drought throughout the prairies, and during the previous several years, the crops were total failures. It was very difficult to make enough money to feed the family. Mother and Dad often argued about moving someplace else, but Dad was afraid he would have a hard time starting over this late in his life. He was 54 years of age at this time. Mother was very unhappy living on the farm under these conditions and finally persuaded Dad to make the move.

Mrs, Detert paid for the hotel and our meals on the trip to Alberta. The Detert's helped and encouraged Dad and Mother to leave the Bench and move to Alberta. At the time, gas was about 15 cents a gallon, and the Ford car averaged about twenty miles per gallon. During the hard times, the family got $29.00 per month from the Government, called "relief" (known today as welfare). As well as the money, they were able to pick up food from Ravenscrag. They also got coal and some feed for their stock. The food consisted of dried smoked fish, cheese, macaroni and sometimes, apples. These payments of money continued for three months after they arrived in Alberta. It seems that since the prairies were in such a bad drought, the Government encouraged people to move and helped them by providing some money and aid to make it possible.

From Suffield, there were no more snow drifts and the driving was easier and faster, so that we arrived at the Schneider's place (Mrs. Detert's in-laws) in the evening, where we stayed for a few days. The Schneider's lived about three miles northeast of Barrhead on the main highway, No. 18.

In the meantime, before leaving the Bench, the Detert's had already rented a farm owned by the Schneiders, in the Freedom district. Mr. Schneider was kind enough to lease a farm to Dad and Mother (on paper only), so that the Government would provide the rail cars for shipping the household furniture, farm equipment and all the stock from Saskatchewan.

The Deterts and our family were able to secure three rail cars for shipping the household furniture, farm equipment and all the stock. The two families shared these rail cars which were loaded in Ravenscrag. All our belongings that were being shipped by rail had to be hauled to Ravenscrag, mostly by wagon and horses. Mr. Detert, his son, Henry, and our brother Harvey, rode the rail cars to supervise and take care of the animals, feeding and watering them when necessary. The rail cars arrived in Manola, Alberta, a couple of days after we arrived by car. The men brought all our belongings and stock to the Detert farm, which was only about four miles from the railroad where the cars were unloaded. The Deterts stored our things in a building on their farm and we stayed with them for about two months until Dad rented a farm from Ernest Duke in the Mellowdale district.

Our lease of the Duke place was to start on April 1, 1938, when the current renters moved out. While we were waiting to move, we briefly stayed in a place not too far away called the Cummings place. It was owned by the Burke family, who became some of our new neighbors. We moved there about the middle of January and stayed until we could move to the Duke place on April 1, 1938. The house was a one room shack (probably a converted chicken coup) that Mother and Dad slept in, and it was also used for a kitchen. Harvey, Irene, Joyce and Raymond slept in a granary nearby in the same yard.

The Duke place was located in the Shoal Lake district. The house was situated on a small hill and overlooked Shoal Lake. It was a small lake about one-half mile from the house. The lake was not very good for anything, because it was bottomless, so they said, and did not even contain any fish. Most of the shoreline was a bog. The scenery was very nice to look at, though. The house had two bedrooms, a large kitchen and large living room with a fireplace (which never worked), a large storage room and one walk-in closet for both bedrooms. Of course, the house had no bathroom, so it came with an outside toilet a few yards from the house. There was also a large attic where the boys slept in the winter time. There was a very large screened-in veranda on the north side of the house where the boys slept during the summer months when it was too hot to sleep in the attic.

When Calvin, Alice and Madge left the Bench farm in April, 1938, leaving Lewis and Robert there, they had saved up enough money to take the train from Piapot, Saskatchewan to Calgary, Alberta. Robert drove them with the horses and Bennett buggy to Piapot. The year before, Calvin had worked in Brooks, Alberta, as farm hand, and managed to save a little money from his wages. He was able to keep $25.00 for himself and the rest he gave to Dad and Mother to use on their trip to Alberta. Elaine, who was working in Vancouver, also helped with the cost of the trip by sending some money home.

To earn more money for their trip to Alberta to join the family, Calvin worked for Uncle Jake and was paid $5.00 a month. Alice worked for Edna and Alex and was paid $3.00 a month. Calvin, Alice and Madge, also played music for the local dances in the area, getting paid anywhere from 50 cents to $1.50 per evening. Calvin played the Violin, Madge played the piano, or corded on the banjo or guitar, and Alice also played the guitar or banjo. They weren't all that great but the local people loved their little band and their music.

Robert stayed on the home farm and continued farming. By this time, he had met a lovely girl from Shaunavon, Gertie Demers. They were married in August, 1938, and they continued to farm the home place and tried to make a go of it. Lewis had rented a place of his own a little north of the farm and ran it as best he could. The weather and the circumstances did not improve so that it was very hard to make a living during the drought, with crop failures every year.

Calvin, Alice and Madge had just enough money to buy train tickets for the three of them as far as Calgary, Alberta. Dad drove from the Duke place to Calgary in his 1928 Model "A" Ford to pick them up. On the way back to the Duke place, they had a small collision with another car at Didsbury, which put the Ford out of commission. They left the car at a local shop for some minor repairs. The four of them had to stay overnight at Didsbury, and in the morning, they pooled their money (Dad had brought a small amount of money with him), bought four bus tickets to Barrhead, and had just enough money left over to buy a cup of coffee and a donut for each for breakfast. That was all they had to eat the whole day. They got off the bus at the Schneider farm in the evening, and they were very hungry by then. The next day, someone in the Schneider family drove them to the Duke place. It was April 10, 1938 when they arrived at the Duke place, Calvin's 19th birthday. Alice was 21 and Madge was 15 years old.

Dad had to return to Didsbury to pick up the car about two weeks later. He took the bus from Barrhead to Didsbury, and after having to pay about $39.00 to have the car fixed, he was able to drive the car back to the Duke place.

In 1938, Elaine came to Barrhead to visit the folks to see what kind of place they lived in. She decided to stay, and she immediately got a job in Barrhead, working as a waitress in the Barrhead Hotel Café.

Lewis, Robert and Gertie gave up farming on the Bench and came to Alberta together in August or September, 1939. Robert and Gertie's daughter, Fern, was born in April, 1939, before they left the Bench. They were able to get the same rail car arrangement from the Government that our family and the Detert family had two years earlier. They brought all the remaining furniture, farm equipment including a tractor, some cows and horses that the family had left there. When the rail cars arrived in Barrhead, everything had to be hauled from the railway station to the Duke farm, a distance of about nine miles. They had shipped about twenty horses and a few cows. The boys had to ride their own horses to town and drive the herd of horses home on the main road. It was quite a job for them to drive these horses because they were inclined to wander off the road and they had to keep rounding them up to keep them on the road.

Lewis and Robert and his family stayed with us on the Duke place for a short time. Lewis found a job working as a farm hand for a local farmer for the next year. Robert also found a job working as a farm hand for the Bender family, who lived not too far away. Their second daughter, Claudette, was born in June, 1941. She was born at home with Mother Bentz acting as the mid-wife. Later that year, after Claudette was born, they moved to the Bender farm and lived in a granary there. They eventually bought their own place. They farmed for a few years and four more children were born: Trevor, born in 1943, Allan in 1946, Dallas in 1947 and Sharon in 1953. They did not have a great deal of success farming, so they gave up the farm and moved to Edmonton. Robert went to work for wages. Two more children were born after they moved to Edmonton, Wesley, born in 1956 and Anthony, born in 1958. They also adopted three children: Rhonda, Lisa and Korine. Besides raising their eleven children, they took welfare children into their home and took care of them. Gertie passed away in May, 1999 and Robert passed away in September, 2002.

There was no school within a reasonable distance from where we lived on the Duke place – the closest was five miles away – so Irene and Joyce had to stay in the town of Barrhead to go to school. Dad rented a room in a rooming house owned by Mrs. Gaines, for $3.00 per month. Joyce started her first school year in Barrhead in September of 1938, and Irene was in grade six.

Madge's first job was very temporary; when she worked for the Roberts family in Manola (they owned a general store), doing housework. She didn't like the job very much and soon moved to Barrhead and started to work as a waitress in the Barrhead Hotel Café along with Elaine. Madge had just turned sixteen at this time.

The next year, 1939, when Raymond started his first year, Dad rented a small two-room apartment upstairs in the Shaper building on the main street of Barrhead. The rent was $5.00 per month. Due to health reasons, Irene had to leave school in 1939 at the end of the school year, after completing grade seven, and she returned to the Duke place to stay with the other members of the family. While Madge and Elaine had been working as waitresses in the Barrhead Hotel Café, they lived in the hotel while they worked there. When the younger kids had to move to this bigger place, Elaine and Madge also moved into this small apartment and they paid the rent instead of Dad. It was quite a small place with a small kitchen and one big room in which there were two double beds and a couch.

In 1940, Dad rented a farm in the Freedom district (about two miles from the Freedom store). It was called the Shortle place. He rented it for Lewis but before Lewis took over the farm, Mother and Dad moved in temporarily, along with Raymond and Joyce, who attended the Freedom School for one school year. Joyce was in grade three and Raymond was in grade two. They had to walk about two miles to the Freedom school. Elaine and Madge still rented the Shaper building apartment and continued their work in Barrhead. Calvin, Harvey, Alice, Irene and Gertie stayed on the Duke place while Mother and Dad lived on the Shortle place. The following year, after the school year ended in June, 1941, Mother and Dad moved back to the Duke place, and when school started again in September, Joyce and Raymond stayed with Elaine and Madge once again, in that very small apartment in Barrhead, and went to school.

In late 1941, Lewis took over the rental of the Shortle place. Lewis had worked at various jobs before he settled on the Shortle place to start farming. Irene went to live with him to keep house, but she soon left and went back home to the Duke place. After Irene arrived back home, Alice went to stay with Lewis for a short while. Then she left and went to Barrhead and got a job as a waitress in the Barrhead Hotel Café, where she worked for the next two years. She moved into the two room apartment with Madge, Joyce and Raymond.

In 1940, Calvin was called up into military service and spent one month in training at Camrose, Alberta. This was compulsory training for all able young men. Harvey was also called into the service, but Dad requested that one of them stay home to help with the farming. It was decided that Harvey would go, and Calvin came home after his training. Harvey spent the war years in the army and for a time was stationed at Kiska in the Aleutian Islands (near Alaska).

Elaine and Madge together rented a house just behind the Red and White Store. The rent was $12.50 per month. They both lived there for a very short time until Elaine and Ed Larkins got married in February, 1942. Elaine and Ed had a very nice wedding supper, which was held at the Shortle place for the family members. Elaine and Ed then took over the rental of the house that Elaine and Madge had shared. Their daughter, Arlene, and their son, Stuart, were born while they lived in this house. Ed ran the local newspaper, the "Barrhead Leader", with his father. Their second daughter, Carol, was born in 1944 after they bought an older house with two lots and lived there until they managed to have a larger home built on the same lots in 1956. They had the misfortune of losing their son, Stuart, who died in May, 1958. He drowned while saving a young girl who had fallen into the Paddle River just south of Barrhead.

In 1942, after Dad was doing better on the Duke place, he went to Edmonton and bought a newer used car, a 1938 Chevrolet. He traded in the 1928 Ford. The new car was very nice and it was the envy of all the neighbors. He kept this 1938 car for many more years. His next car was a brand new Chevrolet that he bought in 1951.

While we lived on the Duke place, Dad did a lot carpentry work for the neighbors, building a house for the Bender family, and building barns and granaries for others. He also built a barn for the Schneider family. The wages were very poor, as he did most of this work for favors.

Before Madge and Alice started to work in Barrhead, Calvin and the two girls played for a few dances in the area. Their first engagement was for a wedding dance in the community of Tiger Lily. They were very lucky if they got paid $1.00 each at these dances. Once the girls started working in Barrhead, Calvin started playing for Carl Johnson and his orchestra. They were very good and had lots of dates to play all over the countryside. They began to make more money, too. Calvin played the piano with this band for quite a few years. It was quite exhausting for him to work on the farm all day and then to go out at night to play at dances, not arriving home until about 3:00 or 4:00 AM in the morning.

Calvin married in December, 1946. He married a very lovely girl, Katherine Metzger, who lived in the Mellowdale area. Calvin had bought his own farm in 1944 in the Camp Creek district. He and Katie lived there for a short time, and then bought a different farm north of Mellowdale. They built a small house on this property, but finally gave up farming this piece of land, rented it out, and in about 1950, they moved to Barrhead. Calvin worked for the Imperial Garage, owned by Fred Tremblay, in the parts department, until 1951 when Fred Tremblay sold the business.

Calvin continued to play with the Carl Johnson orchestra for quite a few years after he and Katie married. In 1952, they decided to go back to farming and bought a farm in the Bloomsbury district, not too far from Barrhead. They built a nice new house and were able to move in just before winter, in 1952. They had four children: Donna, born in 1949, twins Jerry and Jane, born in 1951, and Nancy, born in 1961. Sadly, they lost their eldest daughter, Donna, who passed away in January, 1965 at sixteen years of age. The farming business was not too prosperous for them, so they sold the farm and moved to Kelowna, B. C. in 1973. Katie passed away in May, 1984.

Harvey came back from the service after the war ended, in 1945. He bought a farm next to where Mother and Dad lived and he took up farming on his own. He married Alvina Radke, who lived in the Mellowdale area, in November, 1948. They farmed this land and gradually acquired more land nearby in the next few years. Their one daughter and two sons were born and raised on the farm. Janice was born in 1949, Lorne was born in 1952, and Dale was born in 1956. Harvey passed away in July, 2002 and Alvina passed away in January, 2003.

Lewis gave up farming the Shortle place in 1944 and went to work for the Munsterman family on their farm in the Rossington area. He then joined the Canadian army. After his basic training, he was being sent to Holland for a tour of duty during the war. While they were on the ship crossing the ocean, the war ended, and he then served with the occupation forces in Europe. When he came home after a couple of years, he went into farming in the Barrhead area. He met and married Katie Heberling in 1951, and they had one son, Herbert, who was born in 1953. Katie passed away in October, 1991 and Lewis passed away in September, 1996.

Alice gave up being a waitress and got a job working in the Red and White Store as a clerk, in 1943, and she still lived in the Shaper apartment. Madge got a new job at Mickey O'Brien's Drugstore and Soda Fountain for a short while, and then she took a job at the Barrhead Post Office, where she worked until about 1942.

While Madge was working at the Post Office, she rented a portion of the Schneider house, just a half block from the main street. Joyce and Raymond stayed with her and went to school for the next year. She rented the Kitchen, one bedroom and a closed in porch, which was also used as a bedroom. The house was very large with many nice rooms.

Madge then had an opportunity to move to Edmonton and work in the main Post Office there. At that time, only men were employed in the Post Office, but most of the men had to go into the services during the war. Women were suddenly important enough to take over the men's jobs. However, at the end of the war in 1945, the jobs were all given back to the returning veterans, and Madge had to find another job. She worked at a couple of other jobs, which she didn't like, and this seemed like a good time for her to return to Barrhead. In late 1946, she got a good job working at the Imperial Garage for Fred Tremblay, as a bookkeeper. She rented a small apartment above the old Post Office building for a short time; then in 1947, she rented a small house that was owned by Fred Tremblay, and Joyce and Raymond stayed with her for a short time that same year while going to school. She rented this house until about 1950.

During the time that Alice worked in the Red and While store, she invested in a hairdressing business with her friend, Kay Wilson. The business was not very successful and after a few months, they closed the business. Alice lost her investment.

Alice married Swede (Arthur) Warehime in April, 1946 and they continued to live in the Shaper apartment until their daughter, Myrna, was born. They then moved and rented a house owned by the Pickrell family. Swede was a partner in a trucking business. After their daughter, Lynn was born in 1948, they moved again into a house on Railway Avenue that was owned by the Shapers. Joyce stayed with them for a brief time, as did Swede's sister, Margaret, who also attended school in Barrhead. Raymond stayed with Elaine and Ed for a short time while going to school. In 1952, Alice and Swede tired of city life and moved to a homestead in the Moose Wallow area and took up farming and ranching.

When our family started to farm the Duke place in 1938, they found that the land was run down and hadn't been well taken care of by the previous renters. The first crop was very poor, yielding only 600 bushels, worth about 30 cents per bushel at that time. It took a couple of years of summer fallowing to recondition the land and get it in shape to produce some decent crops. Calvin and Harvey did most of the farm work. They also raised quite a few pigs and did quite well after about two years.

The first year, our neighbor, Mrs. Burke, brought over four or five little piglets because their sow had too many and couldn't feed them all. Mother and Irene fed those little pigs milk from a bottle until they were old enough to be put out in the pen on their own. They grew up very fast. Dad sold some of them and he butchered a couple of them. It was a very nice windfall for our family when we were getting started.

The Burke's were wonderful people and were very nice to us. They were always offering their help when we needed it. Harvey liked to spend time at the Burke home with their sons, Elmer, Herman and Roy. Elmer was an amateur mechanic and inventor, which interested Harvey. Elmer, with Herman's help, built a working tractor and a car from old parts. Elmer was very inventive. The whole family went to the Burke's often to visit.

We had an ice house close to the house. In the winter, the boys use to cut blocks of ice from Shoal Lake and put the blocks into a well dug into the ice house. The ice stayed most of the summer (at least until August), and we kept our milk, cream, butter and meat cool all the time. There was no electricity, and refrigerators were unheard of in those days on the farm. Dad and Mother leased the Duke place for about six years, from 1938 to 1944. Dad then leased a school section from the Government in the Mellowdale district, six miles north and one mile west of Barrhead. No payment was required but he had to show some improvements every year. Years ago, it might have been called a homestead. With Calvin and Harvey's help, he built a new house and farm buildings on the new place. It had never been farmed before, was covered with trees and bush, and took a lot of work to clear some of the land and plough it. Calvin and Harvey worked very hard helping Dad settle on this new place.

The new house was very nice. It had two stories with a kitchen, dining room, living room and one bedroom on the main floor, and three bedrooms and a large hall upstairs. It also had a small cellar. It took a couple of years to build this house during the war years when materials were hard to get, or not always available. Harvey and Calvin worked in the sawmills up north and helped to make some of the lumber that was used in the farm buildings and the house. When the house was partially completed, the family moved in and continued working on it. The house was finally completed in 1946. A large entrance porch was added a few years later.

In 1948, Joyce and Raymond were able to stay at home in Mellowdale and go to the Barrhead school by school bus. Joyce was in grade ten and Raymond in grade nine. The schools in the area were consolidated and a school bus system was implemented to bus all the children to Barrhead.

Irene stayed at home with Mother and Dad most of the time and helped on the farm. In 1948, she went to the next town of Westlock to work in a beauty parlor, and while there she met Gus Stefani. They got married in January, 1949 and purchased a farm through the Veteran's plan. The farm was located in the Eastburg district, which wasn't too far from Westlock. They started their family of two sons: Wayne, born in October, 1949, and Murray, born in 1953. Farming wasn't too successful for them, so in about 1958, Gus wanted a change and decided to re-join the army and continue his military career, which took them to many places in Canada, as well as a tour of duty in Germany. Gus was able to retire from the service in 1974, and they went back to Westlock to retire and they built a new house for their retirement years. Gus passed away in May, 1996. Their son, Wayne, passed away in March, 2000.

Joyce finished her schooling in Barrhead, and in 1950 went to Edmonton to attend a business college for one year. After graduating from the college, she went back to Barrhead and started working her first job at the Bank of Toronto, as a secretary. After finishing high school, Raymond decided to stay on the farm to help Dad with the farm work.

Dad and Mother lived on the farm until 1954. Then they retired and built a new house in Barrhead and moved there. Raymond took over the farm. He married Sheila Dick in 1954 and they continued to live on the farm for the next seventeen years. Their family consisted of six sons, born while they lived on the farm: Marty, born in 1954, Barry in 1955, Neville in 1956, Donald in 1958, Brian in 1959, and David in 1962. In 1972, Raymond and Sheila gave up farming and moved to Calgary, where Raymond started his career of selling farm equipment. They stayed in Calgary for about one year then moved to Edmonton where Raymond continued selling farm equipment.

In 1951, Madge left her job at the Imperial Garage and moved to Edmonton. Her first job was for General Motors Parts, and then she went to a car dealer - South Park Motors - where she worked for several years, until about 1956. She was always in an accounting job. Her next job was for a construction company – McCormick Construction – as a bookkeeper.

Joyce decided to move to Edmonton in 1955. She also worked for a car dealer there – Hood Motors – doing secretarial work. Since both Madge and Joyce were now living in Edmonton, they decided to live together and rented an apartment. It was called the Anamoe Apartments. It was a very old hotel that was converted into apartments. As old as it was, it was still very elegant and a nice place to live.

Joyce left her job in the car business in 1956 and went to work for a trade school. The name of it was Chicago Vocational Training Schools, and she was a secretary there as well as a bookkeeper. This job lasted until 1959, when the company decided to transfer her to their Toronto school. She didn't want to go alone, so Madge quit her job and went along. Madge found a good job at a dealership in Toronto and they lived there for a little more than a year. In 1961, Joyce again accepted a transfer to their Minneapolis school. She wanted Madge to go, too, so Joyce's company sponsored both of them so they could obtain visas to move to Minneapolis. The company also offered Madge a job at the school as a bookkeeper, which she accepted.

They didn't like Minneapolis very much, and after eight or nine months, they decided to quit their jobs and go elsewhere. They decided that California was the place to be, so they took a train from Minneapolis – a long three day journey across the northern States and then down the Pacific Coast to San Francisco. It was a great place! They both found jobs immediately and stayed there for the next twenty-five years. While living there, Joyce met and married Hugh Roesch. Finally, in 1985, Joyce, Madge and Hugh sold their home in California and moved to Kelowna, British Columbia, to retire.

Edna and Alex, who had been living in Saskatchewan with their four sons, Eddie, Ernie, Albert and Clarence, decided to move to Alberta where the farming opportunities were better. They arrived in the Barrhead area in 1948. They were very successful in their farming operations in Alberta, acquiring quite a lot of land. They retired to the town of Barrhead in the 1970's. Alex passed away in July, 1979, and Edna passed away in October, 1995.

John Bentz' Daughter Joyce & her husband Hugh Roesch
on their wedding day in 1964 in San Francisco

John Bentz' Daughters Madge and Joyce (Bentz) & Hugh Roesch – 1985 Kelowna

Madge Bentz & Joyce (Bentz) Roesch – 1985

Joyce and Hugh Roesch – Dec 2007

HISTORY OF JACOB AND ANNIE (PEPPLE) BENTZ

By Dan Bentz and Elizabeth Unrath
(Source: Between and Beyond The Benches - Ravenscrag, Vol. 1 (1981).

Jacob's parents, John and Magdelena (Raile) Bentz Sr. lived near Odessa, Russia, where they had a family of four sons and two daughters, Jacob, John, George, Adolph, Magdalena and Ottilie.

The family immigrated to Harvey and Martin, North Dakota, in 1899, where two more sons, Edward and Bennie, were born.

By the time the Bentz brothers had become young men, almost all the farm land in North Dakota had been settled, so in 1914 and 1915 the three older brothers Jacob (Jake), John Jr., George and a sister Magdalena (Mrs. Adolph Kalk) headed for the Ravenscrag, Saskatchewan area where land was readily available for homesteaders.

Jacob and John settled in the Crossfell District, George and Mr. and Mrs. Adolph Kalk settled in the East Fairwell district. Their brother Edward came later on and also settled in the East Fairwell district. Their parents, John and Magdalena Bentz, and their youngest son, Bennie, remained in North Dakota.

Jake was born on July 23, 1884. He married Annie Pepple of Cathay, North Dakota in November, 1912. She was the fifth child in the Thomas and Marie Pepple family, and was born on December 9, 1890. In 1914, Jake and his brother John came to Saskatchewan, Canada to file a homestead on land in the Crossfell District. Jake's homestead at Crossfell was on the N. E. 1/4 5-8-23. John filed on S. W. 1/4 9-8-23. They returned to North Dakota for a short time, then in early 1915 they returned to Saskatchewan to get the homesteads ready. They built a shack, a barn and some fences to hold the livestock. A month later, Jake's wife, Annie, and their two children, Elizabeth and Walter, arrived in Eastend, Saskatchewan by train.

In 1918, an addition was built onto their original house. Daniel, Violet and Ottilie, who died as an infant, were born on the homestead, with a neighbor lady, Mrs. John Koenig, acting as midwife when Violet was born.

Jake and Annie farmed their homestead for many years, except for the years 1928 to 1930 which was spent farming near Golden Prairie, Saskatchewan.

Annie passed away at the age of thirty-nine on January 3, 1930, but Jake continued to farm the homestead and raise his children with the help of his brother John, and John's wife, Matilda, who lived nearby. Jake passed away on June 21, 1954 at the age of sixty-nine years.

Anna (Pepple), wife of Jacob Bentz – 1920's

Jacob & Anna Bentz' daughter Violet – 1929

Violet's daughter Carol Anderson & husband John and Family – 1982
LR: Troy, John, Carol, Creston & Heidie

John & Carol Anderson and Family – 2003
Back LR: Carol & Creston
Middle LR: Troy, John, Mark & Kyran
Front LR: Trisha, Brianna, Heidie & Emmarae

Jacob Bentz Grandaughter Peggy (Rinkey) & husband John Stelter
LR: Tyson, Kyle & Kristi - 1982

Jacob Bentz' GG Grandson Tyson Stelter and wife Sommer's Wedding -2003

Wedding of Tyson Stelter & Sommer Ellis.

Picture above
Back L-R: Nicholas & Kyle Stelter, Sommer, Tyson, Peggy & Jack Stelter, Kristi Sauter & Craig Sauter. Front L-R: Melanie Stelter holding Markus, Annie Stelter (Jack's mother), Jarod & Justis Sauter.

Wedding Attendees

HISTORY OF AUGUST AND ELIZABETH (BENTZ) UNRATH

(Source: Between and Beyond the Benches - Ravenscrag, Vol. 1 (1981).

On November 15, 1908 Elizabeth Bentz was born in Cathay, North Dakota. Her family immigrated in 1915, to Ravenscrag, Saskatchewan, in the Cypress Hills where they homesteaded ten miles north of town. They built a one-room wooden shack and barn.

In 1919, her father, Jacob rented out the homestead and moved his family to Gascoigne, Saskatchewan, as he had heard that the winters were milder there. Here Elizabeth attended a one-room school by walking the two miles or by driving with horse and buggy. In 1923, the family returned to Ravenscrag, as they could not grow enough wheat to make the payments on their half section of land at Gascoigne.

Elizabeth soon began working for the Dr. Dawson family in Maple Creek, Saskatchewan as a housekeeper. In 1926, she received her certificate from Snow's School of Dressmaking in Anamoose, North Dakota. This was a valued skill as money was scarce. She created many fashions for her friends and family throughout her lifetime.

The Bentz family moved to the Golden Prairie District in 1927. Elizabeth began working for her Uncle Christ and Aunt Martha (Pepple) Martin on their farm at Golden Prairie. Here she met her future husband, August, who had homesteaded two miles from there.

August was born January 10, 1907 in Bessarabia, Russia. His parents, Martin and Ida (Stach) Unrath, immigrated to Canada in 1910, settling on their homestead three miles east and one mile north of Golden Prairie. August grew up on this farm and attended school at the Golden Prairie country school.

He met Elizabeth in 1929 and after a brief courtship; they were married on November 24, 1929 at the Rosenfeld Church in the country. Elizabeth received for her dowry, two horses, a cow and a calf. They had a mixed farming operation on August's homestead, which was located on SW 32-15-26 W3rd at Golden Prairie. Due to poor crops during the depression years, August supplemented his income by joining threshing crews.

They were blessed with three children: Phyllis, born in 1930, Bernice, born in 1935, and Gilbert, born in 1938. To accommodate their growing family, they expanded the original two room wooden house to five rooms. All the children were raised around Golden Prairie. They attended services weekly at the Rosenfeld Baptist Church, where August was the Sunday School Superintendent. During the winter months, they traveled the six miles to church by sleigh using blankets and resting their feet on heated rocks for warmth. Occasionally, the congregation would gather at the Big Stick Lake for baptism by immersion.

For entertainment, they would visit their neighbors and August's sister and brothers at their farms around Golden Prairie. When at home, the family enjoyed playing music on their gramophone and also the radio. The children would surreptitiously listen to "Amos 'n Andy" from the kitchen while doing their homework.

August was a great practical joker. His favorite trick was a comfortable armchair he had rigged with a battery that would give unsuspecting guests a wake up shock. Also for amusement, he was an accomplished escape artist. He would let someone tie his hands behind his back and be able to free himself.

August passed away October 19, 1963 at the farm and Elizabeth then moved to Maple Creek, Saskatchewan, where she worked at the local hospital until she retired. Gilbert took over the family farm. Elizabeth delighted in visiting, playing cards and chauffeuring her friends around Maple Creek and Golden Prairie until her demise on May 19, 1990 at the Maple Creek Hospital.

Elizabeth (Bentz) Unrath – 1920's

Elizabeth (Bentz) & husband August Unrath – 1920's

Elizabeth Unrath – 1920

Elizabeth & August's Daughter Bernice (Unrath)
and her husband Wayne Davies - 2002

Elizabeth & August's Daughter Phyliss (Unrath) and her husband Robert Davy

Elizabeth & August's son Gilbert & wife Marion Unrath & Family – 2000
Back LR: Michelle, Allan, Brad, Janice, Gilbert, Whaylin, Yvette, & Chantelle
Front LR: Leon, Vivian, Marion, Lorraine, Jesse, & Bryce

Elizabeth (Bentz) Unrath 80th Birthday - 1988

HISTORY OF WALTER BENTZ

By Dan Bentz. (Source: Between and Beyond the Benches – Ravenscrag, Vol. 1 (1981))

Walter was born in Martin, North Dakota on April 28, 1914. He stayed with his father to help with the farming operations and also worked for various ranchers and farmers. He was a good worker and very kind hearted. In fact, he was willing to give "the shirt off his back".

The sudden death of his father was a severe shock to him. Walter never married and he made his home in his father's house for many years, although the land had been purchased by his uncle, Edward Bentz.

In 1965, Walter moved to Maple Creek, Saskatchewan, where he passed away on September 9, 1973 at the age of 59 years. He is buried in the Maple Creek Cemetery.

HISTORY OF DAN BENTZ FAMILY

written by Dan Bentz
(Source: Between and Beyond the Benches - Ravenscrag, Vol. 1 (1981).

I was born on my father's homestead N. E. 1/4 5-8-23 in the Crossfell district, Saskatchewan, on December 18, 1918 and attended Crossfell School until the end of grade eight, except for the years 1928 to 1930 when I attended Strausfeld School near Golden Prairie, Saskatchewan.

I remember the hard times of the thirties. All that my father could afford to give me as spending money was one, small, silver, five cent piece. This I kept carefully tied in a handkerchief, shoved deep into my pants pocket, as I rode bareback the sixteen or so miles from home to the Murraydale Stampede. Once there, I competed in every foot-race announced (the dash, the three-legged, the gunny-sack, etc.) so that I would have more five cent pieces or dimes for ice-cream and chocolate bars. I remember well a man by the name of Joe Carson, who was the starter for the races and he would shout: "One, two, three--" many times over, causing many false starts before he finally yelled: "One, Two, Three -- Go!" and go I really did, digging my toes into the earth like a greyhound would. Small as I was at that time, I managed to win often and against boys with longer legs than mine. Sometimes I earned as much as fifty cents before all the races were over.

As I became older, the chief recreation for my friends and I were the dances held in Ravenscrag and Eastend Halls and in the one room schools surrounding us; Crossfell, Kealey Springs, East Fairwell, Murraydale, North Bench, South Fairwell, Black Hill and Star Butte.

The farthest trip I ever made to one of those dances was one night when the temperature was -20d F. That night, my friends Jim Chadwick, Russ Henry, George Singleton and I rode my horse to Star Butte School about thirty miles from home. We left right after noon dinner and arrived at Star Butte at about 8:00 PM. Ahh --, youth!!

During the summers of 1935 and 1936 I worked for Eastern Irrigation District near Duchess and Brooks, Alberta. Later I worked for various ranchers in the Piapot, Saskatchewan area.

When the Second World War came, I joined the Saskatoon Light Infantry on May 26, 1942. The S.L.I. was a support group for the 2nd Canadian Infantry Brigade, Canadian Army Overseas. First I was with the Ack Ack and then with Medium Machine Guns Company. I was in action through Sicily, Italy and Holland. In September, 1979 my wife and I attended the fortieth Anniversary of the S.L.I.

On January 4, 1947 I married Phyllis Hussey of Stewart Valley, Saskatchewan. We lived at Blind Bay, British Columbia. We spent the spring and summer of 1948 on the farm home at Crossfell. From October,1950 to March,1966 we ranched at James River, North of Sundre, Alberta. After selling our ranch, we lived in Sundre for two years, where Phyllis had been teaching school since 1953. We now live on our acreage about two miles east of Sundre.

Our family consists of two sons: Donavon Darrell was born in Maple Creek, Saskatchewan on May 9, 1948. He attended Sundre School and University of Alberta where he obtained his Bachelor of Arts in Recreation. He also has his Master in Education Psychology. He married Marion MacLeod of Spruce Grove, Alberta. They live in Stony Plain, Alberta and have two daughters and one son.

Lloyd James was born October 19, 1951 in Olds, Alberta. He has a bachelor of Physical Education degree. He married Brenda Allen in May, 1980. They live in Edmonton, Alberta and have one son.

Jacob's son Dan Bentz in his hockey playing days – 1930's

Dan & his wife Phyllis Bentz and Family – 1988
Back LR: Marion, Donavon, and Lloyd
Middle LR: Phyllis, Dan, & Brenda
Front LR: Lesley, Kristin, Logan, & David

Dan & Phyllis Bentz on their 60th Wedding Anniversary - 2006

HISTORY OF OTTILIE (BENTZ) AND THOMAS PEPPLE

Thomas Pepple, the third child of Thomas and Marie Pepple, was born November 24, 1885, at Carrington, North Dakota. He grew up on a farm in Wells County, Germantown Township. On November 25, 1911, he married Ottilie (Tillie) Bentz. They took up housekeeping in Wells County on a farm located four miles north of Cathay, North Dakota.

To this union five children were born: Ella, Hayden, Bennie, Adeline and Hilbert. On May 21, 1929, Thomas passed away suddenly and is buried at Germantown Cemetery near Cathay, North Dakota. After his death the family stayed on the farm for several years. After being a widow for several years, Tillie married Ben Ruger. He passed away on April 19, 1957. Tillie died January 16, 1971, in Vancouver, Washington, where she had lived for 16 years. Tillie and Ben are both buried at the Williamette National Cemetery at Portland, Oregon.

Ottilie, Jacob & George Bentz – 1900

Ottilie (Bentz) & Thomas Pepple – Wedding 1911

Ottilie (Bentz) Pepple & Family – 1940-1942

Ottilie (Bentz) Pepple & 2nd husband Ben Ruger & her family – 1945

Ella (Pepple) & husband Bill Picket – 1935

Bill Pickett (son of Ella & Bill)

Ottilie's Son Hilbert (Sonny) Pepple & wife Leila (Lee) - 1981

HISTORY OF GEORGE BENTZ AND THERESA (HASE) BENTZ

Written by Theresa Bentz
(Source: Between and Beyond the Benches - Ravenscrag, Vol. 1 (1981).

George Bentz was born in Neudorf, Russia on December 10, 1892. He moved with his parents to Martin, North Dakota in 1898 and took his schooling there. In 1912 he left his home and went to Ravenscrag, Saskatchewan with his sister, Magdalena and her husband, Adolph Kalk, to take up homesteads. George homesteaded on the N. W. 1/4 24-8-23 W 3rd in the East Fairwell district. He worked for different farmers, going as far east as Regina, Saskatchewan, but always returning to his homestead for the winter months. His greatest joy was breaking horses to ride and then selling them.

When Fred Heth was injured in 1927, George gathered his wife, Mary Heth, and her family together and brought them to the Bill Kalk's homestead because Bill's house was bigger than George's shack. He looked after them for four years until Mr. Heth came back and he moved them to the Kearny place and then eventually to the Christ Webber place.

In 1931, George went back to Martin, North Dakota to visit his parents and we were married there in January 1932. I am the oldest daughter, out of nine, of Amelia and Philip Hase. George and I moved back to the farm in Saskatchewan in 1932. Our daughter Ruby, was born June 12, 1933. We farmed there until 1937 when we moved to Shaunavon, Saskatchewan, where we rented a puffed wheat factory. The town wouldn't allow us to puff the wheat at night because of the terrible noise it made. Because we needed a special kind of wheat, which was very expensive, we could not make a go of it and moved back to the farm a year later. We lived on the Fred Bessie place for a time and eventually moved to the Jack Maclean place.

Times on the farm were very hard. Crops dried up and there was just no money to be had, and when there was a good crop, it still wasn't enough to pay expenses. George was always inventing things, but because of the lack of money, he was always a step behind in getting them patented. He made many broom hangers, but ended up giving them away so they never brought in any profit. In later years he invented a way to make cheaper gas, but he passed away before it could be patented.

We always had our own milk cow, and raised our own chickens and turkeys. We were never without a garden and sometimes we had enough to last over winter, and sometimes not. Although we never really went hungry, there was never any surplus.

Our first truck was a "Rugby", which we could use only a few months of the year. We used Bennett buggies with horses. We then advanced to an old Ford and then a Dodge truck.

George was a hail insurance agent for the government for eight or ten years. He also sold fire insurance.

In about 1957 we began a herd of cattle with just a few cattle, but then had to quit in 1960 because George developed heart trouble. We sold our place to Jack Mackie and moved to Medicine Hat, Alberta. George passed away in 1964.

The first years on the farm were good ones because more people lived there and there was always something to do, but in later years, people moved away and life became lonely with no neighbors nearby.

George & his wife Theresa Bentz – on their wedding day in 1932

HISTORY OF EDWARD BENTZ AND NOVELLA (HETH) BENTZ

By Novella Bentz
(Source: Between and Beyond the Benches - Ravenscrag, Vol. 1 (1981).

Edward Bentz was born at Martin, North Dakota, on October 8, 1901. He was one of eight surviving children born to John Bentz and Magdalena Raile.

When Edward was nineteen, he worked on the Great Northern Railroad for two years. In 1923 he decided to go to Ravenscrag, Saskatchewan to visit his three brothers, George, John and Jake, and his sister Magdalena Kalk, who were all homesteading there. He liked the country, so he decided to stay in Canada. He worked on threshing rigs that fall, going as far as Moose Jaw, Saskatchewan, hauling bundles. The crops were very good at that time. He worked for various farmers and as he never went to town much, he was able to save his wages for some time.

I was born at Anamoose, North Dakota on June 24, 1912 and later my parents moved to Saskatchewan. On October 12, 1935, Edward and I were married in the United Church Manse at Eastend, Saskatchewan. Our Minister was Archibald Peebles and our witnesses were my sister Sophie Heth and a friend, Johnny Schaal.

In 1936 we started farming on the S1/2 of 23-8-24 W3rd. This was the old Bill Kalk place. In September, 1936, Ed became a Canadian Citizen. It was hard to make a living at that time on a half section of land, and as the district was well populated, we couldn't rent any more land. However, eventually people started moving out and we were able to acquire more land.

It was hard work for the women when all the neighbours got together to do the threshing; first one place and then the other. There were early mornings, meals and lunches to be served. I helped with the stooking when crops were good and hauled many a bundle to the threshing machine, and helped fork the hay by hand into racks and from the racks into the hay loft.

While the United Church was still in the Crossfell District, we attended services there, but when it was later moved to Frontier, we held services in our homes or in nearby schools.

For pastime, we travelled to all the entertainments that were held in the school houses, such as whist drives and dances. Christmas concerts were looked forward to and the only decorations on the trees were cranberries and popcorn strung together with a needle and thread, and chains made out of crepe paper. Before we were married, Ed and I used to walk to the places we were going. One night we walked to a dance at Crossfell, four miles there and four miles back. There were no excuses of running out of gas or a flat tire in those days!

Our first transport was a horse-drawn Bennett Buggy and a jumper for the winter months. Our first truck was a 1929 Chevrolet. In 1938 we took the sleigh and horses and drove to the North Bench School. Some folks thought we were crazy as it was forty below, but we were young and the moon and stars were shining. As no musicians showed up, Ed played the organ and we all enjoyed ourselves. We often held dances in our home and Ed played for a few dances at East Fairwell. He played mostly waltzes and two-steps, with his favorites being the "Peek-a-Boo Waltz" and "Red Wing". Ed was also a great baseball fan and played many games. Teams were organized with other districts and they would play each Sunday. Baseball diamonds were situated at Medlock Pond, Ravenscrag and Armstrong Creek. We attended most of the Murraydale Rodeos

Ed worked many years at this rodeo collecting money from people who parked their cars at the fence of the arena.

As we lived only one-half mile from the East Fairwell School, we boarded the last few teachers until the school closed in 1952. As their wages were very small, they paid us only fifteen dollars a month for board to start with.

We bought our groceries in Ravenscrag and were very fortunate to have Mrs. Whitefoot as a storekeeper, as she carried us on credit until we paid her in the fall.

On June 15, 1939, our first daughter, Avalon, was born in the Eastend Union Hospital. Mrs. Howe was Matron and the only nurse at the time. On February 12, 1944 our second daughter, Darlene, was born in the old hospital in Maple Creek, with Dr. Dawson attending. The night Darlene came into the world, we were lucky to have a barbed-wire telephone line, so we called Johnny Schaal to come and take care of Avalon, and Glen Olson to come with his car to take me to Maple Creek. As we had no snow yet, we went through Murraydale, but a blizzard came up unexpectedly causing us to lose our way. Even though we had to back-track to find our way again, we finally made it to the hospital in time. Ten days later, we got a speedy ride home with the team of horses and a sleigh.

On July 1, 1944, Ed and some of the neighbors were doing road work with freznos (heavy scrapers pulled by horses) west of Medlock Pond when a cyclone hit. Because of the severe wind and pounding hailstones, the horses broke away. One man crawled into a culvert, but soon got out when the water rushed in. The others turned a wagon box upside down and crawled under, but the wind soon blew this away leaving the men to face the worst. There were a couple hundred head of cattle behind them and it could have been a disaster if the fence hadn't held them. This cyclone blew the roof off Kearney's barn. Ed was happy to see our house still standing, but the granary next to it had blown to pieces. I was shovelling water out of the house as our west window had broken and there was six inches of water and hailstones inside. Avalon was scared and crying. My turkeys and small chicks were all drowned, as well as many gophers since there hadn't been time for them to go for shelter. After that, whenever a thunderstorm came up, Avalon would run for a pillow to hold against the window and made me get a blanket in case it broke again. The crops came on real good that year, but froze in the fall before the crops could be harvested.

Another incident I shall never forget was while coming home from the hay field, Ed was driving the tractor and I was standing beside him leaning on the fender. We were going up a rough steep side-hill with loose gravel, when the fender broke causing me to hit the pulley and it flipped me under the big wheel. I was in the hospital for two and a half weeks with a cracked pelvis and severe burns and bruises, and on crutches for another week, but lucky to be alive. Ed had been after the District to fix this hill, but it took an accident like this for them to realize it had to be done.

Ed was secretary of the East Fairwell School from May, 1946 until the close of the school in 1952, although meetings were held until 1965. He walked the half mile each morning to do the janitor work and always had the school warm when the teacher and children arrived. Our girls attended school here until it closed and then finished by correspondence. They rode to Armstrong Creek for a few months for extra help, but were unable to go in winter because there were no fence lines to follow. Avalon went to Kealey Springs one winter and boarded with Walter and Lillian Schaal. Darlene rode to the West Bench Colony for three years for extra help.

Times were now better; the girls had their own saddle horses, and we had a truck and a new Case tractor. In 1960, our girls and neighbors surprised us on our 25th wedding anniversary and we never knew we could get so many people into a two-room house. In 1975 we celebrated our 40th anniversary. In 1961 our girls had a double wedding. Avalon married Stanley Hough, and Darlene married Donald Bowles.

In 1966 we discovered Ed had glaucoma and was going blind, so we sold our farm to Stanley and Avalon and we moved to Maple Creek. I worked in the Cypress Lodge for ten years and retired in June 1977.

Edward & Novella Bentz' Daughters Avalon & Darlene – Double Wedding 1961
LR: Lavern Bowles, Bernice Unrath, Stan & Avalon Hough,
Darlene & Don Bowles, Donna May, & Ronnie Bowles

Edward & Novella Bentz – 50th Wedding Anniversary in 1985

HISTORY OF BENJAMIN BENTZ

Benjamin Bentz was born in Martin, N. D. in 1903, and Maleda (Fischer) was born in Odessa, Russia. They were married in 1928 in Martin, North Dakota. They raised four daughters: Alice, born in 1930, Agnes, born in 1931, Eldora, born in 1936, and Wendy, born in 1943.

Alice married Severus Lucas in 1950. Agnes married Glen Schiele in 1949, Eldora married Hugo Johnson in 1960, and Wendy married John Blackburn in 1965.

Ben & Maleda Bentz – on their wedding day in 1928

Ben & Maleda Bentz and daughter (in middle) – 1960

Ben & Maleda's daughter Alice (Bentz) & husband
Severus Lucas – 50th Anniversary 2000

Alice & Severus' son Barry Lucas with wife Sandra & son Brent

Alice & Severus's son Scott & wife Mary Lee (Lesmeister) - 2001
LR: Casey, Scott, Jessica, & Mary Lee)

Alice & Severus' daughter Debra with husband John Tibor and son Lucas - 2001

HISTORY OF GOTTLIEB KALK

Gottlieb Kalk was born March 13, 1862, in Katalue, Dobragea in Romania, which was under Turkish Government at the time. He died at the age of 57 years on October 18, 1919. Magdalena (Derman) Kalk was born on July 25, 1865 in Romania. She died at age 33 years on July 14, 1898. They married in 1883 in Romania, and together they had eight children.

Gottlieb was the oldest in a family of nine. Gottlieb's parents were Wilhelm Kalk and Susana (Liebelt) Kalk. Gottlieb's paternal grandparents were Andreas Liebelt and Eva (Kuehn) Liebelt. Following are the names of Gottlieb's three sisters and one brother:

Eva - Born December 2, 1865 (married Christ Schmidt)
Caroline - Born April 17, 1867 (married Johannes (Raushenberger) Ockert)
Maria - Born May 8, 1874 (married Daniel Derman)
William - Born May 8, 1882 (married five times, only the first wife's name is available - Katherine Kaul. They had two sons and one daughter).
They had four other children, Kristof, Amalia, Wilmina and Christina, but their birth dates are not available.

Magdalena (Derman) Kalk came from a family of four. Her parents were Wolfgang Derman and Annie (Holz) Derman. After Magdalena's father Wolfgang died, her mother Annie remarried a Mr. Radetski. Wolfgang and Annie had these four children:

Mary - Married Thomas Pepple
Magdalena - Gottlieb's wife
Sophia - Married Martin Wagner
Daniel - Married Mary Kalk

In the spring of 1885, Gottlieb and his wife Magdalena (Derman) Kalk left Dobruja, Romania to come to Canada. They arrived in Halifax on April 29, 1885, on the S. S. Brooklyn of the Dominion Line. The ship had sailed from Liverpool on April 16. Their oldest child, Annie, was born in Romania and was just an infant when they arrived in Canada. They travelled across Canada and settled in Belgonie, North West Territories. Belgonie was situated near Regina, Saskatchewan, known then as Pile of Bones (1886). They remained in Belgonie until 1896, and then they moved to Martin City, North Dakota. They were one of the first settlers in Martin, North Dakota.

Gottlieb and Magdalena were married approximately fifteen years, from 1883 until Magdalena's death in 1898. She died just twenty days after giving birth to their eighth child, Susan, born June 24, 1898. Their eight children were:

Annie - Born November 28, 1884
Adolph - Born June 17, 1886
Matilda - Born September 22, 1888
Carl - Born February 12, 1890 (Died at age two)

Mary - Born November 21, 1893
Caroline - Born November 17, 1894
Sophia - Born May 12, 1896
Susan - Born June 24, 1898

Annie, Adolph, Matilda, Carl, Mary and Caroline were all born in Belgonie, N.W.T. and only their last two children, Sophia and Susan, were born in Martin, North Dakota.

After Gottlieb's wife Magdalena died, he married Katrina (Weisser) Bertsch. She had three children when she married Gottlieb, daughters Hattie & Rose, and son August. Then they had seven more children together. These are the names of their seven children:

Daniel - Born September 1, 1900
Gustav - Born December 28, 1901
Benjamin - Born March 28, 1903
Martha - Born March 28, 1904
Ester - Born September 30, 1907
Rueben - Born December 7, 1909
Frederick - Born August 25, 1912

Gottlieb died October 18, 1919 after a car/train accident in which Louis Etter, his son-in-law, was driving the car. Katrina never remarried. She died September 26, 1962 in Seattle, Washington.

HISTORY OF MARTHA KALK AND HER HUSBAND LOUIS ETTER

Louis's first marriage was to Theresia Bertsch in Martin, North Dakota. Theresia was a half sister to his second wife, Martha Kalk. Theresia died in North Dakota and then Louis married Martha. They moved to Polson, Montana in 1937, and then moved to Seattle, Washington in 1941. Louis worked at the shipyards during World War II, and later as a garage mechanic until 1958 when he retired. They then moved back to Polson, Montana where they lived until their deaths.

While living in Polson, Martha was a cook at the "Hut Cafe" and then when they moved to Seattle, she was a cook at one of the hospitals and her mother (Katrina Weisser Kalk) came to live with them. All the kids called her Gramma Coco. She never spoke English, only German. She lived with Louis and Martha until her death in 1962.

Louis and Theresia had three children: Jeannette (died in 1998) and two other children who died at birth (names and dates unknown).

Louis and his second wife Martha had two children: Delane Mildred Etter and Arland Henry Etter.

HISTORY OF ARLAND HENRY ETTER - SON OF LOUIS AUGUST ETTER AND MARTHA (KALK)

Arland Henry Etter enlisted in the Navy on September 23, 1943 in Seattle, Washington, the day before his 18th birthday, and mustered out in October, 1946. He was a Gunners Mate and fire controller. His job was to point and aim the guns. The ship was the LST 223 and was 325 feet long and 50 feet wide. It was a landing ship for tanks, etc.

When Arland mustered out, his classification was FC3, 3rd class fire controller. At one point during the war they took a glancing blow by a boat at New Guinea. It was an American cargo ship. They were in a major battle in the "Battle of the Philippines". No harm was done to the ship.

The following were passengers on the S.S. Brooklyn on that voyage:

ANWEILER		HELM		PEPPLE		Georg	4
Heinrich	30	Jacob	46	Michael	31	Christian	infant
Adolf	18	Catherine	44	Wilhelmina	31	Lena	infant
BANEK		Friedrich	25	Gottlieb	18	SEIBOLD	
Christian	30	Elizabeth	17	Johan	5	Friedrich	44
Marian	28	Jacob	11	Friedrich	3	Sophia	40
Elizabeth	7	Johann	5	Magdalene	infant	Barbara	11
Maria	infant	Phillip	3	PEPPLE		Friedrich	11
Caroline	infant	Peter	infant	Thomas	25	Maria	10
BLUMHAGEN		KALK		Maria	22	Caroline	9
Christian	23	Gottlieb	25	Mathilda	infant	Sophia	7
BUTZ		Magdalene	19	PITT (Piedt?)		Edith	1
Elizabeth	53	Anna	infant	Johann	26	Rosina	infant
Johan	28	KRUEGER		Maria	23	SEIBOLD	
Phillip	26	Bertha	18	** August	8	Jacob	51
Margareta	18	LEIDNER (Leitner?)		Caroline	infant	Lena	48
DERMAN		Franz	25	Elizabeth	infant	Friedrich	16
Sophia	18	Elizabeth	23	ROTHACKER		Catherine	11
EDINGER		Maria	infant	Adam	25	Elizabeth	7
Friedrich	35	LEADNER (Leitner?)		Maria	17	Caroline	5
Susanna	35	Georg	60	RUST		Magdalene	infant
Rosina	11	Christina	48	Ferdinand	18	SEIBOLD	
Jacob	10	• Christian	25	SCHMIDT		Johannes	60
Friedrich	8	Georg	18	Josef	33	Caroline	56
Johan	5	• Jacob	17	Catherine	27	Elizabeth	20
Josef	4	Johan	14	Apolina	26	Johann	15
Ludwig	infant	Friedrich	11	A---t(?)	infant	SEIBOLD	
EDINGER		• Ferdinand	10	SCHMIDT		Johann	27
Josef	25	LUTZ		August	30	Julia	21
Rosina	19	Thomas	53	Emilie	35	Samuel	infant
FECHNER		Anna	52	Maria	10	SEIBOLD	
Adam	32	Thomas	17	Louisa	infant	Johann	25
GENTNER		PEPPLE		SEIBOLD		Christina	18
Friedrich	31	Georg	35	Christian	38		
Anna	25	Maria	32	Minna	35		
Andreas	11	Catherine	11	Friedrich	1		
Maria	7	Jacob	8	Johann	15		
Jacob	5	Caroline	5	Jacob	11	* Ruff	
		Friedrich	infant	Christina	8	** Leitner	
		Magdalene	infant	Wilhelm	5	*** Rust	

—3—

Gotlieb Kalk Ship Manifest – April 16, 1885

92

Name: **Maria Kalk**
Birth: abt 1876
Departure: Liverpool, England and
Queenstown, Ireland
Arrival: 9 Nov 1886 - New York
Destination: Manitoba

Name: **Susanna Kalk**
Birth: abt 1842
Departure: Liverpool, England and
Queenstown, Ireland
Arrival: 9 Nov 1886 - New York
Destination: Manitoba

Name: **Wilhelm Kalk**
Birth: abt 1838
Departure: Liverpool, England and
Queenstown, Ireland
Arrival: 9 Nov 1886 - New York
Destination: Manitoba

Name: **Wilhelm Kalk**
Birth: abt 1882
Departure: Liverpool, England and
Queenstown, Ireland
Arrival: 9 Nov 1886 - New York
Destination: Manitoba

Kalk Immigration Records in 1885

Name:	**Gottlieb KALK**
Year of Record:	**1885**
Source/Event:	**Passenger List: Port of Halifax**
Comments:	**Arrived on the 'Brooklyn'**
Age:	**25**
Reference:	**National Archives of Canada: Microfilm Reel No. C-4512 page 7**

Gottlieb Kalk Immigration Records

Gottlieb Kalk – 1900 North Coast Limited Rail Road (2nd from right)

Gottlieb Kalk & Family – 1903
Back LR: Adolf & Matilda
Middle LR: August, Gotlieb, Caroline, Katrina, Hatti & Rose
Front LR: Gotlieb holding son Dan & Katrina holding son Gustav
Middle Front: Susan

Gottlieb Kalk's 2nd wife Karina with Hattie & August

Gottlieb Kalk's 2nd wife Katrina & Kids
Back LR: Rose, Hattie & August
Front: Katrina

Gottlieb Kalk & his friend Frank Putz – 1917

Gottlieb Kalk's Farm near Martin, ND – 1920's

Gottlieb Kalk's Mother Susana (Liebelt) – 1915

Funeral of Susana (Liebelt) Kalk – 1918

Funeral of Susana Kalk attendees: Pictured on page 97.

1. Gustav Kalk, 2. Emma Pepple, 3 Rose Bertch,
4. Mrs. August Bertch, 5. Gottlieb Kalk,
6. Ms Ortman, 7. Mary Derman, 8. Dan Derman,
9. Caroline Derman, 10. Tom Derman, 11. Mr. Kant,
12. Mrs. Kant, 13 Susan (Kalk) Derman, 14. Mary Pepple,
15. Katherina Kalk. Boy in front, unknown.

Funeral of Susana (attendee names)

Martin, Maerz 9,1918

Lieber Bruder Wilhelm,

Ergreife die Feder um Dir eine Trauer-botschaft zu schreiben und Dir mit-teilen dass unsere Mutter heute Abend um 8 Uhr gestorben ist. Sie war ja schon lange krank und konnte nicht mehr leben. Hat noch sehr viel auszuhalten gehabt bis sie endlich erloesst ist geworden durch den Tod.
Sie hat noch nach Dir gefragt, aber ich sagte ihr dass Du geschrieben haettest Du koenntest nicht kommen weil Du kein Geld haettest.
Die Beerdigung soll bis Dienstag den 12. Maerz sein. Nun es waere ja schoen gewesen Du haettest her kommen koennen, und wir haetten Dich auch Telegraphiert wenn Du nicht geschrieben haettest Dass Du nicht kommen koenntest.

(end of p.one)

Ich habe sie noch in diesen letzten paar Wochen etliche mal besucht, bin auch die letzte 2 Tage bei ihr gewesen. Sie sagte noch zuletzt dass sie sich freute mich noch zu sehen. Hat aber noch gewuenscht Sie koennte ihre anderen Kindern noch sehen, aber es waere ja nicht mehr moeglich hier auf dieser Erde. Sie hoffte aber doch dass sie alle ihre Kinder wieder treffen und sehen koennte drueben. Ihre letzten Worte war ein Gebet zu Gott sie zu erloesen von ihren Schmerzen und sie in den Himmel zu nehmen und gleich darauf ist sie entschlafen.
Nun lieber Bruder sollen wir, weil es ihr letzter Wunsch und auch uns zu unserem besten ist, mit ganzem Ernste danach trachten dahin zu kommen.
Sonst sind wir noch alle gesund, hoffen das selbe von Euch so wie auch die anderen alle. G. Kalk

Martin, March 9, 1918

Dear brother Wilhelm,

I reach for the pen to write you a message of sorrow and want to share with you that our mother died this evening at 8 p.m. She was sick for a long time already and could not live any longer. She has had to suffer a lot yet until she was finally released through death. She asked for you but I told her that you had written that you could not come because you did not have the money. The funeral is on Tuesday the 12th. of March. It would have been good if you could have come here but we would also have sent a telegram to you, had you not written us that you could not come.

(end of p. one)

I have visited her several times during the past couple of weeks and also was with her the last 2 days. In the end she told me yet that she was happy to see me. However, she wished that she could have seen her other children too but that would not have been possible on this earth any more. Although she hoped to see and meet all her children yonder. (over there) Her last words were a prayer to God to release her from her pain and take her to heaven. Upon that she 'fell asleep'. (passed away)
Now dear brother we should, because it was her last wish and also for our best, seriously strive to get there.
Aside from that we are all well and hope the same of you. We greet you as well as all the others.
G. Kalk

Gottlieb Kalk's letter to his brother William regarding the death of their mother. Translated from German to English – March 9, 1918

Gottlieb Kalk's Daughters Mary & Caroline – 1897

Gottlieb Kalk's 2nd Wife Katrina with sons – 1930
LR: Ruben & Fred

Gottlieb Kalk's Daughter Caroline & Family
LR: Ralph Burnett, daughter Yvonne, & Caroline (Kalk) Burnett

Gottlieb Kalk's Daughter Caroline & Husband Ralph Burnett – 1930's

Gottlieb Kalk's Daughter Susan Derman & her son Ronald - 1952

Anna (Kalk) Miley – 1904

Anna (Kalk) Miley – 1914 or 1915

Sophie (Derman) Wagner with Sons Robert (L) and Edwin (R) - 1900

Dan & Mary Derman (adoptive parents to Sophie
Derman Wagner) and Son Thomas – 1900

Dan & Mary (Kalk) Derman and Sophie (Derman) Wagner – 1900

Dan & Mary Derman & Mary's brother William Kalk

Dan & Mary Derman seated

Back LR Thomas & Susan - 1910

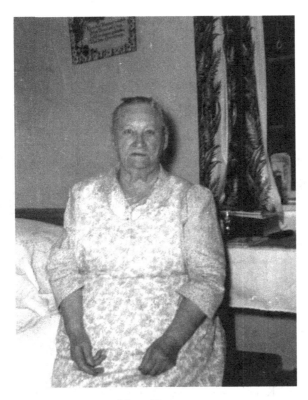

Mary Derman

Mary Derman & her brother William Kalk - 1935

Dan & Rosemary Kalk & Family – 1950
Back LR: Julian, Janet, Louella, Dan, & Rosemary
Front LR: Lorraine, Marvin, Marlene, Natalie, & Barbara

Reuben Kalk and wife Helen – 1955

Reuben & Helen Kalk and Family – on their anniversary in 1987

Katherine Fugere & Lorraine (Kalk) Hooper – taken in 1991

Katherine is Luella Kalk's daughter

HISTORY OF WILLIAM KALK

By Edward Bentz
(Source: Between and Beyond the Benches - Ravenscrag, Vol. 1 (1981).

William (Wilhelm Jr.) immigrated to the United States in 1896 and got his citizenship papers in 1898. He was a carpenter by trade. Bill came to Saskatchewan from Anamoose, North Dakota around 1912 with his nephew, Adolph Kalk. Bill homesteaded the SE1/4 23-823 W3rd. He lived with different people and visited back and forth for a time to Anamoose until 1916, when he built a two-storey house on his land. He broke up eighty acres of land with four horses and a one-bottom plough.

Bill was married in 1903 to Katherine Kaul and they had three children. The oldest boy died in Detroit, Michigan at the age of eighteen from the flu.

In 1914 he married a second time to a girl from the southern states (name unknown). They had no children. Being a carpenter at heart, he built his own house and helped build the Kearney barn, which was the largest barn on the Bench in Saskatchewan.

Bill and his wife found times very hard in Saskatchewan, so they returned to Anamoose, North Dakota where Bill again took up his profession of carpentry. He retired to the Home of the Aged in Bismarck, N. D., in 1957. He was in the hospital six months and passed away September 29, 1958 at the age of 76.

William (Bill) Kalk – 1899

Bill & his wife Katherine (Kaul) Kalk – 1901 or 1902

REPRINT OF A LETTER WRITTEN BY WILLIAM KALK TO HIS NIECE
SOPHIE (KALK) FISHER

St. Louis, Missouri
Feb 18th, 1930

Dear Niece Sophie:

With my best love and good wishes to you and Leona first. I will say that I received your welcome letter and snapshot of yourself and many thanks for same. It looks like you are getting fleshier or maybe it only looks that way on account of the heavy coat you had on. Well, I see the weather conditions are getting better as the days go longer but still only last Friday we had a heavy snow again. But it is all gone again today. We had a real nice day like spring and the snow all disappeared again. No, I have not been working so far as the bad weather practically held everything back. It sure makes things tough when a person is out of work for such a long time and coming nice weather is a Godsend and gives us new hope. I guess there will be plenty of building going on this summer but of course that does not help any this winter and makes it tough going to meet all ends or all bills. I have not heard from Caroline and Ralph for a long time. But I hope they are all fine. Yes, I guess this is a heart breaking time for your Aunt Mary Pepple as three of her dear ones gone in less than a year. Things in this world sure do happen funny as when last I passed there, your sister Mary was already down in bed nerve wrecked and almost anyone thought that saw her at that time that she wouldn't have much longer to live. That is now past seven years, and many healthy ones have gone and she is still alive.

I had a letter from out there saying that Fred was back but that he wants to go to B. C. again. I don't know what will become of them though. Oh, yes, you asked the address of Albert and Freda. Well, Albert's present address is, Albert Kalk, 1517 Harvard Ave., Seattle, Washington and Freda's address is Mrs. Freda Boisvert, 119 - 10 th Ave., N. Seattle, Wash. Her last name is pronounced 'Bovere', her husband is of French decent. Her son, they named him Buster, after Buster Keaton, I guess. And now in regards to relations, my father's name was the same as mine, only he wrote it Wilhelm. My dear girl, you have been away from your relations for so long you almost forgot all their names. Well, yes that will happen. If we could meet only on occasions we then could talk about different things and refresh our memory. No, we had no Adolf and no Herman in our relations as only your brother. My grandfather, that is your Great Grandfather, his name was Ludvig. He lived to a ripe old age as he lived still many years after my father had died. Adolf used to say, my Father's Father's Father is still living. He got to be a grand old man. In his old age he used to make wooden shoes, Holztofd as they are called. When he was past 60 he wore glasses and finally he use two pair of glasses, he put one on top of the other in order to see, but in his later years before he died, he discarded them all and read without any. So I was told he got his second eyesight.

My grandfather had only my father by his first wife and she died then. My grandfather married again, and then came August Kalk, whose family lives in Saskatchewan, Canada, near Earl Gray. Then came Karl but Karl died at the age of 17 with small pox. You had a brother named after him but he died at two years of age of diphtheria, I guess. Then my father had a sister and two more brothers, called Andreas and Michel, but still I don't know what became of them all. This only sister of my father's, she married a man by the name of Duryan, so in years gone by they had gone to Argentina, South America but later they went up to Canada and are now scattered somewhere in Canada with their big family. Andreas and Michel also went to Argentina, South America but I have not heard of them in the later years, if they are still living or if dead by now.

Your father was born in a place in Europe. At the time he was born it was under Turkish Government but later it became Romania. Anyway, after he grew up to manhood he married your mother, but was then drafted into the army for training. In Romania, also Thomas Pepple was married but they could not see it to be married and so do training, and let their wives shift for themselves, so they deserted the Romanian army and fled to America but with them came a chum of your father by the name of Adolf Anviller. This A. Anviller was also a lover of my sister Caroline. Anyway, the three together fled and left their wives and sweethearts behind. Well, later on your father had your mother follow him and your first brother was born in Canada and named after this good friend as a prospective brother-in-law. But to everybody's regret, it never happened. As in the meantime, my sister Caroline was matched up to another boy called Raushenberger, but he got to go under the name of Ockert in Romania on account of him being an adopted son of the old Ockerts, and he got their estate after the old people had died, but still I wished as well as the others had wished that the estate, which was not much, stayed in the Ockert family with Ockerts and that my sister had come along and married the man that loved her, as that Romania has been one damn thing after another, as the Americans say, it is mostly always between life and starvation over there.

My own son, the third born, I had named him Herman but he only lived eleven days and died. We had at that time a minister, his first name was Herman so that is all the Herman's I have ever heard of in our relations. If you have an uncle named George or Herman they are not from the Kalk's side, and I guess you know that your grandmother's name was Holz before she married Derman. She had three girls and your Uncle Dan, Aunt Sophie, Mary and your mother. Then Mr. Derman died by heart stroke and she married Samuel Ratezke, had two more girls, but they died. So you see it would not hardly be there. My mother had one brother living, his name was Michel Liebelt. He died, though, before my mother died. One of my mother's sisters married a Bernt that put me cousins to the Bernts that you got acquainted with.

I will now close or else this letter will be a book of history. People sure do scatter. As I hear, your brother, Adolf, is planning to go to Peace River in the future. With my best love and good wishes to you and Leona from your Uncle.

William Kalk
3631 Botanical Ave
St. Louis, Missouri

HISTORY OF ADOLPH KALK AND MAGDALINA (BENTZ) KALK

(Source: Between and Beyond the Benches - Ravenscrag, Vol. 1 (1981)).

Adolf Kalk was born on June 17, 1886 in Belgonie, North West Territories which was near Regina (known then in 1886 as Pile of Bones). He was the second child in a family of eight. When Adolf was ten years old, in 1896, his parents moved to Minot, North Dakota. From there they went on to homestead land at Martin, North Dakota. This is where Adolph met Magdalena Bentz. Marriage was proposed and on November 7, 1907, they were united in marriage in a double wedding ceremony along with his sister Matilda Kalk, who married John Bentz. It's amazing to think that both couples each raised a family of eleven children.

Magdalena was born in Neudorf, Ukraine, Russia in 1890. Her family immigrated to America, landing in New York in 1899. The whole family had contacted small pox, except Magdalena and her father, John Bentz, Sr. The two of them stayed in a hotel in New York while the remainder of the family, John, George, Jakob and Matilda (Tillie) were in quarantine for one month. The family then moved on by train to North Dakota to homestead. The younger brothers, Adolph, Ed and Ben were born in North Dakota. There apparently were more children in the family who died in infancy.

In 1913, Adolph and Magdalena brought their family of three children to Ravenscrag, Saskatchewan, where they took up a homestead on the SE1/4 24-8-23 W3rd. They had shipped their horses, machinery and other bare necessities by train to Ravenscrag. The oldest three children were Viola, Vernon and Vera. Six more children were born in Ravenscrag Saskatchewan: Adeline, Lorraine, Willard, Bert, Kenneth and Raymond. In 1932 the family moved from the Bench area to Pontrilas, Saskatchewan, where two more children, Eunice and Bruce, were born. Here they purchased a farm and lived there until 1949 when they retired to Victoria, British Columbia. They lived there for about twelve years and then their final years were spent in North Surrey, B. C. They were a well travelled couple and kept very close family ties with their children.

Adolph passed away in August, 1974 at 88 years of age. Magdalena passed away in March, 1976 at 86 years of age. Their youngest son, Bruce, was killed in a car accident at Sooke, British Columbia at 22 years of age.

* * * * *

The following is a poem written by Adolph Kalk,
(Sung to the tune of "Oh My Darling Clementine"),
On the occasion of the 60th Wedding Anniversary of
Adolph and Magdalena on November 7, 1967.
(Source: Between and Beyond the Benches - Ravenscrag, Vol. 1 (1981)).
MR. AND MRS. A. B. KALK FAMILY

HISTORY IN SONG

In the year of nineteen seven
On a cold November day,
Two young people made a promise
To love, cherish and obey.

How we planned and worked together
And we knew of no defeat
On our farm in North Dakota
Milking cows and growing wheat.

So then one day quite unexpected
A visitor from out somewhere
Brought to us a little bundle
And presented to us a little girl.

She was such a lovely baby
With her eyes of brownish blue
Viola Athena we did name her,
She was a comfort for us two.

Oh we were so proud and happy
As we watched our darling grow
Then one day we got a visit
From the stork with number two.

It was a brother for our darling
And a joy to Mom and Dad,
And we named him Vernon Cleveland
A sweeter baby we could never have had.

As time went on we were richly blessed
With three darling baby girls -
Vera, Adeline and Lorraine,
They were all our pride and gain.

As our farming was thriving
We figured some more help should be arriving,
Then it started out with number four.
Bill, Bert, Ken and Ray
So that did balance the score

After ten years of silence
There was no more hope for Mom and Dad,
Then came the best news we ever had,
Eunice and Bruce brought us much pleasure
To us they were a wonderful treasure.

Each little child God sends our way
Is like a piece of soft new clay
'Tis ours to mold and shape and trim
To make it pleasing unto Him.

Each little thing we do or say
Makes an impression day by day,
On every growing mind and heart
Forming a pattern from the start.

Oh what a solemn trust is ours
How we must guard these precious hours,
Too soon this clay will be as stone
Our change is gone - our child is grown.

If we but take the time to pray
And seek God's guidance every day,
He'll give us strength and wisdom too,
To help our family grow strong and true.

So this concludes the family tree --

*   *   *   *   *

MOM AND DAD
(Poem written by Adolph Kalk on their
65th Wedding Anniversary in the year 1972)

We were sure so very happy
But the years have gone so fast
Now we live back in the memories
Of the years long in the past.

Now our family all have left us
Some have children of their own,
But every week they send a message
To their parents who are left alone.

We pray that God will bless our family
And keep them from want and fear.
We hope they will not forget their parents,
As they are getting up in years.

So at last Good Luck we'll add to
What their future will ever be,
But we hope they will remember
That their parents live in B. C.

Adolph & Magdalena (Bentz) Kalk – on their wedding day, November 1907

Magdalena (Bentz) Kalk taken about 1907

Adolf & Magdalena Kalk & Family – 1967
Back LR: Bert, Lorraine, Adaline, Raymond, Viola, Kenneth, Vera, & Eunice

Adolph & Magdalena Kalk – 60th Anniversary 1967

Adolph & Magdalena's Daughter Viola – 1950's
LR: Viola, Einar Erickson, & their daughter Janet Erickson Adkins

Adolph & Magdalena's Sons: L-R Ken, Bert, Ray, & Vernon – 1982

Adolph & Magdalena's Daughter Vera at age 95 - 2006

Adolph & Magdalena's Daughter Lorraine at age 91 - 2007

Adolph & Magdalena's Family

Adolph's Family -1970
LR: Bert, Lorraine, Ken, Eunice, Vernon, Adeline, Ray, and Vera
Front: Aunt Sophie (Kalk) Maples

Willard (Bill) (formerly Kalk) Carlson & wife Caroline –
in their Greenwood B.C. home -1992

Kenneth Kalk (Adolph & Magdalena's son) and wife Edith – Wedding 1944

Kenneth & Edith Kalk & daughters Valerie & Sharon – 1960's

Raymond Kalk (Adolph & Magdalena's Son) and girlfriend Irene
Schellenberg – picture of their band "Irene and the Goodnighters" –
Raymond on far left, Irene on keyboard - 2001

Adolph & Magdalen's granddaughter Louella (Kalk) & her husband
George Denison – 50th Wedding Anniversary in 2006

HISTORY OF ADELINE KALK

FOR MY SONS, GREG AND GLENN
My Biography
By Adeline Dorothy (Kalk) Sutton

I was born in 1915 in a small town called Ravenscrag, in Southern Saskatchewan, Canada. I was the fourth child of eleven children. My father (Adolph Berthold Kalk) was born in 1886 in Belgonie, Saskatchewan, near Regina and at the time it was called "Pile of Bones". My grandparents came from Romania and settled in Saskatchewan which was the North West Territories until 1905. When my dad was ten years old he moved with his parents, in 1896, to Martin, North Dakota, U. S. A.

My mother (Magdalena Bentz) was born in Odessa, Russia in 1890. Because of the revolution in Germany, her great grandparents had moved from Germany to Russia many years before she was born. The family immigrated to the United States in 1899. They landed at Ellis Island in New York, and travelled across the country by train to North Dakota.

My dad and mother met in Martin, North Dakota, and were married in 1907. Mother was seventeen and Dad was twenty one. In 1913 my parents, with their three children, Viola, Vernon and Vera, moved to Ravenscrag, Saskatchewan. This is where I was born. Lorraine, Bill, Bert, Kenneth and Raymond followed me.

My parents received land through a Government Act for $10.00. This was a homestead. My dad was a farmer. He built a two story house and a red barn on the land. He had to acquire horses and machinery. He also invested in cattle, pigs and poultry. We grew all our own vegetables. We required water so a well was dug. Wells were also used for refrigeration. Food was hung in a container down the well near the water to keep it Cool. We had outdoor toilets. Electricity came many years later. A school was built as well as a church. Teachers came from various parts of the province and taught grades one to eight. Lorraine and I sang in the church choir. Dad was the conductor. We all worked hard. We learned to ride horses and milk cows. Dad did very well financially. He later purchased a brick two story house and red barn with more land to farm.

Dad bought a piano and Vera and Lorraine took lessons. Vi could play by ear. She had a special talent. I Liked to sing. The area we lived in was called Cypress Hills. Every summer we would attend a picnic and rodeo at a nearby place called Murrydale. Mother would pack a lunch and Dad gave us all five cents for an ice cream cone - a great treat. Lorraine and I would always win "the three legged race". This is where the left leg of a contestant was tied to the right leg of the other contestant. Vernon was the only one of the family who rode in the rodeo.

In 1929 "the crash" came and we lost everything. This was a difficult time for everyone. There was a drought at this time and crops wouldn't grow and also there were wind storms which blew the land away.

In 1932 we moved to Pontrilas, Saskatchewan, a small town in the northern part of Saskatchewan. My Dad's sister, Aunt Annie, and her husband (Uncle Sam Miley) operated the only hotel in Pontrilas. They gave all our family lodgings until Dad bought land and built a house and barn. We were still farming with horses. In 1935 Dad was able to purchase a tractor and a combine. This was a plus for farmers. Most farmers grew wheat, oats, barley, and rye. I was seventeen when we moved to Pontrilas and I finished high school in Nipawin, a town twelve miles from our home. My dream was to become a teacher but there were no finances for education for any of us. We all worked on the farm. It was very hard work but we enjoyed life the best we could. Lorraine and I joined a softball club. Our team competed in all the nearby towns. Our school teacher was our pitcher. We had a good team and usually won. Lorraine played second base and was our top hitter. I played short stop and batted fourth position. I was a home run hitter. We all had uniforms.

My youngest sister, Eunice, and brother, Bruce, were born in Pontrilas. In 1937 my sister Vi, who previously moved to Longview, Washington, came for a visit with her husband, Einar Ericksen, and their daughter, Janet. She was two years old. In 1990 Janet became ill with Alzheimer's disease and she asked Dr. Kevorkian to assist her to die. She was only fifty four years of age. It was a sad time for all of us.

Lorraine went with Vi and family to Longview. I really missed her as we were so close. We did everything together. We were only seventeen months apart in age. Lorraine never married although she was engaged to a man who loved to gamble. She had a good job so she didn't need a man.

In 1939, when I was twenty four years old, Brother Bill and I went to Longview, Washington, to visit Vi and Lorraine. My brother Vernon went to Longview in 1936. He was working at Weyerhauser, a large lumber company. I stayed in Longview for nine months. I had a visitor's permit. I couldn't work as I wasn't a citizen. Bill went back to Pontrilas. After the nine months when the permit ran out I went to Victoria, British Columbia.

Our cousin, Lucille Miley, was in Victoria. She was a cook for an English millionaire, Mr Opie, who came to Canada many years before. He had a lovely home right on the beach in Oak Bay. It was nice. I was able to stay with Lucille. When Mr Opie's maid got married I got her job. It was a nice easy job. My salary wasn't that much but we had good food. Lucille and I had separate rooms with a bath. There was a living room we were privy to as well. Mr. Opie gave me away when I married your Dad. This is where I met your Dad.

Your Dad lived in Oak Bay not far from where I lived. Your Dad was a friend of our milkman so he asked your Dad to call me. Your Dad was tall, dark and handsome and dressed nicely. We dated about a year and got married on November 15, 1942. We were married at the Baptist Church where I took you boys to Sunday school. This is when my sister Vera came to Victoria with her daughter, Louella, to be my Maid of Honor. Vera raised Louella as a single mother.

In 1956, Louella married George Denison and we had their wedding reception in our home. George was a Police Officer. Lou worked for a finance company for many years. They raised two sons, Brock and Robert. They have had a good marriage.

Your dad's parents were very nice people. I got along with them very well. Your grandmother enjoyed beer, so occasionally she and I would go by bus to a beer parlor. We had a very nice wedding. We went to Vancouver, British Columbia, for a week for our honeymoon. Then we rented an apartment and bought a used car, a 1927 Chevrolet. Your dad was a carpenter and worked with his father and his two brothers, Clavel and Ronald. Their company was called Sutton and Sons. They built mostly houses. Your dad's weekly wage was $50.00. I got a job at a five and dime store called Kresgies, as a salesperson. I was in charge of ordering products. My wages were $15.00 per week.

Before your dad joined the Canadian Navy (the war started in September, 1939), we took a trip to Longview, Washington, so your dad could meet my sisters, Vi and Lorraine. Everyone liked your dad. I was so lucky to have met him. Rather than being drafted your dad joined the Navy in 1943. He had to make a dove-tailed drawer. He passed the test and became a shipwright with a Petty Officer rating. He later got a Chief's rating. He was stationed at Halifax, Nova Scotia. I went to Halifax as well, and was there for two years, 1943 to 1945.

We rented an apartment with another couple, the Pringles. Mr. Pringle was in charge of all the food for the servicemen in the Dockyard. He gave me a job as a manager of the Officers' Canteen. The pay was $20.00 per week. The Government gave me $95.00 per month. Your dad got about $50.00 per month for living expenses. Your dad was sent to Bermuda for six months. I was not allowed to go. I had my job and the Pringles were very good to me. Mr. Pringle did most of the cooking as he was in the restaurant business. We met some very enjoyable Navy people. We would go to dances and enjoyed life as much as we could. While we were in Halifax we took a bus trip to New York. We enjoyed seeing all the sights of interest. Then from Halifax we went to Pontrilas, Saskatchewan so your dad could meet my parents. We only stayed a week as we were anxious to get back to Victoria to start a normal life. As a point of interest, your dad's two brothers, Clavell and Ronald, were in the navy as well. Three of my brothers, Vernon, Bill and Bert, were also in the services. Vernon was in the United States Navy. He was a Gunner on a naval ship and was a Petty Officer. He was stationed mostly in the South Pacific. Bill was in the army stationed in Germany, and Bert, also in the army, was stationed at Regina. He didn't go overseas as he had broken his ankle. Luckily for our families they all survived the war. We were lucky you two boys were not drafted to go to the Vietnam War.

When we arrived back in Victoria in 1945 we lived with your dad's parents in Oak Bay. Your dad worked for his dad and his two brothers, Clavel and Ronald. Your grandfather taught them all carpentry.

Business was good. Your dad bought a lot quite near the downtown area. It only cost $300.00 under the G. I. Bill for servicemen. He built a house with two bedrooms, two bathrooms, with the help of his brothers, in their spare time, on Bank Street. We bought all new furniture and a refrigerator, just new on the market. It was wonderful, after seven years, to have a place of our own.

In 1946 we bought a new Ford car and paid cash for it. That summer we took a trip to San Diego, California. We visited all the places of interest. Gas was reasonable at the time. My sister Vera went with us. We also went to Tijuana, Mexico, which was like another world to us. We liked San Diego. It is hard to believe we have lived here since 1957. At this time we seemed settled and decided to start a family. Greg, you were born on Bank Street in 1949, a cute little baby weighing seven pounds.

In 1949, my dad retired from farming. He and Mother, with Eunice and Bruce, moved to Victoria. Eunice was fourteen and Bruce was twelve. Bruce was killed in a car accident in 1959. He and a friend had been to an "All Sooke Day" and driving home he missed a curve, crashed, and was instantly killed. His friend survived. I came to his funeral from Dan Diego.

My parents bought a home in Victoria. Dad bought and sold real estate. He did very well. He was a smart business man. It was so nice to have my parents living in Victoria. Mother was so good to help with you two little guys.

We sold our home on Bank Street and bought a home that needed many repairs, on Lovett Street. Your dad being the carpenter he was, made many improvements. This was in 1952 where you, Glenn, were born. You were a cute little guy and weighed seven pounds.

In 1954 we sold the home on Lovett Street and your dad built a lovely home in Oak Bay on Plumer Street. This is where you went to school, Greg. Then in 1957, we sold everything and moved to San Diego, California. Greg, you were eight years old and Glenn, you were five. Your dad bought a station wagon in Portland, Oregon, so we took a few belongings and not much money. We arrived in San Diego in August, 1957. We booked into a hotel with a kitchen. We then bought a home in Allied Gardens. It was affordable for us, and near a school.

Before leaving Canada we had to apply for visas to live and work in the U. S. We had to live in the U. S. for five years before we could become citizens. We took classes to learn about the government. You boys automatically became citizens. You both went to school at Lewis Elementary; grades one to eight. Greg, you went to Hoover High and Glenn, to Patrick Henry. We soon made friends with our neighbours, mostly young people raising families. Both of you went to the Y.M.C.A to learn to swim and joined the Swim Club. I was able to take you to the swim meets mostly every weekend, as by this time; we had purchased a second car, a lavender 1965 Chevrolet convertible. It was a lovely car. Over the years your dad prided himself in buying nice cars.

Your dad joined the Carpenters' Union and had no trouble getting a job with Hart & Sons. Later he worked for American Housing Guild doing maintenance. This was an enjoyable job and he also did maintenance for the owner, who was Jewish and amicable. He had come from New York and bought up property, mostly for track homes. After twenty five years on the job, and at age sixty two, your dad retired. He received a pension from the Carpenters Union and Social Security for both of us. At age sixty five, we also got a pension from Canada based on the number of years we had lived there.

I was a stay-at-home Mom for most of the time. I did alterations for a cleaning firm. I also sold Emmons Jewellery. I did this by going from door to door. I also sold Avon Products in Dal Cerro. I kept busy and tried to be a good Mom to both of you. Greg, when you graduated from Hoover, we gave you a down payment on a new 1968 red Mustang. You met Pat at a Junior College and you and Pat took a trip to Canada to visit relatives. You married Pat in 1969. You were twenty years old and you made a good life with Pat, raising two very lovely children, Carrie and Daniel.

I am sure you remember all the swim meets we went to during the summers as you were growing up. We had nice times together. We also visited a lot of amusing places in Southern California, like Disneyland, etc.

Greg, you also worked as a life guard during the summer months. Glenn, when you graduated from Patrick Henry High, we gave you a down payment on a green van. You liked music and took guitar lessons, and it paid off as you are currently teaching music in Poway, where you live. You have been good sons and I love you both.

We bought an Airstream Travel Trailer in 1975. We toured most of the U.S.A. and a lot of Western Canada. A lot of our relatives live in Victoria. My brother, Ken, lives in Langley, B.C., and Brothers Bert and Ray live in Saskatchewan. We travelled for twenty five years with our travel trailer and also took several cruises. For our 50th Wedding Anniversary, we took a cruise through the Panama Canal. The Canal was one of the highlights of our many cruises. We visited the Hawaiian Islands four times. They are beautiful. We also went to Bermuda.

In 1979, we sold our home on 49th Street and bought a triple-wide mobile home in Santee, California. We bought new furniture and, your dad being so talented added many extras. We have enjoyed living there. It is an accommodating park. In 1981, your dad retired and we took several more trips with our trailer. We pulled the trailer with a Ford truck. After your dad retired, we took a trip to Graceland and the Grand Ol' Opry in Tennessee. In 1992 we sold our truck and trailer and bought a Buick. We also took several trips. It was quite a change staying in motels and eating in restaurants.

One very nice trip we took was flying to New York and taking a bus tour to Niagara Falls and Toronto, Canada.

As I write this, it is now 2006, and I just want to say a few things about your dad. He is a wonderful husband to me. We have now been married for 63 years. Your dad never got irritable or angry. Almost every day he tells me how much he loves me.

I hope you both realize what a wonderful dad you have. We both tried to be good parents and we love you so very much.

Your Mother, Adeline

Adolph & Magdalena's daughter Adeline (Kalk) & her husband
Frederick (Mack) Sutton – On their wedding day in 1942

Adeline (Kalk) & Mack Sutton - 1991

HISTORY OF EUNICE KALK CATTERALL

EUNICE'S MEMOIRS

On November 7, 1907, our parents, Adolph Kalk and Magdalena Bentz got married. On the same day John Bentz and Matilda Kalk were wed in a double wedding ceremony. Their marriages took place in Harvey, North Dakota. It's nice to remember that both families had a reunion in 1982, and there were 206 family relatives present. There were many who were absent. This reunion took place in a small community called Summerdale, near Barrhead, Alberta, where the Bentz family lived after moving from Ravenscrag, Saskatchewan. The two families each had eleven children so they have the same relatives.

My mother's dowry was four cows. My parents farmed in North Dakota. Their children, Vi, Vern and Vera were born there. They then moved to Ravenscrag, Saskatchewan in 1914. They farmed near Ravenscrag. Their next children, Adeline, Lorraine, Bill, Bert, Kenneth and Raymond were born there on the farm. After a few years of drought conditions on the prairies, they moved further north to Pontrilas, Saskatchewan in May, 1932.

Dad bought a quarter of land a mile south of Pontrilas. The family stayed at Uncle Sam and Aunt Annie's hotel in Pontrilas until a house was built on the farm. Adeline, Lorraine, Bill, Bert, Ray and Ken were home at that time.

I was born at Armley, Saskatchewan, just six miles from Pontrilas. I was the first member of our family to be born in a hospital. It seemed strange to be the tenth of eleven children and our family was never all home at one time. My young brother, Bruce, was born in 1936.

In 1937, Mom, Dad, Ken, Ray, Adeline, Bruce and I drove to North Dakota to see my mother's parents. Dad had a very old truck at the time. Ken and Ray had to ride in the back of the truck. I don't know how we all fit into the front of the truck, but we managed. The trip was very long from where we lived. In those days not too many of the roads were paved. They were mostly gravelled roads.

Vern came to Pontrilas from Ravenscrag with the family in 1932, and he and Cliff Reese stayed in a shack on the property that dad had bought. The shack is still on the farm and Ray, who now lives on the property, uses it for storage.

In 1934, dad bought a house from Shindles and Vern moved the house with horses to the farm, no easy job, I'm sure. This was a lovely two story home. The bedrooms were all upstairs. There was one big bedroom where the boys slept. There was no running water and, of course, there was an outhouse. This was not rare as this is how everyone lived.

Vern worked for the Boxhall family for a short time and then he left in 1935 and went to Longview, Washington. In Longview he worked for Longbell and Weyerhaeuser. He joined the American Navy in 1941 and spent the war years in the Navy. In 1947, he met and married Rosella Kluthe. He and Rosella bought a 17 acre farm in Beaverton, near Portland, in the mid 1950's. Vern had a garbage route and also raised cattle. We all have many wonderful memories of the years we visited them while they were on that farm.

They adopted their son, Ernie, in 1961. Then in 1965 they bought the Bell Motel in Bellingham, which they owned and operated for several years. Then they sold the motel and bought a home in Bellingham where they lived until 1992. Then they moved to a retirement complex in Bellingham and lived there until Vern passed away in October, 2004. Rosella passed away in 2007.

Earlier, my sisters Vera and Vi had gone to see Aunt Caroline in Montana. Vera came to Pontrilas and then in the early part of 1934 went to Moose Jaw, Saskatchewan. Vi ended up in Longview where Aunt Sophie was living. In 1937, Vi, her husband, Einar, and their daughter, Janet, came to Pontrilas to visit, and took Lorraine and Bill with them when they returned to Longview, Washington. Lorraine and Vern boarded together when she moved there. Vera moved from Moose Jaw to Rosetown, Saskatchewan with her daughter, Louella, and lived there until 1942 when they moved to Victoria, B. C., as Adeline had asked Vera to come and be her bridesmaid at her wedding.

Sister Vi was a marvel! There wasn't anything that she couldn't do. She had many jobs during her working years. She took a course in barbering. She always said she could work like a man. She worked as a welder during the war. Vi and her husband, Einar, had a lovely home in Portland. Vi could sew beautifully. She was a painter of homes. She also did waitress work. She worked in a hospital doing menial jobs for sometime.

In 1944, Mom, Dad, Bruce and I took a train from Regina to Victoria, B. C. On the way we visited so many of Mom and Dad's "old" friends. They seemed so old to me since I was only nine years old, but they were people our parents knew from years gone by.

We visited Vera and Lou in Victoria. Mom was always so kind to we kids, and she would buy things for us that we wanted, within her meager finances, of course. In Regina Mom bought me a pair of high heeled shoes and overshoes. Vera threw them away as she felt it was embarrassing to see me with these adult shoes. I was so heart broken.

Then we took a bus to Portland. We stayed from November to April with Vi, Einar and Janet. While we were there, Dad worked for Montgomery Ward, a department store. He would get special buys. I can remember a pair of shoes that he brought home for me. They were "almost" the same as the other pair, although a bit too small, but I wore them anyway. He also bought two dresses - one for me and one for Janet. They were a pretty blue. Janet's fit her just right and mine had to be shortened. There was a beautiful flower near the bottom and it had to be turned over half way to be hemmed up. Janet and I had so many laughs about that as I was so jealous of her. She was eight months younger than I was.

We saw a lot of relatives that winter. Bruce and I went to school during our time in Portland. The school had shifts. We started at 8:00 AM until 1:00 PM. We finally had to leave and arrived back home in Pontrilas on April 24, 1945, the day that President Roosevelt died. We soon got back to our "normal" living.

Janet and I, and our families, enjoyed seeing each other through the years. We had so much in common as we each had three boys when we married. Each time we went to Portland where Janet, her husband, Ron, and sons, Neil, Norman and Ronald lived, we would stay with them and have such a good time. What an "up" person Janet was. Janet loved for me to get into her kitchen and prepare meals for the whole gang. Vi and Lorraine would be with us a lot, too. We had such good discussions and conversations, and a lot of times we played games.

Janet and Ron were married in 1955. In 1957 they went to France as Ron was in the army and he played for an army band. Their first son, Neil, was born in Orleans, France, in 1958. After two years in France they went back home to Portland. They loved France and went back for a visit in the 1980's. Neil went to Paris to attend university when he was through high school.

Their second son, Norman, was born in 1961 and their youngest son, Ronald, was born in 1964. Janet died in 1990. She was Dr. Kevorkian's first patient. There was much controversy about that case. She had told us she would be doing something to end her life as she had Alzheimer's disease and didn't want her children and grandchildren to see her the way she would be in a matter of time. She is so missed by all who knew her. My husband, John, and I went to Portland the day that Neil told us Janet was gone. We had to tell Janet's mother, Vi. This was very hard on Vi, who was living in an apartment at the time, caring for herself. Her husband, Einar, passed away in the year 1975. Several years later Vi went to live in a nursing home and passed away in 1996, at the age of 88.

Vi had a son, Ralph, at a very early age and the father and his family raised Ralph. Our mother said she would raise him but she had just had baby, Ken, and she was talked out of keeping the child. Ralph was 30 when he found Vi. He was married with two children. Ralph's marriage ended and he moved to Portland. He did commercial landscaping in the Portland area and did very well at it. He was very good to Vi. One time he took Vi to Hawaii, which must have been a wonderful trip for both of them. Unfortunately and very sadly, Ralph was murdered in Portland a few years later. It was very mysterious until a suspect finally admitted that he had killed Ralph. The suspect was in a jail in California where a "stoolie" was put into the same cell with him and the suspect admitted his deadly deed. I don't remember the details but I do believe that the "suspect" got time for the murder. It was a very sad ending for Ralph and another devastating blow to Vi. Poor Vi wasn't dealt the best hand in her life as both her children had such sad endings.

It was wonderful that Vi had Janet and Vera had Lou, as they produced playmates for me. Ken and his wife, Edith, had two daughters, Valerie and Sharon, and we all had such good times together. All my cousins are special. Adeline's two sons, Greg and Glenn are two great guys, and so are Bert's three sons, Larry, Don and Brent. I have a great rapport with all my nieces and nephews. Unfortunately we didn't see Bill's family when they were growing up. We weren't around Ray's children, Woody and Shay, as they grew up in Saskatchewan. But I would probably have taken them in hand, too, if we had lived near them.

Lorraine, who lived in Longview, Washington, was very close to Janet's family and her sister, Vi. They all spent many weekends together, as Lorraine was still working. Lorraine had moved to Longview, Washington in 1937. She did house work for a short time, then moved into the Baltimore Hotel where she worked as a waitress. In 1938 she worked at Weyerhaeuser for $5.00 a day. She worked at the planer mill, and she worked with lumber that was stacked six high. This was done with electric machines which tied the ends with twine. She got a bonus each month for putting through the most tied stacks.

Lorraine also taught piano for eight years. This she did on weekends and evenings, depending on her working shifts at Weyerhaeuser. She received $1.50 for a 45 minute lesson per student. Then in 1946 she quit Weyerhaeuser and went to work for Longview Fiber, in the office. After working there for 35 years she retired in 1981.

That year our son, Bruce, was stationed in Petawawa, Ontario. He was in the army and taking paramedics. He came home to pick up our 1974 Oldsmobile, and Lorraine drove back East with him. On the way, they stopped at Pontrilas to see Ray and his wife, Dot, and Bert and his wife, Lois. They had a wonderful trip and saw many sites in Eastern Canada.

Our parents celebrated their 50th Wedding Anniversary in 1957 in Victoria, with many Baptist Church people attending. Another gathering for their celebration was held in Portland. We had a dinner at Paul Robert's Restaurant and then a party at Vern and Rosella's. Many relatives attended and all the family was there, except Bruce and Bill.

Ten years later, in 1967, they celebrated their 60th Anniversary, which was held in Surrey, B. C. Many friends and relatives gathered. Three of Dad's sisters, Aunt Tilda, Aunt Sophie and Aunt Susan came to attend the celebration. After the dinner most of the guests came back to our home in Coquitlam. Our mother was very upset that we didn't invite her and dad. We thought they were too tired. Mom said that they wanted to be where the "action" was.

In 1972 Mom and Dad's 65th Anniversary was held at Vern and Rosella's in Bellingham. Many relatives and family members came. At the same time we were celebrating Vern and Rosella's 25th Anniversary.

In 1939 Adeline went to Victoria and worked with Cousin Lucille Miley in a millionaire's home. Lucille was the cook, and Adeline had the job as a maid. They were very nice people to work for and good to their employees. Adeline met her future husband, Mack Sutton, in Victoria and they married in 1942. They moved to Halifax for almost two years while Mack was in the Navy. On their way back from Halifax, they stopped at Pontrilas for a visit and I can recall how handsome Mack looked in his uniform. They returned to Victoria to live. Their two sons, Greg and Glenn were born in Victoria. They then moved to San Diego in 1957 where Mack was employed as a finish carpenter. He stayed with the same company until he retired. He was an expert cabinet maker. He also built many ship models, and some in bottles.

We went to visit them many times in their nice home. Then they moved to a retirement complex in the 1980's. They loved to travel and took many trips and cruises. They never missed a family function up in Canada. They had an Airstream trailer that they travelled in for many years. They would go to Portland to visit with Vi and Lorraine and then continue on up to Vancouver. Lorraine travelled with them on special occasions.

Bill and Bert went into the army in 1942. Ken and Edith got married in 1944 and that left Ray, Bruce and I at home. When Bill got out of the army, he purchased Kalk's Store in Pontrilas and ran it until he left in 1946. Bill was always so kind to me. I will always cherish the times we spent together. He would always take me along when he dated girls from the area. That was only in the day time. Whereas, Ken and Ray spent a lot of time teasing me. They would hang me down a well by my feet. They loved to hear me squawk. Ken would tell me I should have been a dog, and when I asked, "why", he'd say, "Because you have such nice hair". I never had a chance to get an ego. The boys always said that the folks got me from the Indians, and I believed them. There was a lot of bush by the railroad tracks and Ken and Ray would tell me there was a big black bear there. I had to walk that way to school and I always worried that the bear was going to come after me. Bert was our quiet brother. He did a lot of thinking and was very clever. He was a great poker player.

Ken and his wife, Edith, lived one mile west of Pontrilas and farmed there. Their daughters were born in Nipawin; Sharon in 1945 and Valerie in 1950. They moved to Nipawin in the 1950's where Ken worked for Edith's brother, Cliff, at a cement plant. In 1956 they moved to Walley, B. C. where Ken went to work in a saw mill on the afternoon shift. At the same time he and Edith built a duplex in Surrey. They also finished a suite in the downstairs where they lived. They were both very adept at working, and Edith had a job outside the home as well. A friend of Ken's once said, "Ken works hard and he plays hard"!

In 1966 they built another duplex very near their first one. They now had four rentals. Ken then worked installing overhead doors for many years. In 1980 they retired and sold the duplex they lived in and moved to Langley, B. C. By this time their daughters had settled out on their own. Sharon married and has two children, Dana and Kenneth. Sharon has since divorced and lives in the same complex in Langley as Edith and Ken. Valerie is a teacher's assistant and lives in Vancouver with Sam. Those two girls are the most fun-loving girls one could ever meet.

When Edith and Ken moved to Langley, Ken started his own business of renovating. He remodeled our kitchen and den. What a wonderful job he did! He was so fast and thorough. They enjoy their retirement and are involved in their church as well as the park where they live.

During the early years on the farm, dad had Shetland ponies. They were very unmanageable. Ray was the only one who could really handle them. Their names were Fairwell and Patrick. They produced a colt. On my first day of school, I was put on this very stubborn colt in a saddle and dad came along in the car and honked the horn. Naturally it startled the colt and it started to run. I slipped off and hung onto the saddle and somehow skinned both my knees. I was taken home and was bandaged up with torn sheets and camphor salve. I got the last seat in school right behind Harry Martin, or "Pigpen" as they called him. He never smelled too good but perhaps the camphor salve may have smelled worse.

I always loved harvest time as there were so many workers hustling to get the grain fields harvested. Mom had to work hard to get all the food prepared. She would stay up until 3:00 in the morning making pies and then she was up again at 5:00 to get breakfast for the gang. Fortunately, it was only at harvest time when the women had to work so hard on preparing the meals. Adeline and Lorraine were there to help. I remember going to the field with Adeline in the truck to take coffee, sandwiches and cake to the workers for their morning and afternoon breaks. Mom had to make many loaves of bread to feed these hungry people during that time. Adeline was a great help to mom. My sisters and I learned to be very good cooks, having learned from mom during our early years of growing up. Our mother was an excellent cook.

In 1940 Mom was standing on a chair to clean the soot out of the stove pipes, and when stepping down from the chair, she fell and broke her ankle. Bert drove her to Tisdale, which was thirty miles from where we lived, with a team of horses and the van. The doctor she went to didn't do a good job of setting her ankle bone and she had trouble with that foot for many years.

One time, Bert, Mom and I went to Pontrilas with the van and team of horses for mom to go to a Mission Circle Meeting. Both Mom and I had new coats from Eaton's catalogue. On the way home Bert was driving and the team got a fright and ran. The van tipped over and the fire in the little stove in the van sent ashes onto our new coats and burned holes in them. Bert retrieved the horses and off we went on home, but feeling very sorry about our ruined coats.

When I was six years old, Mom went to see her parents who lived in North Dakota. I stayed with Uncle Sam and Aunt Vera at the hotel in Pontrilas. Vera was Uncle Sam's second wife. This was in the wintertime and it was so cold, I shared the bed with Alfred Seckinger to keep warm. Alfred was in his twenties and was the son of very good friends of Mom and Dad's. These friends lived about a mile and a half from Pontrilas. Alfred worked in Pontrilas and sometimes stayed at the hotel.

I always thought it was great growing up on the farm. I remember how quickly Mom could milk a cow. She taught me to milk one of the gentler cows. She was such a hard worker and would do inside and outside work. Our mother was definitely a Saint! She raised turkeys and chickens. She could grab a chicken and cut off its head with an axe faster than anyone, and make sure it didn't get away to run around the yard without a head before it died. She would pluck it and have it in the pot in short order. I remember the clothes on the line in the winter that was frozen stiff as boards. Washing clothes was an ordeal as all the water had to be carried in from the well, and then the washing machine and tubs had to be set up. Clothes were boiled in the copper washtub on top of the stove. Bluing was used for rinsing. The clothes seemed so clean after using the home made soap that was made from lye and lard. The soap was very strong and would take your skin off, if you weren't careful, but it didn't seem to hurt the clothes.

Dad and the boys built a huge barn on the farm. Bill, Bert and Ken worked in a sawmill for a couple of years to earn the lumber for this barn. And, yes, they painted it red. It housed many cattle and Percheron horses. These horses were big and black - as I remember them. Dad bought a Case tractor with lugs in 1937 and a Case plough. Ray still has this antique plough today. Bert drove the tractor until he went into the service. In the 1940's Dad bought a self-propelled combine. This sure helped with harvesting the crops.

Dad bought a 1936 Chevrolet sedan when I was ten years old. Bert, Ken and Ray taught me to drive the grain trucks, so I asked Dad if I could drive the car into town thinking I could sit on his lap (I just wanted to steer). Dad said, "If you want to drive, drive." I got in and stripped a few gears and came near to the ditch a lot times, but I finally got to town. Dad just sat there and didn't say a word. It wasn't long before I could take the car out by myself, especially out to the fields to take food to the boys when they were either summer-fallowing or harvesting.

In the winter months, Dad had bought a shack in Pontrilas where Bruce and I could stay when going to school. We kept warm with an air-tight heater and a huge eiderdown quilt. Mom stayed on the farm with Ray and Bert. Dad peddled fish and he kept them frozen under our beds, which were in a lean-to abutting the shack. The fish were pickerel and white fish. He kept them in large gunny sacks. Dad would go north of our place to purchase the fish from people who spent their time fishing in the lakes. Dad had a team of horses and a sleigh. He would fill the sleigh with frozen fish and then he went from farm to farm selling the fish. He probably sold some locally to the town people as well.

The school in Pontrilas had two rooms. Grades one to six were in one room and grades seven to twelve were in the other room. There was a hall on Main Street. It was an all purpose hall. It held Lutheran and Baptist church services, meetings and dances and social events. Eventually, there was a Baptist Church built which our family attended. I went to Sunday school and also church services. I played the organ for Sunday school, and if Mrs. Lancaster, our regular organist was away, I would play for Church. I played only by ear so sometimes one couldn't tell what I was playing, but there was a good beat. If one was a true Baptist you didn't drink, smoke, go to movies, dance or wear makeup, or hardly breathe. Once in awhile we had revival meetings, held in tents, put on by an Evangelist who was high on salvation. I don't know to this day if I am saved, and I don't know from what!

The shack we lived in was fixed up into a nice little house, in which Mom, Dad, Bruce and I lived until we left in 1949 for Victoria, B. C. Bert and his wife, Lois, lived in this same shack when they got married in September, 1949.

Ray and his wife, Dorothy, got married in the very same month in 1949. Bert and Lois farmed until 2005 and then they moved to Nipawin. They had three sons; Larry born in 1951, Don in 1956, and Brent in 1966. Larry and Don married and live in Hinton, Alberta. They have lived there for many years. Larry and his wife, Bonnie, have two daughters, Bekki and Kristi. Don and his wife, Cindy, have two daughters, Ashley and Brittany. Brent joined the Navy and has made that his career. He and his wife, Karen, have one son, Aiden, and they live in Esquimalt, B. C.

In 1946, Bill took a bus to Saskatoon. We never saw him again until 1990. He had had a lot of issues that didn't seem to get resolved. He knew that Ray and Bert were still in Pontrilas. He got information from the Saskatchewan Government and called Ray from Regina. He called on our Mother's birthday, February 6, 1990. No one could believe that he had turned up after all these years. We didn't know if he was dead or alive. The family looked very hard for him when our parents celebrated their 50th anniversary in 1957, and then again in 1967 when they had been married 60 years. No one knew that Bill had changed his name to "Carlson". We tried to use army data to find him to no avail.

When Bill left, he had a daughter, Judy, in Saskatoon, who went with her mother after the separation. Bill hadn't seen Judy until his wife, Caroline, found her in about 1999. She joined the rest of the family and was close to Bill until his passing in October, 2005.

What a wonderful time we all had at our first family reunion in 1990 in Portland. Norman, Janet and Ron Adkins's second son, got married in October, 1990 and this occasion brought us all together. There were ten of us together for the first time. Bill had married his wife, Caroline, in 1954 and they had five children; Richard, Raymond, Robert, Ralph and Judy. We held a family reunion in 1990 at Bill and Caroline's place in Greenwood, B. C. Eight members of the family attended. Lou and I did a skit. We dressed as two cousins and when we were announced this surprised most because we wore wigs, sunglasses and old dresses and weren't easily recognized.

In 1947, Mom, Dad, Bert, Ray, Bruce and I went to the Calgary Stampede. The Calgary Stampede was world famous and we really enjoyed being there. We also visited Barrhead, North of Edmonton, and saw all the Bentz relatives. They were all so hospitable to us. I especially remember Robert Bentz and his wife, Gertie. They wanted to entertain us royally so they just caught a few chickens from the yard and cooked them up, and Gertie made a wonderful chocolate cake. There were a lot of us visiting and it couldn't have been easy to get that much food ready in such a short time. I remember Mom and Aunt Tilda went to the beer parlour in Barrhead and after one beer they laughed a lot.

When Ray was about seventeen, he was a jockey and rode in many races in Saskatchewan and Manitoba. Dad bought a Sawmill about twenty miles North of Pontrilas that was no longer running. There were some shacks at the mill that Ken and Ray tore down for lumber. Ray said there were lots of mosquitoes and bulldog flies.

Dad had bought a quarter section of land with a house on it about 1945. The house was moved to Nipawin. Ray and a neighbour, Trapper Johnson, dug out the basement with a team of horses and a scraper. After it was completed, Dad sold it.

Ray went to Victoria in 1947 and worked at Leechtown. He and his wife, Dot, came out to the coast many winters and stayed with us. They both worked during the months they were in Victoria, and then in the spring went back home to Pontrilas. Ray took over the home place in Pontrilas when he and Dot got married in 1949. They adopted two children, Woody and Shayla. Dot passed away in 1993. They had seven grandchildren.

Ray still farms. Ray was always very musical. He plays the violin and Saxophone. He and his friend, Irene, formed a band and they go all over Saskatchewan and some places in Manitoba to play music for dances and other events. Irene plays the piano and keyboard. They named their band "Irene and the Goodnighters". They make sweet music together.

Ray is a collector of antiques. He frequents auction sales and it's amazing what he finds as treasures. He has a shelf all around his garage which holds toy farm implements. He has a collection of small cars which he keeps in his basement in cases. He has old stoves, lamps, saws, clocks, watches, elephants and anything else that may be of value. At one time he had nine old tractors but he sold them. At present he is having an auctioneer come to look at his treasures as he wants to sell out completely, including the living area and the land. I believe he has two quarters left to sell.

In 1949 when we left Pontrilas, Dad, Mom, Bruce and I were driving a 1946 Mercury, pulling a homemade silver trailer that Dad had made, which looked a bit like a bullet. It held our piano and some of our wares. When we got to Quappelle Valley, there was a very steep hill we had to descend. Mom wasn't going to take any chances and she got out the car and walked down the hill. The second gear on the car went out and we drove the rest of trip with two gears. I did most of the driving. I didn't have a driver's license so Dad drove through the cities. When we stopped at night, Dad and Mom slept in the trailer and Bruce and I slept on the seats in the car. When we started out we had a big hunk of bologna, a whole watermelon and a loaf of bread. We did stop at one restaurant for a meal and Dad said we could all have soup and to load up on crackers, which we did.

We arrived in Sidney, B. C. via Washington. Vera, Lou, Mack and Adeline (large with their first child, Greg), met us as we got off the ferry. Lou was so embarrassed as we all looked like hillbillies. Mom always blamed Lou for trying to "citify" me. I had a blue dress that I had ordered from Eaton's catalogue before we left home (I have to admit now that it was very weird). I also had orange shoes that had straps that wrapped way up my legs. I thought I looked really dressy! In those days there was no television to keep us up-to-date.

Dad had bought a house the year before when we visited Victoria in the winter of 1948. Vera and Lou lived in the house and they stayed with us after we moved in. Then Dad bought a house closer to Victoria. Vera and Lou moved to James Bay in Victoria after having lived with us for a year. I really missed Lou. We were so close; it was like my right arm had been cut off.

I went to Mount View High School. That is where I first met John Catterall. We were both fourteen. Then I moved to Victoria High, where Lou was going, and I didn't see John for the next eleven years. High school years were great! Lou and I were inseparable. Eventually, we both married policemen and had sons. Through the years we have travelled together and have had many gatherings. We keep in close contact with each other.

I am so glad that Vera had Lou. Lou is definitely a friend/relative. John always said, "We are given our relatives, thank goodness we can choose our friends".

Vera was a very hard working girl. She worked at the Catterall Gardens in Victoria for many years and then she worked in a fish packing plant. She retired and lived in James Bay in a lovely condo, which was so very neatly furnished.

Adlolph & Magdalena's Daughter Eunice Kalk – taken in 1937 (sorry Eunice J)

Eunice (Kalk) & John Catterall – on their wedding day in 1960

Eunice (Kalk) Catterall & Family
LR: John, Blake, Bruce, Wade, & Eunice - 2004

HISTORY OF VERNON KALK

MEMORIES, By Vernon Kalk
(Source: Between and Beyond the Benches - Ravenscrag, Vol. 1 (1981).

I was born on October 3, 1909 in Martin, North Dakota. My two older sisters, Viola and Vera were also born in North Dakota. In 1912 my parents moved to Saskatchewan with their family of three children and took up a homestead near Ravenscrag. My sisters Adeline and Lorraine and my brothers Bill, Bert, Kenneth and Raymond were born in the years following. We older children attended school at East Fairwell. Dad served on the school board from 1917 to 1923 and was the first Secretary-Treasurer.

Viola, Vera and I attended Crossfell School one year, and we also attended school in Ravenscrag one winter. I only attended East Fairwell about five years as it was not ready until 1917.

In the fall of 1931 I broke a three year old horse which turned out to be real intelligent rope horse. The saddle was purchased in 1928 and put on display at Pontrillas' Homecoming in 1976.

In 1926 a Community United Church was built east of our place, and I hauled the lumber for it from Eastend - the nearest lumber retail yard at that time. Dad, Uncle John Bentz, John Kessel and Roy Wilderman used to preach the Gospel and did a fair job of it.

I rode in the bareback competition at the Murraydale Stampede somewhere around the age of fifteen or sixteen and also attended a few dances at Ravenscrag.

We moved from our homestead on the Bench in 1932 to Pontrillas, Saskatchewan where two more children, Eunice and Bruce were born. Here my folks purchased a farm and lived there until 1949 when they retired and moved to Victoria, British Columbia. They lived there for about twelve years and then moved to Surrey, British Columbia.

I was in the U. S. Navy during the years 1942 to 1945. I was on the destroyer "Lewis", on escort duty for six months from Panama Canal to Quontanimo Bay, Cuba, one of the big navy bases. I waited there for oil tankers to join the convoy from Trinidad, where we got most of our crude oil. From Guontanimo we proceeded to all parts on the east coast. I got a leave from Brooklyn Navy yard, caught a troop ship out of Richmond, California and took a load of troops to India, and came back to Australia. We were pulled off for a replacement gun crew for the aircraft carrier, "Rudyard Bay". I felt good being one of the top gunner's mates. After my discharge in 1945, I received all my records.

Rosella Kluthe and I got married on June 29, 1947. We settled in Bellingham, Washington and have one son, Ernie.

Adolph & Magdalena's son Vernon Kalk – at age 21 - 1928

Vernon & his wife Rosella (Kluthe) Kalk – 1947

Vernon's wife Rosella (Kluthe) Kalk – 1990

FROM THE PEN OF LEN

It's me again, Len with the pen,
I'm losing my know-how but still have the yen.
I'll use some words from an old song, put in some
Childhood reminiscing and add a school story.
Folk who were raised in the country will understand.
I hope the remainder will tolerate.

It's been a long time now, but it seems like only yesterday
GEE! ain't it funny how time slips away.

I remember as a kid, I was sent to milk the cow.
Rather boring but I knew that I'd get by somehow.
I'd have some fun doin' things, I tell you where it's at,
Like squirting milk in the open mouth of our big old grey tom cat.

They sent me out to feed the pigs, we called it "slop the hogs".
'I'd wind up giving some of it to our big old friendly dogs.

There were chickens needed plucking,
The ones that just stopped clucking,
They were the toughest birds in our whole brood.
But after special cleaning, they'd come out just a gleaming,
With the taste of Ambrosia, after being stewed.

Go feed the horses, that's what they'd say
From up in the loft, there's plenty of hay.
But when I climbed up to the loft, it was mostly just to play.

141

Go pump some water, they'd tell me, the cows are getting thirsty.
I realized right there and then, I had them at my mercy.
I'd make a puddle, just by pumping water on the ground
Jump in bare footed, make a dirty mess by sloshing water all around.

I wasn't all that bad you know, I did some things in earnest.
Like in the winter, going to school, lighting up the furnace.
Our fuel back then, from the local mine, was soggy lignite coal.
The furnace in our little School, had a great big fire bowl.
One day I filled the bowl right up, just like water in an urn,
With dampish lignite coal, you know, just hoping it would burn.
There was a flicker but mostly smoke, it looked to me like one big joke.

Just at that time quite suddenly, I had to leave the room,
But when I stepped outside the door, there was this "roaring boom"!
I stepped back inside, with great dismay, and all I could see
Were stove pipes, coal and ashes, with great piles of debris.

I must admit, I lost my job, in a subtle sort of way.
But worst of all, they took my wage, which was just ten cents a day!

But you get used to it, yeah, you get used to it.
The early days of ones young life,
Are often filled with toils and strife.
But it's wonderful, you get to like it more and more and more!
You get used to it, then when you get use to it,
You'll do things, exactly as you did before.

Written by Len Heth (1920-2013)

POEM WRITTEN BY LEN HETH

To Friends And Family Whom I love

When my time has come, release me, I must go,
To do the things, undone, from long ago.
Please do not flood yourself with many tears,
Be happy that we've shared so many years.

We've shared our love and you can only guess
How much you've given me in happiness.
I thank you for the love each one has shown,
And now 'tis time to travel on my own.

Just grieve a moment for me, if you must,
Then let your grief be silenced by the trust,
That time will tell how long we'll be apart.
And bless the memories that lie within your heart.

Life goes on, and I'll be ever near.
Just listen closely and you may even hear,
You cannot see or touch me, as we are apart.
You will feel the love around you from your heart.

And then when you must come this way alone,
My smile and hug will tell you, "Welcome Home".

Len Heth
March 9, 1920 – August 3, 2013

Heth Sisters: Left Johnny & Sophia (Heth) Schaal, Right Walter
& Lilian (Heth) Schaal – double-wedding day 1938

Sophia & Johnny Schaal – 50th Wedding Anniversary 1988

Lillian & Walter Schaal – 50th Wedding Anniversary 1988

Heth Family Siblings – 1988 (mother: Mary Kalk; father: Fred Heth)
LR: Len, Lillian, Novella, Sophia, and Arthur

Len Heth and wife Winifred – 1980's

Len (the Pen) Heth – 1990's

HISTORY OF KALK FAMILY

MY FAMILY
WRITTEN BY GUST KALK:

My father, Gottlieb Kalk, was born in Europe. He came to Saskatchewan, Canada in 1888 and settled at Edenwald, near Regina where he farmed, but when he found out that there was land to be had in North Dakota, he decided to look into it. So in March 1896, my father and Fred Putz, Sr. hitched a team of horses to a wagon and started out for North Dakota. There was still snow on the ground.

They arrived at Harvey, North Dakota about ten days too late. All the good properties were taken; so they picked their claim about eight miles West of Harvey near what is now the town of Martin. Gottlieb Kalk filed the land that is now the Tillie Kost farm (our farm), and Fred Putz, Sr. filed the land on the North side of the railroad tracks. After they had staked their land, they had to drive to Devils Lake, which was the nearest land office, to file their claims. So they drove back to Edenwald, Saskatchewan in time to plant a crop.

After the crop was planted they hitched up their wagons and haying equipment and drove to North Dakota again to put up some hay for the coming winter and also built a 12' X 16' claim shack as was required. In the meantime, others came down from Canada to this area.

After the shack was built and the hay was put up they started to drive back to Edenwald. They got back there in time to harvest their crop. It was a very small crop because it was a very dry year. After this crop was in, along with some other families they loaded their wagons again with their belongings and their families. They drove the cattle behind the wagons and started out for North Dakota, for the third time. They got as far as Portal, North Dakota and ran into a snow storm so they loaded their belongings and cattle into railroad cars and shipped them the rest of the way. When they arrived at their destination, a foot of snow was on the ground, and it turned out to be one of the worst winters in history, but they came through it all right.

There was a place called Casselman about a mile East from where they filed, but it was only a depot and elevator, so they had to go to Harvey for supplies. Harvey was already in existence. There was a store, lumber yard, and some businesses. So they started to build up their farms and in 1898 the town of Martin was started. Chris Herr started a grocery store and a Minneapolis firm built a grain elevator. My father, Gottlieb Kalk, managed the elevator for the first year, and then started an implement business. In the meantime, the Mollendorf's, Nicklaus's and the Fiesel's started a hardware store and then the Mollendorf's started a general store and a hotel, so that is how the town of Martin started.

That is the way I heard it from my father and my father-in-law, Fred Putz, Sr. I was born in 1901 and pretty much grew up in Martin.

HISTORY OF ELLA PUTZ AND GUST KALK

Ella and Gust knew each other all their lives, having grown up on neighboring farms. Their courtship Began in 1920, but they didn't marry until November 24, 1927. Marriage had to wait because Gust had to take over the farming operation for his mother when his father died. Gust's father, Gottlieb Kalk, and Ella's father, Fred Putz, Sr., were the two men who had travelled together from Canada to the United States to lay their claim for land, the first claims made in the Martin area.

When they married, Ella and Gust moved to Minot where Gust worked as a carpenter for the Olson Orheim Construction Co. The first night in Minot was spent in a hotel. The next morning they turned on their radio and heard that a man had been stabbed in the heart and died in the business place across the street from their hotel.

They moved into a home that week and Gust continued on this job that gave him experience in building. His work sent him to many locations, including Harvey, where they were building an addition to the grade school. Ella moved with him to an upstairs apartment and there they had visits from Martin relatives. In 1948 Gust began his own construction business in Minot, building and remodelling homes and business buildings, until his retirement in 1968.

Gust and Ella had no children, and when Gust's sister, Esther, died, her husband asked them to care for his baby daughter named Marlene. They consented and immediately became very attached to this beautiful and talented child, who was one year and nine months old. Later, her father agreed to her adoption by Gust and Ella. She took vocal, piano and tap dancing lessons. As a child, Marlene spent a lot of time playing with her 'Putz' cousins, Les Putz, Claire Ann Walker and Audrey Walker, who lived only a block from her home.

Her pianist abilities continued and she began giving piano lessons until recent years, when she completed 27 years in this field. In addition to her music interests, Marlene had been involved in church organizations, scouts, brownies, and was an avid bowler for 30 years.

Marlene had been the organizer of the yearly family potluck picnics. Relatives from all over the country attended. Ella is known for her cooking abilities and a spotless home. Her candy, cookies, homemade soups and German dishes are still served to visiting relatives. She makes her own sauerkraut and caps it for future use and continues to entertain.

The Kalk home was available when anyone needed a room. Bennie Kalk, Gust's brother, lived with them when he was employed in Minot; and Dorothy and Betty (nieces) came from Martin and stayed there while attending the Minot fair. During that time, Ella would take them to the coulee a few blocks from her home to pick juneberries so she could bake them a fresh juneberry pie. A few who picked berries got poison ivy, but her delicious pies were worth the risk.

They purchased a cabin at Lake Metigoshe, which they later enlarged. This was another place for Putz relatives to gather. Each day they would awaken to a large breakfast consisting of ham, eggs, hash brown, fruit, kuchen, and sometimes pancakes, too, followed by a fishing expedition early in the morning when the fish were biting best.

The day would continue with a nap and then more food and fishing. The outdoor "bif" was called "the pink house". It was painted pink and had seats from indoor bathrooms. This comfortable outhouse was located behind the cabin in a secluded area that had many trees and shrubs to give it a lot of privacy.

One day Gust and Ella were ending a day of good fishing when the propeller of the boat suddenly dropped off the boat into the lake. There was quite a bit of excitement, but luckily they were near the dock and managed to row to shore.

When Marlene married and grandchildren began to arrive, Ella and Gust's love for children continued. Anytime Marlene needed a baby sitter, or just came to visit, Ella would put her work on hold and play with the grandchildren. They were free to roam the house and bring out all the toys she had for them. As the grandchildren grew up and married, they still visited the grandparents and offered their help whenever Gust or Ella needed something.

Some of Gust's pastime after retirement, in addition to fishing trips to Lake Metigoshe, included curling at the Minot Curling Rink. He and his friends also attended baseball games when the Minot Mallards team played in Minot. When the umpires walked out on to the field, the group would sing, "Three Blind Mice". Ella and Gust enjoyed playing cribbage, and when grandson Donny played cribbage with Grandpa, Donny gave him some competition.

They celebrated their 50th anniversary on November 24, 1977 at an open house at Emmanuel Baptist Church, and their 60th anniversary in 1987 was celebrated at an open house that Marlene planned at her home.

REPRINT OF AN ARTICLE WHICH APPEARED IN THE MINOT, NORTH DAKOTA, NEWSPAPER, by Jill Schramm, Daily News Staff Writer. Date: 1991.

When Gust Kalk took his first construction job in 1923, he promised himself he would direct the show someday. A few years later, he was heading up some of Western North Dakota's building projects as construction foreman. His handiwork is evident in Minot in Trinity and St. Joseph's Hospitals, Leo's school, Sunnyside School, St. Mark's Lutheran Church, Minot Model School and the former Union National Bank and State Theater. His buildings stand in 22 communities, including courthouses in Minot, Mohall, Linton and Bowbells.

Kalk, 90, spent 45 years in construction, including 20 years working on his own. A native of Martin, Kalk was seventeen when his father died. Kalk ran the family farm for five years, then sold out and moved to Minot. "I gave everything to mother and I took off. I took off with only the belongings I had in my suitcase and a $20 bill in my pocket," Kalk said.

He took interest in the erection of a Minot school and applied for a job. The job with Olson Construction - later Olson and Orheim, and eventually Orheim and Alm - lasted for 25 years. "Pretty soon I got all the big jobs out of town. The boss would send me because I was the most dependable man, I guess," Kalk said. "I ran a lot of jobs in my life and some big ones, too, and I never made any mistake ever that cost over 100 bucks." He figures his time spent out of town would add up to ten and half years. And in those days, cars weren't such that one went home often.

Kalk and his wife, Ella, still live in Minot in the first house he ever built. "I shingled the roof at 22 below zero," he said. The Kalks moved in during construction, hosting a neighbor until his own home was built. "In the 20's, you couldn't get a place to live in town. We were paying $50 a month and, shucks, we were only getting 75 cents an hour," Kalk said. His worst years were 1931 and 1932. "I only worked about three months in the two years. There was no work," Kalk said.

In 1928, he was laid up a month with a fractured skull. He was working on the Ellison or Fair building downtown when he fell eighteen feet down an elevator shaft. The crew put him on the back of the truck, not knowing whether he was dead for alive, and took him to the hospital, he said. Among the worst of his construction injuries was a broken back that he said was caused by trying to prove how much he could lift. "Like a fool, I picked up three pieces of plywood. I fell over backwards and broke my back," Kalk said. During demolition of the old Ward County Courthouse, a floor accidently caved in. "We buried a couple of guys in there, but luckily enough, they didn't get hurt very bad," Kalk said. Early day construction was done without much equipment. During construction of the Ward County Courthouse in 1929, the crew used a wooden hoist and poles with ropes and winches. The only modern equipment was a borrowed power shovel from a paving company in town on another project. "It was all done by hand work and we did the job in twelve months. I would say to this day, with all the equipment they have, they wouldn't do the job in less time than that," he said. "It was unbelievable what we could do in those days without anything."

Kalk retired in 1968. His interest in construction hasn't waned, though. Having heard about cracks in the roof membrane at Minot State University's Dome, Kalk planned to take a look. No fan of domes, Kalk believes them unsafe in North Dakota wind and snow. Kalk approves of the renovations and expansions of some of his buildings, with one exception. He opposed the tuck-pointing of the Courthouse a few years ago. The bottom of the building was moisture damaged and needed joint work, but there was no need for tuck-pointing the entire Courthouse, Kalk said. The work actually will turn out to be detrimental down the road, he predicted.

Gustav (Gust) & Ella (Putz) Kalk – 50th Anniversary 1977

HISTORY OF MY FAMILY, BY SOPHIE KALK

In the year 1885, quite a few families immigrated from Katalui and Tultscha, Romania to Canada, where they took up homesteads north of Belgonie, Saskatchewan (known as Northwest Territories in those years). Among these families were Phillip Putz, father of Fred Putz, Gottlieb Kalk, Henry Fiesel Sr., father of Martin Fiesel, Jacob Rust Sr., father of the Rust brothers of Martin, North Dakota, John Rust, brother of Jacob Rust Sr., S. Radezki, and many others.

They remained in Canada for about ten years, where most of them were converted under the Baptist Minister, Rev. Klaus Phoelman. Some were converted later under the leadership of Rev. R. Fenshe, and became members of the Edenwald Baptist Church of Saskatchewan, Canada.

Due to severe winters in Canada and the early frost, which often ruined their best crops, they became discouraged, and when they heard that there was land to be had in North Dakota, where the climate was somewhat milder, many of them decided to move to the United States. Some moved to North Dakota in 1896, and in 1897 still more moved to North Dakota to file for land. They decided to settle near Casselman, North Dakota, which is now called Martin. Among the first settlers were Phillip Putz, Frank Putz, Jacob Rust Sr., John Rust, Gottlieb Kalk, Jacob Buntus, Henry Fiesel Sr., S. Radezki, and others.

After each one had located a homestead which appealed to him, they began to build their sod houses as pioneers of North Dakota. They had to struggle with much poverty and hardship, but they trusted God would help them in every way, and God did. After each family had built a temporary sod house, they assembled for prayer meetings in the different homes.

God answered their prayers and blessed their meetings and also their handiwork, and enabled them to earn their daily bread. Their numbers increased and their sod houses soon became too small for their meetings on Sundays. Their children needed a school also, so in 1897 they built a school house, which was also used for Church services on Sundays. At this same time they started Sunday school. God added his blessings and many souls were won for Christ.

Sophie's parents moved to Martin, North Dakota when she was six weeks old. In 1915 she married Charley Fisher. They had a ranch together in Jordan, Montana, until his death in 1928. In 1930 she moved to Longview, Washington, where she met and married James Maples. They bought the old Carroll's Church and converted it into their home. Mr. Maples died in 1959. Sophie worked at Long-Bell Lumber Company during World War II.

Her greatest joys were gardening, cooking and her family. She always took care of people, and taught her grandchildren the joy of their family. She lived at Campus Towers, in Longview, for twenty one years. Her memberships included Northlake Baptist Church and the Rebekah Lodge.

SOURCES:
LIFE: HISTORY OF the Martin Baptist Church, July 18, 1897-1947. Sophie Maples.

MY LITTLE ROOM, by Sophie Maples, written in 1974

It overlooks the city wide and all the mountain peaks - my cozy little room,
Where early morning sun creeps in to chase away the gloom,
With pictures of my family all around the wall
I've lots of lovely little things, dear treasures all my own, of friends that I have known.
I read and write and sew some days to pass away the time.
The very large impressive house in which I use to dwell
Could never bring contentment like this room I love so well.
In all my gay and younger days we needed space to roam –
When age has overtaken us, one room can be our home.

Gottlieb Kalk's daughter Sophia (Kalk) (Fisher) Maples– 100 yrs old 1996

Sophia's daughter Leone (Fisher) Olson on her Nursing graduation in 1935

Outline Descendant Report for Johannes Benz

1 Johannes Benz (1786 - 1869) b: 1786 in Mettenzimmern, Ludwigsburg, Wurttemberg, Germany, d: 25 Mar 1869 in Odesa, Ukraine, Russia

... + Christine Wetzler (1784 - 1869) b: 1784 in Mettenzimmern, Ludwigsburg, Wurttemberg, Germany, m: Unknown in Mettenzimmern, Ludwigsburg, Wurttemberg, Germany, d: 1869 in Odesa, Ukraine, Russia

......2 Johann Jakob Benz (1810 -) b: 1810 in Odesa, Ukraine, Russia, d: Odesa, Ukraine, Russia

...... + Juliane Henne (1811 -) b: 1811 in Odesa, Ukraine, Russia, m: Odesa, Ukraine, Russia, d: Odesa, Ukraine, Russia

.........3 George Friedrich Benz (1832 - 1921) b: 23 Sep 1832 in Neudorf, Odessa Region, S. Russia, d: 18 Mar 1921 in Fairfax, South Dakota

.........3 Johann Bentz (1834 - Unknown) b: 1834 in Odessa, Ukraine, Russia, d: Unknown in Odessa, Ukraine, Russia

.... + Magdalena Stroh (1837 - Unknown) b: 1837 in Odesa, Ukraine, Russia, m: Unknown in Odessa, Ukraine, Russia, d: Unknown in Odesa, Ukraine, Russia

............4 Christine Bentz (1858 -) b: 03 Jan 1858 in Neudorf, Odessa Region, S. Russia, d:

............4 Johann Bentz (1859 - 1941) b: 26 Nov 1859 in Odesa, Ukraine, Russia, d: 30 Jun 1941 in unknown

.... + Magdalena Raille (1858 - 1944) b: 12 Nov 1858 in Odesa, Ukraine, Russia, m: 10 Nov 1881 in Odesa, Ukraine, Russia, d: 09 Dec 1944 in unknown

...............5 John Adam Bentz (1883 - 1967) b: 15 Mar 1883 in Odesa, Ukraine, Russia, d: 02 May 1967 in Barrhead, Alberta, Canada

.... + Matilda Kalk (1888 - 1979) b: 22 Sep 1888 in Belgonie, NWT, Canada, m: 07 Nov 1907 in unknown, d: 25 May 1979 in Barrhead, Alberta, Canada

..................6 Edna Rachael Bentz (1908 - 1995) b: 26 Jan 1908 in Harvey, Cavalier, North Dakota, USA, d: 29 Oct 1995 in Barrhead, Alberta, Canada

.... + Alexander Ernst (1901 - 1979) b: 08 May 1901 in Odesa, Ukraine, Russia, m: 02 Apr 1931 in Eastend, Saskatchewan, Canada, d: 07 Jul 1979 in Barrhead, Alberta, Canada

.....................7 Edwin Albert Ernst (1931 -) b: 04 Jul 1931 in Eastend, Saskatchewan, Canada

.... + Audrey Patricia Airlie (1927 -) b: 21 Mar 1927 in Albert Park, Alberta, m: 09 Jul 1960 in Calgary, Alberta, Canada

........................8 Riley Alexander Ernst (1961 -) b: 29 Nov 1961 in Calgary, Alberta, Canada

.... + Nadine Marianne Eadle (1967 -) b: 08 Jun 1967 in Winnipeg, Manitoba, Canada, m: 20 May 1989 in Calgary, Alberta, Canada

...........................9 Randi Mae Ernst (1992 -) b: 06 Jan 1992 in Calgary, Alberta, Canada

...........................9 Wyatt Daniel Ernst (1993 -) b: 06 Apr 1993 in Calgary, Alberta, Canada

........................8 Kelly Patrick Ernst (1963 -) b: 04 Apr 1963 in Calgary, Alberta, Canada

.... + Angel Dunphy (1963 -) b: 04 Apr 1963 in Calgary, Alberta, Canada, m: 1981 in Calgary, Alberta, Canada

........................8 Shauna Mary Ernst (1966 -) b: 16 Sep 1966 in Calgary, Alberta, Canada

.... + Jeffrey Thomas Mostowich (1960 -) b: 02 Jun 1960 in Calgary, Alberta, Canada, m: 15 Aug 1993 in Calgary, Alberta, Canada

...........................9 Liam Edward Mostowich (2002 -) b: 26 Jul 2002 in Calgary, Alberta, Canada

...........................9 Lucas Samuel Mostowich (2004 -) b: 30 Sep 2004 in Calgary, Alberta, Canada

........................8 Tara Patricia Ernst (1968 -) b: 26 Jun 1968 in Calgary, Alberta, Canada

.... + Roger Siemens (15 Nov -) b: 15 Nov in Calgary, Alberta, Canada, m: 19 Feb 2005 in Calgary, Alberta, Canada

...........................9 Aiden Rowan Siemens (2008 -) b: 18 Aug 2008 in Calgary, Alberta, Canada

.....................7 Ernest Lloyd Ernst (1932 -) b: 02 Sep 1932 in Eastend, Saskatchewan, Canada

.... + Ethel May Anderson (1942 - 1991) b: 12 Jul 1942 in Barrhead, Alberta, Canada, m: 21 Oct 1961 in Barrhead, Alberta, Canada, d: 23 Apr 1991 in Westlock, Alberta, Canada

........................8 Roselyn Gail Ernst (1962 -) b: 15 Dec 1962 in Barrhead, Alberta, Canada

.... + David Stewart Anderson (1962 -) b: 03 Dec 1962 in Magrath, Alberta, Canada, m: 12 Oct 1985 in Westlock, Alberta, Canada

...........................9 Kylie Nicole Anderson (1989 -) b: 26 Aug 1989 in Westlock, Alberta, Canada

...........................9 Lindsey Joline Anderson (1990 -) b: 27 Sep 1990 in Edmonton, Alberta, Canada
...........................9 Breanna June Anderson (1994 -) b: 29 Dec 1994 in Westlock, Alberta, Canada
...........................9 Karalee Rose Anderson (1998 -) b: 19 Mar 1998 in Westlock, Alberta, Canada
........................8 Joanne Deane Ernst (1964 -) b: 26 Apr 1964 in Barrhead, Alberta, Canada
.... + Donald Eric Galloway (1955 -) b: 20 Sep 1955 in Edmonton, Alberta, Canada, m: 10 Apr 1993 in Edmonton, Alberta, Canada
...........................9 Devon Dayle Galloway (1994 -) b: 10 Feb 1994 in Edmonton, Alberta, Canada
...........................9 Alexa Rae Galloway (1996 -) b: 06 Jan 1996 in Edmonton, Alberta, Canada
........................8 Lorine May Ernst (1969 -) b: 20 Mar 1969 in Barrhead, Alberta, Canada
.... + Norman Kelly (1967 -) b: 05 Jun 1967 in Scotland, m: 14 Sep 1996 in Westlock, Alberta, Canada
.... + Betty Jean Emsley (1930 -) b: 22 Dec 1930 in Rochester, Alberta, m: 21 Mar 1992 in Westlock, Alberta, Canada
...................7 Albert Alexander Ernst (1934 - 2009) b: 28 May 1934 in Eastend, Saskatchewan, Canada, d: 02 Jun 2009 in Westlock, Alberta, Canada
.... + Alice Petruchik (1932 -) b: 03 May 1932 in Lunford, Alberta, Canada, m: 12 Jul 1954 in Barrhead, Alberta, Canada
........................8 Norman Albert Ernst (1955 -) b: 05 Mar 1955 in Barrhead, Alberta, Canada
.... + Sandra Jean Frost (1959 -) b: 19 Jun 1959 in Sundridge, Ontario, m: 30 Dec 1975 in Golden, British Columbia
...........................9 Gordon Norman Ernst (1976 -) b: 12 Aug 1976 in Golden, British Columbia
.... + Rebecca Louise Young (1979 -) b: 30 Jan 1979 in Brighton, England, m: 24 Jul 1999 in Calgary, Alberta, Canada
..............................10 Noah Gordon Ernst (1997 -) b: 10 Oct 1997 in Calgary, Alberta, Canada
...........................9 Crystal Robin Ernst (1978 -) b: 02 Dec 1978 in Golden, British Columbia
..............................10 Levi Emanuel Ernst (1995 -) b: 10 Nov 1995 in Calgary, Alberta, Canada
..............................10 Mica Angelo Ernst (2000 -) b: 28 Nov 2000 in Cranbrook, British Columbia
...........................9 Bethany Ann Ernst (1985 -) b: 30 Mar 1985 in Calgary, Alberta, Canada
.... + Vivian Janet Horrick (1954 -) b: 15 Jul 1954 in Vegreville, Alberta, Canada, m: 29 Jun 1996 in Westlock, Alberta, Canada
...........................9 Lucinda Anne Browne (1987 -) b: 15 Dec 1987 in Westlock, Alberta, Canada
........................8 Delores Alice Ernst (1964 -) b: 01 Apr 1964 in Toronto, Ontario, Canada
.... + Alec Frederick McRae (1959 -) b: 19 Jun 1959 in Montréal, Quebec, Canada, m: 30 Aug 1986 in Calgary, Alberta, Canada
...........................9 Danielle Elizabeth McRae (1989 -) b: 06 Apr 1989 in Calgary, Alberta, Canada
...........................9 Aaron Francis McRae (1992 -) b: 21 Jan 1992 in Calgary, Alberta, Canada
...................7 Calvin Clarence Ernst (1937 -) b: 14 Oct 1937 in Eastend, Saskatchewan, Canada
.... + Myrtle Alicia Craft (1940 -) b: 24 May 1940 in Barrhead, Alberta, Canada, m: 07 Jul 1960 in Barrhead, Alberta, Canada
........................8 Roger Kevin Ernst (1962 -) b: 11 Nov 1962 in Barrhead, Alberta, Canada
.... + Daylene Karole Devins (1965 -) b: 30 Dec 1965 in Barrhead, Alberta, Canada, m: 24 May 1997 in Whitecourt, Alberta
...........................9 Dustin Leon Devins (1983 -) b: 30 Jul 1983 in Barrhead, Alberta, Canada
...........................9 Jerhomey Paul Devins (1986 -) b: 07 Aug 1986 in Hinton, Alberta, Canada
...........................9 Chase Roger Ernst (1993 -) b: 18 Dec 1993 in Red Deer, Alberta
........................8 Michael Scott Ernst (1965 -) b: 06 Apr 1965 in Barrhead, Alberta, Canada
.... + Desiree Emperingham b: unknown, m: 18 Dec 1992 in Whitecourt, Alberta
...........................9 Alicia Courtney Ernst (1992 -) b: 19 Jun 1992 in Whitecourt, Alberta
.... + Phyllis Irene Lassesen (1940 -) b: 25 Nov 1940 in Camrose, Alberta, Canada, m: 29 Nov 1980 in Barrhead, Alberta, Canada
........................8 David Charles Greig (1962 -) b: 25 May 1962 in Barrhead, Alberta, Canada
.... + Marlene Martin (1964 -) b: 18 Jan 1964 in Barrhead, Alberta, Canada, m: 08 Jan 1983 in Barrhead, Alberta, Canada
...........................9 Christopher David Greig (1982 -) b: 08 Sep 1982 in Edmonton, Alberta, Canada
...........................9 Kimberly Lynn Greig (1985 -) b: 12 Aug 1985 in Barrhead, Alberta, Canada

........................8 Donald James Greig (1964 -) b: 17 Jan 1964 in Edmonton, Alberta, Canada
.... + Alfred James Dodgson (1908 - 1994) b: 06 Nov 1908 in Cardston, Alberta, Canada, m: 06 Feb 1982 in Barrhead, Alberta, Canada, d: 23 Dec 1994 in Barrhead, Alberta, Canada
................6 Elaine Ruby Bentz (1909 - 2008) b: 16 Dec 1909 in Harvey, Cavalier, North Dakota, USA, d: 12 Jun 2008 in Barrhead, Alberta, Canada
.... + Edward Arthur Larkins (1911 - 1981) b: 02 Jun 1911 in Mundare, Alberta, Canada, m: 24 Feb 1941 in Barrhead, Alberta, Canada, d: 03 Mar 1981 in Barrhead, Alberta, Canada
....................7 Arlene Joan Larkins (1942 -) b: 22 Jan 1942 in Barrhead, Alberta, Canada
.... + Leroy Claude Christianson (1940 -) b: 19 Jul 1940 in Barrhead, Alberta, Canada, m: 25 Aug 1959 in Edmonton, Alberta, Canada
....................8 Cheryl Dene Christianson (1959 -) b: 18 Jan 1959 in Barrhead, Alberta, Canada
.... + Fred Eric Preuss (1956 - 2002) b: 22 Sep 1956 in Barrhead, Alberta, Canada, m: 30 Aug 1975 in Barrhead, Alberta, Canada, d: 10 Jun 2002 in Barrhead, Alberta, Canada
....................9 Trina Lisa Preuss (1976 -) b: 14 Apr 1976 in Barrhead, Alberta, Canada
.... + Joseph DaCosta (1974 -) b: 25 Feb 1974 in Edmonton, Alberta, Canada, m: 09 Jul 1994 in St. Albert, Alberta, Canada
....................10 Kayla Jasmine Maria DaCosta (1994 -) b: 02 Oct 1994 in St. Albert, Alberta, Canada
.... + Michael Jarrard (1971 -) b: 03 Feb 1971 in Vancouver, British Columbia, Canada, m: 24 Jul 2010 in Coquitlam, British Columbia, Canada
....................10 Braydon Jarrard (2006 -) b: 31 Jul 2006 in Coquitlam, British Columbia, Canada
....................10 Chanel Jarrard (2008 -) b: 26 Aug 2008 in Coquitlam, British Columbia, Canada
....................9 Troy Dean Preuss (1977 -) b: 09 Nov 1977 in Barrhead, Alberta, Canada
.... + Melissa Gail Bates (1980 -) b: 23 Feb 1980 in Barrhead, Alberta, Canada
....................10 Ashlyn Jade Preuss (2001 -) b: 30 Sep 2001 in Barrhead, Alberta, Canada
....................10 Tray Wyatt Preuss (2005 -) b: 16 Oct 2005 in Barrhead, Alberta, Canada
.... + Robert Miller (1960 -) b: 28 Oct 1960 in Edmonton, Alberta, Canada, m: 03 Sep 1988 in Calihoo, Alberta, Canada
.... + Rodney William Sopiwnyk (1964 -) b: 03 Mar 1964 in Winnipeg, Manitoba, Canada, m: 20 May 2000 in Edmonton, Alberta, Canada
....................9 Mathew Kyle Sopiwnyk (1990 -) b: 21 Nov 1990 in Edmonton, Alberta, Canada
....................8 Vance Jackie Christianson (1960 -) b: 22 Feb 1960 in Barrhead, Alberta, Canada
.... + Joanne Kathleen Zarry (1959 -) b: 30 Jun 1959 in Edmonton, Alberta, Canada, m: 21 Jun 1980 in Barrhead, Alberta, Canada
....................9 Jason Murray Christianson (1980 -) b: 12 Dec 1980 in Fort St. John, British Columbia, Canada
.... + Carly Perkins (1981 -) b: 29 May 1981 in Daysland, Alberta, Canada, m: 02 Jun 2005 in Fort St. John, British Columbia, Canada
....................10 Skyler Anne Christianson (2005 -) b: 02 Nov 2005 in Edmonton, Alberta, Canada
....................10 Samantha Kathleen Christianson (2008 -) b: 04 Sep 2008 in Edmonton, Alberta, Canada
....................10 Quinn Arlene Christianson (2010 -) b: 03 Mar 2010 in Edmonton, Alberta, Canada
....................9 Jessica Dawn Christianson (1982 -) b: 25 Jun 1982 in Fort St. John, British Columbia, Canada
.... + Shawn Nicolaas Van Wyk (1982 -) b: 21 Oct 1982 in Nanimo, B.C., m: 01 Jul 2008 in Las Vegas, Clark, Nevada, USA
....................10 Austin Van Wyk (2004 -) b: 19 May 2004 in Ft. St. John, B. C. Canada
....................10 Declan Van Wyk (2007 -) b: 03 Jul 2007 in Ft. St. John, B.C. Canada
....................9 Joel Anthony Christianson (1987 -) b: 03 Jun 1987 in Fort St. John, British Columbia, Canada
....................8 Colleen Elaine Christianson (1962 -) b: 25 Nov 1962 in Barrhead, Alberta, Canada
.... + William Michael Dobney (1960 -) b: 12 Jul 1960 in Sherwood Park, Alberta, m: 01 Sep 1984 in Barrhead, Alberta, Canada
....................9 Stuart William Dobney (1987 -) b: 12 Feb 1987 in St. Albert, Alberta
.... + Rachelle Volden (Unknown -) b: Unknown in Unknown, m: Unknown in Unknown

...........................9 Blaine Michael Dobney (1990 -) b: 20 Mar 1990 in St. Albert, Alberta

.... + Danny Olson (1972 -) b: 21 May 1972 in Barrhead, Alberta, Canada

.....................7 Stuart Floyd Larkins (1943 - 1958) b: 31 May 1943 in Barrhead, Alberta, Canada, d: 19 May 1958 in Barrhead, Alberta, Canada

.....................7 Carol Alice Larkins (1944 -) b: 11 Dec 1944 in Barrhead, Alberta, Canada

.... + Charles William Sutherland (1940 -) b: 03 Dec 1940 in Barrhead, Alberta, Canada, m: 25 Mar 1967 in Barrhead, Alberta, Canada

.........................8 Christopher Jason Sutherland (1972 -) b: 26 Dec 1972 in Barrhead, Alberta, Canada

.... + Elizabeth Eva Shield (1980 -) b: 05 Mar 1980 in Barrhead, Alberta, Canada, m: 15 Aug 2009 in Barrhead, Alberta, Canada

.........................9 1 Kiran Dax Sutherland (2014 -) b: 13 Jul 2014 in Barrhead, Alberta, Canada

.........................8 Sharla Kae Sutherland (1975 -) b: 22 Jul 1975 in Barrhead, Alberta, Canada

.... + Shaheed Merani (1980 -) b: 11 Dec 1980 in Edmonton, Alberta, Canada, m: 29 Sep 2007 in Edmonton, Alberta, Canada

..................6 Lewis Bentz (1911 - 1996) b: 13 Nov 1911 in Harvey, Cavalier, North Dakota, USA, d: 11 Sep 1996 in Barrhead, Alberta, Canada

.... + Katie Heberling (1910 - 1991) b: 11 Dec 1910 in Mlinska, Hungary, m: 04 Mar 1951 in Barrhead, Alberta, Canada, d: 05 Oct 1991 in Barrhead, Alberta, Canada

.....................7 Herbert Walter Bentz (1953 -) b: 10 May 1953 in Barrhead, Alberta, Canada

.... + Jacqueline Ann Johnstone (1950 -) b: 21 Apr 1950 in Urmston, Lancashire, England (Now part of Manchester), m: 27 Dec 1986 in Vancouver, British Columbia, Canada

.........................8 Julia Leanna Bentz (1987 -) b: 21 Sep 1987 in Vancouver, British Columbia, Canada

.........................8 Simon Alexander Bentz (1990 -) b: 14 Jul 1990 in Vancouver, British Columbia, Canada

..................6 Robert Alloys Bentz (1914 - 2002) b: 22 Oct 1914 in unknown, d: 27 Sep 2002 in Edmonton, Alberta, Canada

.... + Marie Gertrude Demers (1915 - 1999) b: 21 May 1915 in Lyster, Quebec, Canada, m: 01 Aug 1938 in Medicine Hat, Alberta, Canada, d: 22 May 1999 in Edmonton, Alberta, Canada

.....................7 Fern Anna Bentz (1939 -) b: 17 Apr 1939 in Ravenscrag. Saskatchewan, Canada

.....................7 Claudette Delores Bentz (1941 -) b: 02 Jun 1941 in Barrhead, Alberta, Canada

.....................7 Trevor Robert Bentz (1943 -) b: 09 Jan 1943 in Barrhead, Alberta, Canada

.... + Linda Anne Smaha (1945 -) b: 30 Aug 1945 in Hazelton, British Columbia, m: 28 Dec 1963 in Unknown

.........................8 Steven Trevor Bentz (1965 -) b: 15 Jun 1965 in Terrace, British Columbia

.... + Lauri Marie Geddes (1968 -) b: 17 Oct 1968 in Edmonton, Alberta, Canada, m: 16 Jul 1993 in Kamloops, British Columbia, Canada

.........................9 Reade Robert John Bentz (1997 -) b: 09 Mar 1997 in Kamloops, British Columbia

.........................9 Kelsy Trevor Geddis Bentz (2000 -) b: 02 Oct 2000 in Kamloops, British Columbia

.........................8 Warren John Bentz (1969 -) b: 31 May 1969 in Terrace, British Columbia, Canada

.... + Melinda Funk (1973 -) b: 18 Oct 1973 in Nanaimo, British Columbia, Canada

.........................9 Adam John Alan Bentz Funk (1994 -) b: 10 Sep 1994 in Kamloops, British Columbia, Canada

.....................7 Allan Harvey Bentz (1946 -) b: 27 Apr 1946 in Barrhead, Alberta, Canada

.... + Margaret Ann McQuire (1947 -) b: 29 Apr 1947 in Edmonton, Alberta, Canada, m: 05 Feb 1965 in Edmonton, Alberta, Canada

.........................8 Tammy Ann Bentz (1966 -) b: 18 Jun 1966 in Edmonton, Alberta, Canada

.... + Trevor Charles James Hansen (1963 -) b: 10 Oct 1963 in Ottawa, Ontario, Canada, m: 10 Oct 1987 in Morinville, Alberta, Canada

.........................9 Dane Thomas Hansen (2002 -) b: 26 Jun 2002 in Vancouver, British Columbia, Canada

.........................8 Casey Allan Bentz (1967 -) b: 26 Jul 1967 in Edmonton, Alberta, Canada

.... + Tamie Alma Froment (1973 -) b: 16 Jun 1973 in St. Albert, Alberta, m: 17 Jul 1993 in Morinville, Alberta, Canada

.........................9 Maguire Casavant Bentz (2000 -) b: 07 Jun 2000 in St. Albert, Alberta

.........................8 Gregory Robert Bentz (1974 -) b: 28 Jan 1974 in St. Albert, Alberta, Canada

.... + Lynne Marie Froment (1978 -) b: 02 Jun 1978 in St. Albert, Alberta, m: 01 Aug 2001 in Morinville, Alberta, Canada

......................7 Dallas Wayne Bentz (1947 -) b: 02 May 1947 in Barrhead, Alberta, Canada

.... + Karen Kathleen Klukus (1950 -) b: 07 Apr 1950 in Edmonton, Alberta, Canada, m: 19 Jul 1969 in Edmonton, Alberta, Canada

......................8 Brenton Powell Bentz (1971 -) b: 01 Apr 1971 in Edmonton, Alberta, Canada

.... + Monica Kuebler (1978 -) b: 03 Mar 1978 in Ontario, m: 16 Sep 2006 in Edmonton, Alberta, Canada

......................8 Christopher Wade Bentz (1972 -) b: 28 Nov 1972 in Edmonton, Alberta, Canada

......................8 Jason Willis Bentz (1974 -) b: 06 Mar 1974 in Edmonton, Alberta, Canada

.... + Kimberly Tomm (1975 -) b: 24 Jul 1975 in Edmonton, Alberta, Canada, m: 27 Jul 2003 in Edmonton, Alberta, Canada

.........................9 Griffin Bentz (2007 -) b: 03 Aug 2007 in Edmonton, Alberta, Canada

...........................10 Calvin Bentz (2010 -) b: 05 Aug 2010 in Edmonton, Alberta, Canada

.........................9 Calvin Bentz (2010 -) b: 05 Aug 2010 in Edmonton, Alberta, Canada

....................7 Sharon Vaughn Bentz (1953 -) b: 19 Jul 1953 in Barrhead, Alberta, Canada

.... + Dennis Robert Gunn (1947 - 1996) b: 19 Feb 1947 in Medford, Oregon, USA, m: 16 May 1974 in Edmonton, Alberta, Canada, d: 1996 in Whittiker, California

....................8 Matthew Robert Jonathan Gunn (1978 -) b: 16 May 1978 in Edmonton, Alberta, Canada

.... + Lisa Wagner (Unknown -) b: Unknown in Unknown, m: Unknown in Unknown

.......................9 Parker Robert Gunn (2005 -) b: 18 May 2005 in Edmonton, Alberta, Canada

.... + Tish Shelby Claughton (1980 -) b: 01 Aug 1980 in Edmonton, Alberta, Canada

.......................9 Lavender Shelby Gunn (2013 -) b: 05 Mar 2013 in Edmonton, Alberta, Canada

....................7 Wesley Alloys Bentz (1956 -) b: 23 Oct 1956 in Edmonton, Alberta, Canada

.... + Jennifer Gail Clark (1963 -) b: 07 Sep 1963 in Burnaby, British Columbia, Canada

....................8 Huxley Clark Bentz (1994 -) b: 16 Feb 1994 in Edmonton, Alberta, Canada

....................8 Elliott Johann Bentz (1999 -) b: 28 Sep 1999 in Edmonton, Alberta, Canada

....................7 Anthony Gerard Vincent Bentz (1958 -) b: 11 Dec 1958 in Edmonton, Alberta, Canada

.... + Katherine Lynne Cotton (1962 -) b: 08 Sep 1962 in Winnipeg, Manitoba, Canada, m: 08 Aug 1985 in Edmonton, Alberta, Canada

....................8 Melissa Diane Bentz (1987 -) b: 17 Apr 1987 in Edmonton, Alberta, Canada

.... + Ian Phillipchuk (Unknown -) b: Unknown in Unknown, m: 15 Sep 2012 in Edmonton, Alberta, Canada

....................8 Kristen May Bentz (1990 -) b: 21 Sep 1990 in Edmonton, Alberta, Canada

....................7 Rhonda Jean Bentz (1959 -) b: 05 Oct 1959 in Edmonton, Alberta, Canada

.... + Donald Ray Littlejohn (1955 -) b: 09 Sep 1955 in Edmonton, Alberta, Canada, m: 25 Oct 1978 in Edmonton, Alberta, Canada

....................8 James Robert Littlejohn (1978 -) b: 16 Apr 1978 in Edmonton, Alberta, Canada

....................8 Roberta Jean Littlejohn (1979 -) b: 17 Aug 1979 in Edmonton, Alberta, Canada

.........................9 Savanah Rebecca Littlejohn (1997 -) b: 17 Apr 1997 in Edmonton, Alberta, Canada

....................7 Lisa Marie Bentz (1962 -) b: 01 Jul 1962 in Edmonton, Alberta, Canada

.... + Tony Fortney b: unknown, m: 28 Dec 1980 in Shaunavon, Saskatchewan, Canada

....................8 Nickolas Anthony Fortney (1980 -) b: 05 Jul 1980 in Shaunavon, Saskatchewan, Canada

....................8 Terra Lyn Fortney (1982 -) b: 28 Feb 1982 in Shaunavon, Saskatchewan, Canada

....................8 Joshua Robert Fortney (1984 -) b: 26 Dec 1984 in Shaunavon, Saskatchewan, Canada

.... + Douglas Steven Tymchuk

....................8 Aaron Jackson Tymchuk

....................8 Dustin Steven Tymchuk

....................7 Korrine Octa Bentz (1962 -) b: 19 Sep 1962 in Edmonton, Alberta, Canada

.... + Richard Wayne Pigeon (1961 -) b: 19 Jul 1961 in Edmonton, Alberta, Canada, m: 08 Mar 1980 in Edmonton, Alberta, Canada

....................8 Christopher Richard Pigeon (1980 -) b: 03 May 1980 in Edmonton, Alberta, Canada

.... + Unknown

.................9 Brandon Pigeon (2002 -) b: 21 Jul 2002 in Edmonton, Alberta, Canada

.................8 Jessica Marie Pigeon (1982 -) b: 19 Aug 1982 in Edmonton, Alberta, Canada

.... + Unknown

.................9 Jayde Pigeon (1999 -) b: 14 May 1999 in Edmonton, Alberta, Canada

.... + Vincent Arthur Michaud (1958 -) b: 03 Apr 1958 in Edmonton, Alberta, Canada, m: Unknown in Uknown

.................7 Cheryl Ann Widynowski (1966 -) b: 04 Jul 1966 in Edmonton, Alberta, Canada

.................7 Daryl Shepherd (1970 -) b: 17 May 1970 in Edmonton, Alberta, Canada

.................7 Jamie El-Khatib (1974 -) b: 09 Jun 1974 in Edmonton, Alberta, Canada

...............6 Alice Gertrude Bentz (1917 -) b: 31 Mar 1917 in Ravenscrag. Saskatchewan, Canada

.... + Arthur Farquhar Warehime (1919 - 2006) b: 05 Aug 1919 in Barrhead, Alberta, Canada, m: 27 Apr 1946 in Barrhead, Alberta, Canada, d: 07 Dec 2006 in Barrhead, Alberta, Canada

.................7 Myrna Alice Warehime (1946 -) b: 12 Nov 1946 in Barrhead, Alberta, Canada

.... + Albert Lee Chadd (1940 -) b: 04 Mar 1940 in Barrhead, Alberta, Canada, m: 12 Nov 1966 in Barrhead, Alberta, Canada

.................8 Zene Ross Chadd (1967 -) b: 19 Sep 1967 in Barrhead, Alberta, Canada

.... + Jodi Leanne Arnal (1967 -) b: 25 Mar 1967 in Barrhead, Alberta, Canada, m: 29 Nov 1986 in Barrhead, Alberta, Canada

.................9 Jimy Lee Chadd (1986 -) b: 22 Jul 1986 in Barrhead, Alberta, Canada

.... + Crystal Gail McIntosh (1981 -) b: 30 Nov 1981 in Barrhead, Alberta, Canada, m: 13 Jun 2009 in Tiger Lily, Alberta, Canada

.................10 Wyatt James Arthur Chadd (2007 -) b: 12 Apr 2007 in Barrhead, Alberta, Canada

.................10 Damien Michael Travis Chadd (2010 -) b: 11 Aug 2010 in Barrhead, Alberta, Canada

.................9 Michael Zene Chadd (1989 -) b: 27 Jan 1989 in Barrhead, Alberta, Canada

.................9 Kaylee Nicole Chadd (1991 -) b: 28 Feb 1991 in Barrhead, Alberta, Canada

.... + Tracy Mary Devolt b: Whitecourt, Alberta

.................9 Dominic Devolt (1999 -) b: 15 Jan 1999 in Whitecourt, Alberta

.................9 Abigal Frances Chadd (2005 -) b: 07 Jun 2005 in Whitecourt, Alberta, Canada

.................8 Lonnie Wade Chadd (1969 -) b: 03 Nov 1969 in Barrhead, Alberta, Canada

.... + Louise Elaine Cowley (1976 -) b: 27 Jan 1976 in Mayerthorpe, Alberta, Canada, m: 10 Sep 1994 in Mayerthorpe, Alberta, Canada

.................9 Tre Ty Chadd (1999 -) b: 06 Oct 1999 in Barrhead, Alberta, Canada

.................9 Logan Grant Chadd (2005 -) b: 22 Apr 2005 in Edmonton, Alberta, Canada

.................8 Lowell Jason Chadd (1970 -) b: 28 Dec 1970 in Barrhead, Alberta, Canada

.... + Lolita Irene Properzi (1972 -) b: 28 Jul 1972 in Westlock, Alberta, Canada, m: 11 Aug 1990 in Barrhead, Alberta, Canada

.................9 Trinity Kathleen Chadd (1991 -) b: 24 Aug 1991 in Barrhead, Alberta, Canada

.................9 Xayna Myrene Chadd (1994 -) b: 24 May 1994 in Barrhead, Alberta, Canada

.................9 Erin Lee Chadd (1995 -) b: 07 Dec 1995 in Barrhead, Alberta, Canada

.................8 Dana Lee Chadd (1971 -) b: 08 May 1971 in Barrhead, Alberta, Canada

.... + Tania Lee White (1973 -) b: 21 Aug 1973 in Mayerthorpe, Alberta, Canada, m: 12 Nov 1994 in Mayerthorpe, Alberta, Canada

.................9 Kasandra Margaret Chadd (1996 -) b: 17 Sep 1996 in Edmonton, Alberta, Canada

.... + Kimberly Ann Gauthier (1980 -) b: 10 Aug 1980 in Nanaimo, British Columbia, Canada, m: 21 Sep 2002 in Barrhead, Alberta, Canada

.................9 Vincent Elmond Chadd (2005 -) b: 06 Oct 2005 in Barrhead, Alberta, Canada

.................9 Anna Marie Chadd (2008 -) b: 08 Dec 2008 in Barrhead, Alberta, Canada

.................8 Quentin Arthur Chadd (1981 -) b: 08 Nov 1981 in Barrhead, Alberta, Canada

.... + Lacey Rebecca Barbara Pringle (1981 -) b: 17 Nov 1981 in Swift Current, Saskatchewan, Canada, m: 25 May 2002 in Tiger Lily, Alberta, Canada

.................9 Cameron Chadd (2002 -) b: 03 Mar 2002 in Edmonton, Alberta, Canada

.................9 Emily Mary Ellen Chadd (2005 -) b: 02 May 2005 in Barrhead, Alberta, Canada

...........................9 Luke Zene Chadd (2009 -) b: 10 Nov 2009 in Barrhead, Alberta, Canada

....................7 Lynn Shari Warehime (1948 -) b: 18 May 1948 in Barrhead, Alberta, Canada

....   + Lowell Clarence Cramer (1948 - 1992) b: 10 Apr 1948 in Barrhead, Alberta, Canada, m: 11 May 1968 in Barrhead, Alberta, Canada, d: 05 Aug 1992 in Barrhead, Alberta, Canada

........................8 Rechelle Alice Cramer (1969 -) b: 30 Mar 1969 in Barrhead, Alberta, Canada

....   + Todd William Koehler (1965 -) b: 21 Oct 1965 in Rivers, Manitoba, Canada, m: 15 Apr 1989 in Barrhead, Alberta, Canada

...........................9 Dylan Lowell Koehler (1990 -) b: 18 Oct 1990 in Barrhead, Alberta, Canada

...........................9 Chelsea Lynn Koehler (1993 -) b: 23 Mar 1993 in Barrhead, Alberta, Canada

...........................9 DevinTodd Koehler (1994 -) b: 14 Dec 1994 in Barrhead, Alberta, Canada

........................8 Robin Lowell Cramer (1971 -) b: 12 Mar 1971 in Barrhead, Alberta, Canada

....   + Dawn Mae Holowaychuk (1976 -) b: 19 Jul 1976 in Edmonton, Alberta, Canada, m: 20 Aug 1999 in Barrhead, Alberta, Canada

...........................9 Jaydon Dawn Cramer (2002 -) b: 07 Aug 2002 in Barrhead, Alberta, Canada

...........................9 Kiera Robin Cramer (2004 -) b: 04 Aug 2004 in Barrhead, Alberta, Canada

........................8 Tammy Lynn Margaret Cramer (1973 -) b: 16 Apr 1973 in Barrhead, Alberta, Canada

....   + Shawn Doyle Kinden (1974 -) b: 08 Apr 1974 in St John's, Newfoundland and Labrador, Canada

...........................9 Laura Anne Kinden (2005 -) b: 30 Oct 2005 in Grande Prairie, Alberta, Canada

........................8 Christina Noreen Cramer (1976 -) b: 08 Jun 1976 in Barrhead, Alberta, Canada

..................6 Calvin Paul Bentz (1919 - 2005) b: 10 Apr 1919 in Eastend, Saskatchewan, Canada, d: 02 Feb 2005 in Vegreville, Alberta

....   + Katherine Hannah Metzger (1928 - 1984) b: 14 Sep 1928 in Barrhead, Alberta, Canada, m: 17 Dec 1946 in Mellowdale, Alberta, Canada, d: 14 May 1984 in Kelowna, British Columbia, Canada

....................7 Donna Shirley Bentz (1949 - 1965) b: 30 Mar 1949 in Barrhead, Alberta, Canada, d: 27 Jan 1965 in Barrhead, Alberta, Canada

....................7 Jerry Allan Bentz (1951 -) b: 21 Nov 1951 in Barrhead, Alberta, Canada

....   + Jane Elizabeth Matheson (1952 -) b: 21 Dec 1952 in Edmonton, Alberta, Canada, m: 16 Aug 1974 in Edmonton, Alberta, Canada

........................8 Sarah Katherine Bentz (1978 -) b: 09 Dec 1978 in Edmonton, Alberta, Canada

....   + Chad Ryan Paul Schulz (1974 -) b: 31 Oct 1974 in Lahr, Germany, Europe, m: 09 Jun 2007 in Edmonton, Alberta, Canada

........................8 Andrea Heather Bentz (1980 -) b: 10 Dec 1980 in Edmonton, Alberta, Canada

....   + Ryan Freehan b: Edmonton, Alberta, Canada, m: Edmonton, Alberta, Canada

........................8 Lisa Marie Bentz (1983 -) b: 19 Mar 1983 in Edmonton, Alberta, Canada

....................7 Jane Kathleen Bentz (1951 -) b: 21 Nov 1951 in Barrhead, Alberta, Canada

....   + Joseph Paul Hoffman (1950 -) b: 05 Dec 1950 in Barrhead, Alberta, Canada, m: 31 Aug 1970 in Barrhead, Alberta, Canada

........................8 Charlene Crystal Hoffman (1973 -) b: 24 Nov 1973 in Vegreville, Alberta, Alberta, Canada

....   + Garett Hromada (1971 -) b: 06 Jul 1971 in Edmonton, Alberta, Canada, m: 30 Sep 2006 in Edmonton, Alberta, Canada

...........................9 Jake Garett Hromada (2008 -) b: 02 Jun 2008 in St Albert, Alberta, Canada

...........................9 Gavin Carl Joe Hromada (2011 -) b: 28 Jul 2011 in St Albert, Alberta, Canada

........................8 Christy Lynn Hoffman (1977 -) b: 08 Feb 1977 in Vegreville, Alberta, Canada

....   + Michael Le-Roy Webb (1975 -) b: 31 Aug 1975 in Balfast, Ireland, m: 01 Sep 2001 in Vegreville, Alberta, Canada

...........................9 Connor Joseph Webb (2005 -) b: 27 Apr 2005 in Vegreville, Alberta

...........................9 Kenneday Jane Webb (2006 -) b: 21 Nov 2006 in Vegreville, Alberta

....................7 Nancy Ann Bentz (1961 -) b: 11 Nov 1961 in Barrhead, Alberta, Canada

....   + Mauri Kalevi Saura (1955 -) b: 07 May 1955 in Finland, Europe, m: 29 May 1982 in Kelowna, British Columbia, Canada

...........................8 Amanda Katherine Saura (1985 -) b: 06 Jun 1985 in Victoria, British Columbia, Canada

.... + Nelson Lindahl m: 02 Oct 2004 in Kelowna, British Columbia, Canada

...........................9 Allie Katherine Lindahl (2012 -) b: 24 Feb 2012 in Kelowna, British Columbia, Canada

...........................9 Ava Marie Lindahl (2013 -) b: 20 Dec 2013 in Kelowna, British Columbia, Canada

...........................8 Jessica Leal Saura (1994 -) b: 28 Feb 1994 in Revelstoke, British Columbia, Canada

.... + Harvey Melvin Kilbrie (1951 -) b: 10 Sep 1951 in Winnipeg, Manitoba, Canada, m: 06 Oct 2012 in Kelowna, British Columbia, Canada

.......................7 John Bentz (1951 - 1951) b: 21 Nov 1951 in Barrhead, Alberta, Canada, d: 21 Nov 1951 in Barrhead, Alberta, Canada

...................6 Harvey Harold Bentz (1921 - 2002) b: 30 Jan 1921 in Ravenscrag. Saskatchewan, Canada, d: 30 Jul 2002 in Barrhead, Alberta, Canada

.... + Alvina Radke (1921 - 2002) b: 23 Sep 1921 in Barrhead, Alberta, Canada, m: 11 Nov 1948 in Mellowdale, Alberta, Canada, d: 30 Jul 2002 in Barrhead, Alberta, Canada

.......................7 Janice Lee Bentz (1949 -) b: 11 Dec 1949 in Barrhead, Alberta, Canada

.... + Robert Ernest Maxwell (1942 -) b: 08 Aug 1942 in Duncan, British Columbia, Canada, m: 06 Oct 1972 in Mellowdale, Alberta, Canada

...........................8 Melanie Leah Maxwell (1979 -) b: 06 Sep 1979 in Vancouver, British Columbia, Canada

.......................7 Lorne Douglas Bentz (1952 -) b: 20 Mar 1952 in Barrhead, Alberta, Canada

.... + Judith Yvone King (1957 - 1983) b: 26 Jul 1957 in Barrhead, Alberta, Canada, m: 08 May 1976 in Barrhead, Alberta, Canada, d: 03 Jun 1983 in Barrhead, Alberta, Canada

...........................8 Bradley Douglas Bentz (1979 -) b: 23 Mar 1979 in Edmonton, Alberta, Canada

.... + Melinda Larson (1982 -) b: 23 Mar 1982 in Barrhead, Alberta, Canada, m: 13 Aug 2005 in Barrhead, Alberta, Canada

...........................9 Hunter Riley Bentz (2007 -) b: 18 Oct 2007 in Edmonton, Alberta, Canada

...........................9 Cole Douglas Bentz (2009 -) b: 19 Nov 2009 in Barrhead, Alberta, Canada

...........................8 Michael James Bentz (1981 -) b: 19 Jul 1981 in Barrhead, Alberta, Canada

.... + Alicia Torey Schmidt (1984 -) b: 15 Jul 1984 in Westlock, Alberta, Canada, m: 18 Jul 2009 in Barrhead, Alberta, Canada

...........................9 Mason Dane Bentz (2011 -) b: 12 Aug 2011 in St. Albert, Alberta

.... + Judy Anne Baron (1954 -) b: 29 Jun 1954 in Barrhead, Alberta, Canada, m: 20 Feb 1999 in Mellowdale, Alberta, Canada

.......................7 Dale Keith Bentz (1956 -) b: 17 Apr 1956 in Barrhead, Alberta, Canada

.... + Laurie Gail Geis (1957 -) b: 25 Sep 1957 in Barrhead, Alberta, Canada, m: 21 Mar 1981 in Mellowdale, Alberta, Canada

...................6 Magdalena Bentz (1922 - 2003) b: 22 Dec 1922 in Eastend, Saskatchewan, Canada, d: 07 Aug 2003 in Kelowna, British Columbia, Canada

...................6 Irene Evelyn Bentz (1926 - 2012) b: 03 Jan 1926 in Eastend, Saskatchewan, Canada, d: 27 May 2012 in Barrhead, Alberta, Canada

.... + Gustav Stefani (1923 - 1996) b: 11 Nov 1923 in Poland, Europe, m: 03 Jan 1949 in Barrhead, Alberta, Canada, d: 05 May 1996 in Westlock, Alberta, Canada

.......................7 Wayne Ronald Stefani (1949 - 2000) b: 25 Oct 1949 in Westlock, Alberta, Canada, d: 06 Mar 2000 in Richmond, British Columbia, Canada

.... + Cheryl MacDonald (Unknown -) b: Unknown in Vancouver, British Columbia, Canada, m: 07 Nov 1969 in Vancouver, British Columbia, Canada

...........................8 Mark Kenneth Stefani (1970 -) b: 25 Mar 1970 in Vancouver, British Columbia, Canada

.... + Bonnie Soroke (Unknown -) b: Unknown in Vancouver, British Columbia, Canada, m: Unknown in Unknown

...........................8 Joel Stefani Soroke (1990 -) b: 05 May 1990 in Vancouver, British Columbia, Canada

.... + Katherine McElroy Zanner (Unknown -) b: Unknown in Vancouver, British Columbia, Canada, m: Unknown in Unknown

...........................8 Ryan Ronald Zanner (1982 -) b: 24 Dec 1982 in Vancouver, British Columbia, Canada

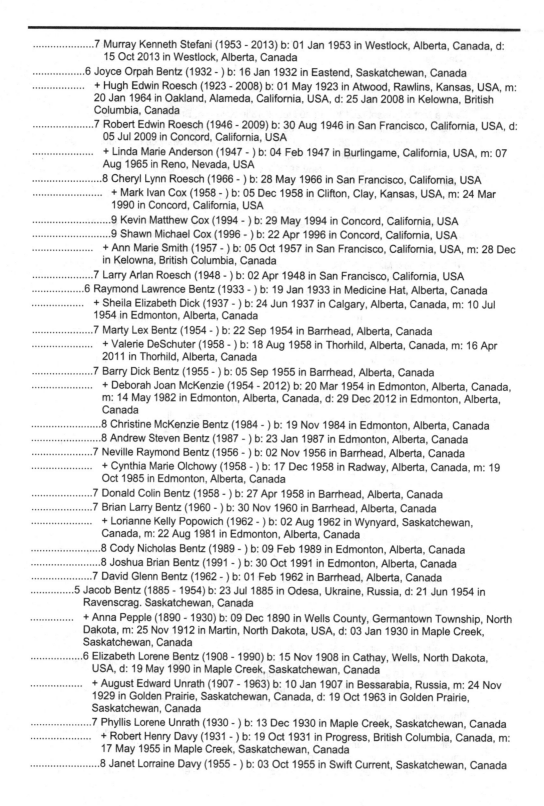

....................7 Murray Kenneth Stefani (1953 - 2013) b: 01 Jan 1953 in Westlock, Alberta, Canada, d: 15 Oct 2013 in Westlock, Alberta, Canada

.................6 Joyce Orpah Bentz (1932 -) b: 16 Jan 1932 in Eastend, Saskatchewan, Canada

.... + Hugh Edwin Roesch (1923 - 2008) b: 01 May 1923 in Atwood, Rawlins, Kansas, USA, m: 20 Jan 1964 in Oakland, Alameda, California, USA, d: 25 Jan 2008 in Kelowna, British Columbia, Canada

....................7 Robert Edwin Roesch (1946 - 2009) b: 30 Aug 1946 in San Francisco, California, USA, d: 05 Jul 2009 in Concord, California, USA

.... + Linda Marie Anderson (1947 -) b: 04 Feb 1947 in Burlingame, California, USA, m: 07 Aug 1965 in Reno, Nevada, USA

........................8 Cheryl Lynn Roesch (1966 -) b: 28 May 1966 in San Francisco, California, USA

.... + Mark Ivan Cox (1958 -) b: 05 Dec 1958 in Clifton, Clay, Kansas, USA, m: 24 Mar 1990 in Concord, California, USA

...........................9 Kevin Matthew Cox (1994 -) b: 29 May 1994 in Concord, California, USA

...........................9 Shawn Michael Cox (1996 -) b: 22 Apr 1996 in Concord, California, USA

.... + Ann Marie Smith (1957 -) b: 05 Oct 1957 in San Francisco, California, USA, m: 28 Dec in Kelowna, British Columbia, Canada

....................7 Larry Arlan Roesch (1948 -) b: 02 Apr 1948 in San Francisco, California, USA

.................6 Raymond Lawrence Bentz (1933 -) b: 19 Jan 1933 in Medicine Hat, Alberta, Canada

.... + Sheila Elizabeth Dick (1937 -) b: 24 Jun 1937 in Calgary, Alberta, Canada, m: 10 Jul 1954 in Edmonton, Alberta, Canada

....................7 Marty Lex Bentz (1954 -) b: 22 Sep 1954 in Barrhead, Alberta, Canada

.... + Valerie DeSchuter (1958 -) b: 18 Aug 1958 in Thorhild, Alberta, Canada, m: 16 Apr 2011 in Thorhild, Alberta, Canada

....................7 Barry Dick Bentz (1955 -) b: 05 Sep 1955 in Barrhead, Alberta, Canada

.... + Deborah Joan McKenzie (1954 - 2012) b: 20 Mar 1954 in Edmonton, Alberta, Canada, m: 14 May 1982 in Edmonton, Alberta, Canada, d: 29 Dec 2012 in Edmonton, Alberta, Canada

........................8 Christine McKenzie Bentz (1984 -) b: 19 Nov 1984 in Edmonton, Alberta, Canada

........................8 Andrew Steven Bentz (1987 -) b: 23 Jan 1987 in Edmonton, Alberta, Canada

....................7 Neville Raymond Bentz (1956 -) b: 02 Nov 1956 in Barrhead, Alberta, Canada

.... + Cynthia Marie Olchowy (1958 -) b: 17 Dec 1958 in Radway, Alberta, Canada, m: 19 Oct 1985 in Edmonton, Alberta, Canada

....................7 Donald Colin Bentz (1958 -) b: 27 Apr 1958 in Barrhead, Alberta, Canada

....................7 Brian Larry Bentz (1960 -) b: 30 Nov 1960 in Barrhead, Alberta, Canada

.... + Lorianne Kelly Popowich (1962 -) b: 02 Aug 1962 in Wynyard, Saskatchewan, Canada, m: 22 Aug 1981 in Edmonton, Alberta, Canada

........................8 Cody Nicholas Bentz (1989 -) b: 09 Feb 1989 in Edmonton, Alberta, Canada

........................8 Joshua Brian Bentz (1991 -) b: 30 Oct 1991 in Edmonton, Alberta, Canada

....................7 David Glenn Bentz (1962 -) b: 01 Feb 1962 in Barrhead, Alberta, Canada

..............5 Jacob Bentz (1885 - 1954) b: 23 Jul 1885 in Odesa, Ukraine, Russia, d: 21 Jun 1954 in Ravenscrag. Saskatchewan, Canada

.... + Anna Pepple (1890 - 1930) b: 09 Dec 1890 in Wells County, Germantown Township, North Dakota, m: 25 Nov 1912 in Martin, North Dakota, USA, d: 03 Jan 1930 in Maple Creek, Saskatchewan, Canada

.................6 Elizabeth Lorene Bentz (1908 - 1990) b: 15 Nov 1908 in Cathay, Wells, North Dakota, USA, d: 19 May 1990 in Maple Creek, Saskatchewan, Canada

.... + August Edward Unrath (1907 - 1963) b: 10 Jan 1907 in Bessarabia, Russia, m: 24 Nov 1929 in Golden Prairie, Saskatchewan, Canada, d: 19 Oct 1963 in Golden Prairie, Saskatchewan, Canada

....................7 Phyllis Lorene Unrath (1930 -) b: 13 Dec 1930 in Maple Creek, Saskatchewan, Canada

.... + Robert Henry Davy (1931 -) b: 19 Oct 1931 in Progress, British Columbia, Canada, m: 17 May 1955 in Maple Creek, Saskatchewan, Canada

........................8 Janet Lorraine Davy (1955 -) b: 03 Oct 1955 in Swift Current, Saskatchewan, Canada

.... + Terry Dale McKinley (1951 - 1999) b: 04 Apr 1951 in Grande Pairie, Alberta, Canada, m: 29 Jun 1979 in Calgary, Alberta, Canada, d: 08 Sep 1999 in Calgary, Alberta, Canada

................8 Karen Lynn Davy (1961 -) b: 11 Nov 1961 in Swift Current, Saskatchewan, Canada

.... + Mervyn William Newton (1961 -) b: 29 Apr 1961 in Saskatoon, Saskatchewan, Canada, m: 21 Mar 1987 in Saskatoon, Saskatchewan, Canada

................9 Julia Lauren Newton (1991 -) b: 09 Nov 1991 in Saskatoon, Saskatchewan, Canada

................9 Treena Louise Newton (1993 -) b: 02 Nov 1993 in Saskatoon, Saskatchewan, Canada

................9 Yvonne Lorraine Newton (1996 -) b: 17 May 1996 in Calgary, Alberta, Canada

................7 Bernice Annie Unrath (1935 - 2011) b: 01 Jun 1935 in Golden Prairie, Saskatchewan, Canada, d: 17 Sep 2011 in Medicine Hat, Alberta, Canada

.... + Wayne Leonard Davies (1933 - 2010) b: 20 Feb 1933 in Coronach, Saskatchewan, m: 18 Jul 1962 in Golden Prairie, Saskatchewan, Canada, d: 14 Aug 2010 in Medicine Hat, Alberta, Canada

................8 Thomas Joseph Davies (1966 -) b: 19 May 1966 in Bienfait, Saskatchewan, Canada

.... + Tracey Deanne Smith (1971 -) b: 07 May 1971 in Kamloops, British Columbia, m: 08 May 1993 in Calgary, Alberta, Canada

................9 Braeden Allen Davies (1994 -) b: 15 Aug 1994 in Calgary, Alberta, Canada

................8 Timothy Dale Davies (1967 -) b: 02 Nov 1967 in Bienfait, Saskatchewan, Canada

.... + Dana Marie North (1967 -) b: 17 Jan 1967 in Sudbury, Ontario, Canada, m: 21 Dec 1991 in Sudbury, Ontario, Canada

.... + Mary Ann Vandenburg (1973 -) b: 12 Nov 1973 in St Thomas, Ontario, m: 22 Nov 2000 in Montego Bay, Jamaica

................7 Gilbert Norman Unrath (1938 - 2011) b: 03 May 1938 in Golden Prairie, Saskatchewan, Canada, d: 30 Sep 2011 in Medicine Hat, Alberta, Canada

.... + Marion Edith Unsworth (1941 -) b: 08 Apr 1941 in Maple Creek, Saskatchewan, Canada, m: 28 Oct 1960 in Maple Creek, Saskatchewan, Canada

................8 Allan Gilbert Unrath (1960 -) b: 23 Oct 1960 in Maple Creek, Saskatchewan, Canada

.... + Michele Marie Vandenameele (1968 -) b: 27 Sep 1968 in Langenburg, Saskatchewan, m: 03 Jul 1993 in Langenburg, Saskatchewan

................9 Boston Unrath (2003 -) b: 29 Jul 2003 in Regina, Saskatchewan, Canada

................9 Taylor Unrath (2003 -) b: 29 Jul 2003 in Regina, Saskatchewan, Canada

................8 Vivian Jean Unrath (1961 -) b: 12 Nov 1961 in Maple Creek, Saskatchewan, Canada

.... + Leon Harvey Peter Moch (1960 -) b: 23 Dec 1960 in Maple Creek, Saskatchewan, Canada, m: 22 Jul 1978 in Maple Creek, Saskatchewan, Canada

................9 Brad Leon Moch (1978 -) b: 23 Jul 1978 in Medicine Hat, Alberta, Canada

.... + Janelle Katherine Gizen (1979 -) b: 17 Sep 1979 in Leader, Saskatchewan, Canada, m: 04 Jun 2006 in Medicine Hat, Alberta, Canada

................10 Cade Jacob Moch (2006 -) b: 01 Nov 2006 in Medicine Hat, Alberta, Canada

................10 Lucy June Moch (2009 -) b: 18 Aug 2009 in Medicine Hat, Alberta, Canada

................9 Janice Jean Moch (1982 -) b: 29 Mar 1982 in Medicine Hat, Alberta, Canada

.... + Richard Charles Humphrey (1978 -) b: 09 Feb 1978 in Lima, Ohio, USA, m: 09 Oct 2011 in Medicine Hat, Alberta, Canada

................8 Lorraine Gwen Unrath (1962 -) b: 25 Nov 1962 in Maple Creek, Saskatchewan, Canada

.... + Delmer Dwayne Beck (1955 -) b: 29 May 1955 in Golden Prairie, Saskatchewan, Canada, m: 12 Mar 1982 in Medicine Hat, Alberta, Canada

................9 Whaylin Delmar Beck (1983 -) b: 28 Sep 1983 in Medicine Hat, Alberta, Canada

.... + Frank William Hilgendorf (1961 -) b: 08 May 1961 in Medicine Hat, Alberta, Canada, m: 13 Oct 2013 in Medicine Hat, Alberta, Canada

................8 Bryce Norman Unrath (1964 -) b: 14 Jan 1964 in Maple Creek, Saskatchewan, Canada

.... + Yvette Marie Koch (1967 -) b: 15 Aug 1967 in Medicine Hat, Alberta, Canada, m: 25 Apr 1987 in Medicine Hat, Alberta, Canada

................9 Chantelle Rae Unrath (1987 -) b: 19 Sep 1987 in Medicine Hat, Alberta, Canada

...........................9 Jesse Jerome Bryce Gilbert Unrath (1989 -) b: 04 Oct 1989 in Medicine Hat, Alberta, Canada

.................6 Walter Bentz (1914 - 1973) b: 28 Apr 1914 in unknown, d: 09 Sep 1973 in Maple Creek, Saskatchewan, Canada

.................6 Daniel Bentz (1918 - 2008) b: 18 Dec 1918 in Ravenscrag. Saskatchewan, Canada, d: 13 Feb 2008 in Sundre, Alberta, Canada

.... + Phyllis Leona Hussey (1916 - 2013) b: 04 Nov 1916 in Swift Current, Saskatchewan, Canada, m: 04 Jan 1947 in Ravenscrag. Saskatchewan, Canada, d: 01 Dec 2013 in High River, Alberta Canada

....................7 Donavon Darrell Bentz (1948 -) b: 09 May 1948 in Maple Creek, Saskatchewan, Canada

.... + Marion Elsie MacLeod (1950 -) b: 09 Jun 1950 in Bassano, Alberta, Canada, m: 03 Mar 1973 in Calgary, Alberta, Canada

.......................8 Lesley Kathleen Bentz (1978 -) b: 24 Dec 1978 in Edmonton, Alberta, Canada

.... + Aubrey Bradley Dekok (1978 -) b: 07 Sep 1978 in Calgary, Alberta, Canada, m: 20 May 2006 in unknown

..........................9 Willem Benjamin Dekok (2009 -) b: 19 May 2009 in Calgary, Alberta, Canada

..........................9 Katherine Jordan Dekok (2010 -) b: 19 Sep 2010 in Calgary, Alberta, Canada

..........................9 Coen Daniel Dekok (2012 -) b: 21 Sep 2012 in High Riverr, Alberta, Canada

.......................8 Kristin Janet Bentz (1981 -) b: 23 Jul 1981 in Edmonton, Alberta, Canada

.......................8 David Daniel Bentz (1984 -) b: 03 Mar 1984 in Edmonton, Alberta, Canada

....................7 Lloyd James Bentz (1951 -) b: 19 Oct 1951 in Olds, Alberta, Canada

.... + Brenda Diane Allen (1953 -) b: 31 May 1953 in Paradise Hill, Saskatchewan, m: 10 May 1980 in Edmonton, Alberta, Canada

.......................8 Logan James Bentz (1980 -) b: 25 Oct 1980 in Edmonton, Alberta, Canada

.................6 Violet Leona Bentz (1923 - 1975) b: 11 Dec 1923 in Ravenscrag. Saskatchewan, Canada, d: 04 Apr 1975 in Medicine Hat, Alberta, Canada

.... + Edwin Rinkey (1916 - 1974) b: 19 Nov 1916 in Irvine, Alberta, Canada, m: 06 Nov 1948 in Medicine Hat, Alberta, Canada, d: 11 Nov 1974 in Calgary, Alberta, Canada

....................7 Peggy Ann Rinkey (1949 -) b: 22 Sep 1949 in Medicine Hat, Alberta, Canada

.... + John Wayne Stelter (1949 -) b: 23 Feb 1949 in Empress, Alberta, Canada, m: 04 Mar 1972 in Empress, Alberta, Canada

.......................8 Kyle John Stelter (1973 -) b: 21 Jun 1973 in Empress, Alberta

.... + Melanie Chantalle Verrier (1973 -) b: 10 Jul 1973 in Calgary, Alberta, Canada, m: 22 May 1999 in Victoria, British Columbia, Canada

..........................9 Nicholas John Stelter (2001 -) b: 25 Mar 2001 in Vancouver, British Columbia, Canada

..........................9 Markus Alexander Stelter (2003 -) b: 18 Mar 2003 in Chiliwack, British Columbia, Canada

.......................8 Tyson Edwin Stelter (1975 -) b: 23 Nov 1975 in Empress, Alberta

.... + Sommer Rose Ellis (1976 -) b: 02 Aug 1976 in Medicine Hat, Alberta, Canada, m: 13 Sep 2003 in Medicine Hat, Alberta, Canada

..........................9 Tryton John Stelter (2004 -) b: 03 Sep 2004 in Medicine Hat, Alberta, Canada

.......................8 Kristi Carol Stelter (1979 -) b: 11 Aug 1979 in Empress, Alberta, Canada

.... + Craig Sauter (1969 -) b: 26 Dec 1969 in Medicine Hat, Alberta, Canada, m: 06 Jul 2002 in Empress, Alberta, Canada

..........................9 Jarod Sauter (1995 -) b: 28 Mar 1995 in Irvine, Alberta, Canada

..........................9 Justis Sauter (1998 -) b: 21 Jan 1998 in Irvine, Alberta, Canada

....................7 Carol Diane Rinkey (1951 -) b: 19 Jul 1951 in Medicine Hat, Alberta, Canada

.... + John Victor Andersen (1946 -) b: 07 Sep 1946 in Empress, Alberta, Canada, m: 19 Nov 1976 in Medicine Hat, Alberta, Canada

.......................8 Heide Ann Leona Andersen (1976 -) b: 04 Sep 1976 in Medicine Hat, Alberta, Canada

.... + Mark Adrian Bowyer (1974 -) b: 16 Dec 1974 in Maple Creek, Saskatchewan, Canada, m: 09 Oct 1999 in Medicine Hat, Alberta, Canada

..........................9 Brianna Adrianna Carol Bowyer (1995 -) b: 31 Dec 1995 in Medicine Hat, Alberta, Canada

...................9 Kyran John Phillip Bowyer (1998 -) b: 23 Apr 1998 in Medicine Hat, Alberta, Canada

...................9 Emmarae Madsen Bowyer (2000 -) b: 02 Oct 2000 in Medicine Hat, Alberta, Canada

...................8 Troy John Peter Andersen (1978 -) b: 12 Sep 1978 in Medicine Hat, Alberta, Canada

.... + Patricia Marie Barrack (1978 -) b: 07 Sep 1978 in Calgary, Alberta, Canada, m: 18 May 2002 in Oyen, Alberta, Canada

...................9 Karter William Andersen (2004 -) b: 08 Oct 2004 in Grande Prairie, Alberta, Alberta

...................8 Cresten Edwin Andersen (1980 -) b: 16 Feb 1980 in Medicine Hat, Alberta, Canada

.............5 Magdalena Bentz (1890 - 1976) b: 06 Feb 1890 in Odesa, Ukraine, Russia, d: 06 Mar 1976 in North Surrey, British Columbia

.... + Adolph Berthold Kalk (1886 - 1974) b: 17 Jun 1886 in Belgonie, NWT, Canada, m: 07 Nov 1907 in Minot, Ward, North Dakota, USA, d: 21 Aug 1974 in North Surrey, British Columbia,Canada

...............6 Viola Eugene Kalk (1908 - 1995) b: 27 Feb 1908 in unknown, d: 11 Oct 1995 in Portland, Clackamas, Oregon, USA

.... + Einar Ericksen (1907 - 1975) b: 13 Jan 1907 in Trondheim, Sor-Trondelag, Norway, m: 25 Jan 1934 in Longview, Cowlitz, Washington, USA, d: 1975 in Portland, Clackamas, Oregon, USA

...................7 Janet Elaine Ericksen (1935 - 1990) b: 10 Sep 1935 in Longview, Cowlitz, Washington, USA, d: 04 Jun 1990 in Portland, Clackamas, Oregon, USA

.... + Senior Ronald Leroy Adkins (1932 -) b: 19 Sep 1932 in Portland, Clackamas, Oregon, USA, m: 06 Aug 1955 in Portland, Clackamas, Oregon, USA

...................8 Neil Thomas Adkins (1958 -) b: 10 Jan 1958 in Orléans, Loiret, Centre, France

...................8 Norman James Adkins (1961 -) b: 20 Oct 1961 in Forest Grove, Washington, Oregon, USA

.... + Tami Jo Denise Drangstvelt (1961 - 2010) b: 21 May 1961 in Grand Forks, North Dakota, USA, m: 06 Oct 1990 in Portland, Clackamas, Oregon, USA, d: 01 Feb 2010 in Portland, Clackamas, Oregon, USA

...................9 Lance Adkins (1993 -) b: 1993 in Portland, Clackamas, Oregon, USA

...................10 Kyler Adkins (1994 -) b: 1994 in Portland, Oregon, USA

...................10 Carson Adkins (1995 -) b: 1995

...................8 Junior Ronald William Adkins (1964 -) b: 23 Feb 1964 in Forest Grove, Washington, Oregon, USA

...............6 Vernon Cleveland Kalk (1909 - 2004) b: 03 Oct 1909 in unknown, d: 22 Sep 2004 in Bellingham, Whatcom, Washington, USA

.... + Rosella Kluthe (1918 - 2007) b: 28 Apr 1918 in Whitefish, South Dakota, USA, m: 29 Jun 1947 in Bellingham, Whatcom, Washington, USA, d: 03 Mar 2007 in Bellingham, Whatcom, Washington, USA

...................7 Ernest Joseph Kalk (1961 -) b: 01 Jan 1961 in Portland, Clackamas, Oregon, USA

...................8 Jimmy Kalk (1985 -) b: 01 Jan 1985 in Portland, Clackamas, Oregon, USA

...............6 Vera Grace Kalk (1911 - 2010) b: 09 Aug 1911 in unknown, d: 08 Jan 2010 in Victoria, British Columbia, Canada

...................7 Louella Grace Kalk (1934 -) b: 12 Mar 1934 in Moose Jaw, Saskatchewan, Canada

.... + George Brock Denison (1935 -) b: 29 May 1935 in Ottawa, Ontario, Canada, m: 30 Jun 1956 in Victoria, British Colmbia, Canada

...................8 Brock George Denison (1959 -) b: 20 Jun 1959 in Victoria, British Columbia, Canada

.... + Alexis Denise Smart (1962 -) b: 11 May 1962 in Victoria, British Columbia, Canada, m: 05 Sep 1987 in Victoria, British Colmbia, Canada

...................9 Brooklyn Ashley Denison (1991 -) b: 09 May 1991 in Victoria, British Columbia, Canada

...................9 Tessa Annie Denison (1993 -) b: 02 Dec 1993 in Victoria, British Columbia, Canada

...................8 Robert David Denison (1964 -) b: 25 Jun 1964 in Victoria, British Columbia, Canada

.... + Margaret Lorraine Straw (1963 -) b: 31 Jul 1963 in Dawson Creek, British Columbia, Canada, m: 24 Jan 1982 in Victoria, British Colmbia, Canada

...................9 Tyler David Denison (1997 -) b: 24 May 1997 in Victoria, British Columbia, Canada

...................9 Eryn Lorrell Denison (2000 -) b: 25 May 2000 in Victoria, British Columbia, Canada

...............6 Adeline Dorothy Kalk (1915 -) b: 18 Feb 1915 in Ravenscrag. Saskatchewan, Canada

.... + Frederick Macklin Sutton (1919 - 2012) b: 25 Jan 1919 in Victoria, British Columbia, Canada, m: 25 Nov 1942 in Victoria, British Colmbia, Canada, d: 27 Jul 2012 in Santee, San Diego, California, USA

.....................7 Gregory Allan Sutton (1949 -) b: 04 Oct 1949 in Victoria, British Columbia, Canada

.... + Patricia Anne Kaliruer (1949 -) b: 04 Apr 1949 in Norfolk, Virginia, USA, m: 30 Sep 1969 in San Diego, California, USA

.....................8 Carrie Lynn Sutton (1976 -) b: 27 Dec 1976 in San Diego, California, USA

.....................8 Daniel Christopher Sutton (1978 -) b: 30 Sep 1978 in San Diego, California, USA

....................7 Glenn Howard Sutton (1952 -) b: 15 Jul 1952 in Victoria, British Columbia, Canada

..................6 Lorraine Florence Kalk (1916 - 2013) b: 25 Sep 1916 in Ravenscrag. Saskatchewan, Canada, d: 07 Jan 2013 in Longview, Cowlitz, Washington, USA

..................6 Willard Edwin Carlson (1918 - 2005) b: 09 Apr 1918 in Ravenscrag. Saskatchewan, Canada, d: 20 Oct 2005 in Greenwood, British Columbia, Canada

.... + Caroline Mary Tibbetts (1926 - 2001) b: 22 Jul 1926 in Simcoe, Ontario, Canada, m: 30 Sep 1955 in Simcoe, Ontario, Canada, d: 18 Oct 2001 in Greenwood, British Columbia, Canada

.....................7 Richard Edwin Carlson (1956 -) b: 05 May 1956 in Atikokan, Ontario, Canada

.... + Karen Audrey Butcher b: Atikokan, Ontario, Canada

.....................8 Clinton Scott Carlson (1986 -) b: 12 Aug 1986 in Atikokan, Ontario, Canada

.....................7 Raymond Alan Carlson (1957 -) b: 06 Jul 1957 in Atikokan, Ontario, Canada

.... + Katherine Elizabeth Larson (1962 -) b: 09 Mar 1962 in Kenora, Ontario, Canada, m: 13 Aug 1982 in Kenora, Ontario, Canada

.....................8 Jeffrey Alan Carlson (1985 -) b: 07 Apr 1985 in Atikokan, Ontario, Canada

.....................8 Kimber Nicole Carlson (1988 -) b: 19 Jul 1988 in Atikokan, Ontario, Canada

....................7 Robert Dale Carlson (1958 -) b: 08 Nov 1958 in Atikokan, Ontario, Canada

.... + Catherine Anne Albrecht (1962 -) b: 1962 in Atikokan, Ontario, Canada

.....................8 Benjamin Robert Carlson (1984 -) b: 10 Sep 1984 in Atikokan, Ontario, Canada

.....................8 Andrew Alfred Carlson (1988 -) b: 20 Jul 1988 in Atikokan, Ontario, Canada

.... + Lorri Verfterzoff (Unknown -) b: Unknown in Atikokan, Ontario, Canada, m: Unknown in Unknown

.....................8 Rebecca Caroline Carlson (1994 -) b: 18 Oct 1994

....................7 Willard Ralph Carlson (1961 -) b: 21 Dec 1961 in Atikokan, Ontario, Canada

.... + Candice Jean Fraser (1966 -) b: 12 Jun 1966 in Atikokan, Ontario, Canada, m: 23 Sep 1984 in Thunder Bay, Ontario, Canada

.....................8 Summer Lynn Carlson (1986 -) b: 30 Apr 1986 in Thunder Bay, Ontario, Canada

....................7 Judith Leigh Carlson (1965 -) b: 22 Aug 1965 in Atikokan, Ontario, Canada

.... + Alex Patrick Bailey (1955 -) b: 07 Oct 1955 in Bracebridge, Ontario, Canada, m: 01 Jun 1988 in Atikokan, Ontario, Canada

.....................8 Patrick James Bailey (1987 - 1987) b: 12 Jan 1987 in Atikokan, Ontario, Canada, d: 02 Jul 1987 in Atikokan, Ontario, Canada

.....................8 Matthew Michael Bailey (1988 -) b: 09 Aug 1988 in Ontario, Canada

...................7 Judy Caroline Klub (1948 -) b: 06 Jan 1948 in Vanguard, Saskatchewan, Canada

.... + Carl Ernest Jautz (1940 -) b: 20 May 1940 in Humboldt, Saskatchewan, Canada, m: 08 Oct 1966 in Humboldt, Saskatchewan, Canada

.....................8 Lori Lynn Jautz (1969 - 1997) b: 21 Jul 1969 in Calgary, Alberta, Canada, d: 02 Dec 1997 in Calgary, Alberta, Canada

.... + Edward Neighbours (Unknown -) b: Unknown in Calgary, Alberta, Canada, m: 08 Jul 1995 in Unknown

.....................8 Monty Carl Jautz (1971 -) b: 01 Jan 1971 in Regina, Saskatchewan, Canada

.... + Wynette Lynn Neighbors (1975 -) b: 23 Jul 1975 in Melfort, Saskatchewan, Canada, m: 10 May 1998 in Unknown

.....................9 Britany Ashley Jautz (1998 -) b: 27 Oct 1998 in Calgary, Alberta, Canada

.... + Stewart Arthur McNeil (1952 -) b: 07 Nov 1952 in Calgary, Alberta, Canada, m: 07 May 1983 in Calgary, Alberta, Canada

.... + Caroline Klub b: unknown, d: Greenwood, British Columbia, Canada

...................7 Judy Caroline Klub (1948 -) b: 06 Jan 1948 in Vanguard, Saskatchewan, Canada
.... + Carl Ernest Jautz (1940 -) b: 20 May 1940 in Humboldt, Saskatchewan, Canada, m: 08 Oct 1966 in Humboldt, Saskatchewan, Canada
.......................8 Lori Lynn Jautz (1969 - 1997) b: 21 Jul 1969 in Calgary, Alberta, Canada, d: 02 Dec 1997 in Calgary, Alberta, Canada
.... + Edward Neighbours (Unknown -) b: Unknown in Calgary, Alberta, Canada, m: 08 Jul 1995 in Unknown
.......................8 Monty Carl Jautz (1971 -) b: 01 Jan 1971 in Regina, Saskatchewan, Canada
.... + Wynette Lynn Neighbors (1975 -) b: 23 Jul 1975 in Melfort, Saskatchewan, Canada, m: 10 May 1998 in Unknown
.........................9 Britany Ashley Jautz (1998 -) b: 27 Oct 1998 in Calgary, Alberta, Canada
.... + Stewart Arthur McNeil (1952 -) b: 07 Nov 1952 in Calgary, Alberta, Canada, m: 07 May 1983 in Calgary, Alberta, Canada
.................6 Bert Edward Kalk (1920 - 2007) b: 10 Feb 1920 in Ravenscrag. Saskatchewan, Canada, d: 14 Nov 2007 in Nipawin, Saskatchewan, Canada
.... + Lois Edna Dobell (1927 -) b: 04 Jun 1927 in Pontrilas, Saskatchewan, Canada, m: 02 Sep 1949 in Nipawin, Saskatchewan, Canada
...................7 Larry Wayne Kalk (1951 -) b: 14 Mar 1951 in Nipawin, Saskatchewan, Canada
.... + Bonnie Lynn Dymterko (1952 -) b: 03 Jun 1952 in Nipawin, Saskatchewan, Canada, m: 29 Mar 1978 in Hinton, Alberta, Canada
.......................8 Kristy Lee Kalk (1978 -) b: 12 Aug 1978 in Hinton, Alberta, Canada
.......................8 Beckki Lynn Kalk (1981 -) b: 29 Mar 1981 in Hinton, Alberta, Canada
...................7 Donald Bert Kalk (1956 -) b: 17 Jan 1956 in Nipawin, Saskatchewan, Canada
.... + Cindy Lou Boxall (1960 -) b: 03 Oct 1960 in Nipawin, Saskatchewan, Canada, m: 11 Nov 1983 in Nipawin, Saskatchewan, Canada
.......................8 Ashley Dawn Kalk (1984 -) b: 30 Aug 1984 in Hinton, Alberta, Canada
.......................8 Brittney Erin Kalk (1989 -) b: 20 Jan 1989 in Hinton, Alberta, Canada
...................7 Allan Brent Kalk (1966 -) b: 11 Jun 1966 in Nipawin, Saskatchewan, Canada
.... + Kelly Gay Trainor (1964 -) b: 06 Feb 1964 in Nipawin, Saskatchewan, Canada, m: 21 Dec 1988 in Nipawin, Saskatchewan, Canada
.......................8 Aiden Bret Kalk (1993 -) b: 24 Jul 1993 in Virctoria, British Columbia, Canada
.................6 Kenneth Fredrick Kalk (1924 - 2010) b: 15 Jun 1924 in Ravenscrag. Saskatchewan, Canada, d: 28 Jul 2010 in Langley, British Columbia, Canada
.... + Edith Laura Becker (1925 -) b: 12 Feb 1925 in Middle Lake, Saskatchewan, Canada, m: 01 Nov 1944 in Middle Lake, Saskatchewan, Canada
...................7 Sharon Diane Kalk (1945 -) b: 03 Jul 1945 in Nipawin, Saskatchewan, Canada
.... + Robert Patrick Marshall (1941 -) b: 24 Sep 1941 in British Columbia, Canada, m: 30 Apr 1971 in British Columbia, Canada
.......................8 Dana Claire Railey (1973 -) b: 25 Jul 1973 in Calgary, Alberta, Canada
.......................8 Kenneth Railey Marshall (1976 -) b: 25 Mar 1976 in Calgary, Alberta, Canada
...................7 Valerie Jean Kalk (1950 -) b: 25 Jun 1950 in Nipawin, Saskatchewan, Canada
.... + Norman Rowlings (Unknown -) b: Unknown in British Columbia, m: 1970 in British Columbia, Canada
.... + Sam Kwan (1952 -) b: 26 Sep 1952 in Vancouver, British Columbia, Canada
.................6 Raymond Sidney Kalk (1926 -) b: 17 Mar 1926 in Maple Creek, Saskatchewan, Canada
.... + Dorothy Bigelow (1930 - 1994) b: 02 Apr 1930 in Spoonville, Meuse, Lorraine, France, m: 23 Sep 1949 in Nipawin, Saskatchewan, Canada, d: 26 Aug 1994 in Nipawin, Saskatchewan, Canada
...................7 Blaine Woodrow Kalk (1966 -) b: 30 Jul 1966 in Saskatoon, Saskatchewan, Canada
.... + Jodie Lynn Graham (1968 -) b: 30 Mar 1968 in Regina, Saskatchewan, Canada, m: 21 May 1994 in Saskatoon, Saskatchewan, Canada
.......................8 Janelle Marie Dorothy Kalk (1996 -) b: 27 Jun 1996 in Saskatoon, Saskatchewan, Canada
.......................8 Seline Marie Antoinette Kalk (1998 -) b: 14 Oct 1998 in Calgary, Alberta, Canada
.......................8 Allysa Marie Magdalina Kalk (2000 -) b: 21 Apr 2000 in Calgary, Alberta, Canada

.....................7 Shayla Lorraine Kalk (1969 -) b: 20 Dec 1969 in Maple Creek, Saskatchewan, Canada

.... + Benny Roy Geisbrecht b: Fort St. John, British Columbia, Canada, m: 31 Jul 1994 in Maple Creek, Saskatchewan, Canada

.......................8 Jonathan Mark Kalk (1989 -) b: 20 Apr 1989 in Saskatoon, Saskatchewan, Canada

.......................8 Gerald Blaine Kalk (1991 -) b: 15 Jan 1991 in Grand Pairie, Alberta, Canada

.......................8 Wyatt Raymond Kalk (1993 -) b: 12 Oct 1993 in Grande Prairie, Alberta, Canada

.......................8 Diedra Mae Kalk (1995 -) b: 25 Oct 1995 in Grand Pairie, Alberta, Canada

.................6 Eunice Eileen Kalk (1935 -) b: 13 Feb 1935 in Armley, Saskatchewan, Canada

.... + John Walter Herbert Catterall (1935 -) b: 01 Jan 1935 in Victoria, British Columbia, Canada, m: 11 Nov 1960 in Victoria, British Colmbia, Canada

.....................7 Roydon Blake Catterall (1962 -) b: 29 Jan 1962 in Victoria, British Columbia, Canada

.... + Rebecca Lynn Ross (1960 -) b: 10 Jul 1960 in Denver, Colorado, USA, m: 04 Jun 1983 in Victoria, British Colmbia, Canada

.......................8 Candace Suzanne Catterall (1990 -) b: 14 Sep 1990 in Aurora, Colorado, USA

.......................8 Connor Ross Catterall (1993 -) b: 20 May 1993 in Aurora, Colorado, USA

.....................7 Bruce John Catterall (1963 -) b: 13 Jan 1963 in Victoria, British Columbia, Canada

.... + Donna Hebert (1962 -) b: 08 May 1962 in White Horse, Yukon, Canada

.....................7 Wade Vincent Catterall (1966 -) b: 17 Mar 1966 in New Westminster, British Columbia, Canada

.... + Karen Nestor (1949 -) b: 14 Nov 1949 in Cardston, Alberta, Canada, m: 01 Feb 1998 in Cobble Hill, British Columbia, Canada

.................6 Bruce Lenard Kalk (1934 - 1959) b: 26 Dec 1934 in Nipawin, Saskatchewan, Canada, d: 18 Aug 1959 in Victoria, British Columbia, Canada

...............5 George E. Bentz (1892 - 1964) b: 10 Dec 1892 in Odesa, Ukraine, Russia, d: 06 Dec 1964 in Medicine Hat, Alberta, Canada

.... + Theresa Haas (1903 - 1987) b: 25 Feb 1903 in unknown, m: 14 Jan 1932 in Medicine Hat, Alberta, Canada, d: 03 May 1987 in Medicine Hat, Alberta, Canada

.................6 Ruby June Bentz (1933 -) b: 12 Jun 1933 in Eastend, Saskatchewan, Canada

.... + David Wutzke (1925 - 2007) b: 25 Sep 1925 in Woolchester, Alberta, m: 10 Nov 1952 in Medicine Hat, Alberta, Canada, d: 19 Nov 2007 in Medicine Hat, Alberta, Canada

.....................7 Eileen Enez Wutzke (1954 -) b: 16 Mar 1954 in Medicine Hat, Alberta, Canada

.... + Fred John Brannan (1948 -) b: 04 Nov 1948 in Pembroke, Ontario, Canada, m: 18 Dec 1972 in Medicine Hat, Alberta, Canada

.......................8 Jeffery Dwayne Brannan (1971 -) b: 01 Mar 1971 in Medicine Hat, Alberta, Canada

.... + April Marie Lernar (1978 -) b: 05 Apr 1978 in Medicine Hat, Alberta, Canada, m: 1993 in Medicine Hat, Alberta, Canada

.........................9 Cole Dwayne Lernar Brannan (1994 -) b: 08 Aug 1994 in Medicine Hat, Alberta, Canada

.........................9 Chazz Jeffery Lernar Brannan (2000 -) b: 17 Oct 2000 in Medicine Hat, Alberta, Canada

.......................8 Keven Dwight Brannan (1972 -) b: 01 May 1972 in Pembroke, Ontario, Canada

.... + Glen Robert Sletvold (1955 -) b: 30 Oct 1955 in Medicine Hat, Alberta, Canada, m: 28 Jan 1995 in Medicine Hat, Alberta, Canada

.....................7 Dianna Lee Wutzke (1956 -) b: 17 Oct 1956 in Medicine Hat, Alberta, Canada

.... + William Henry Hoffman (1953 -) b: 07 Sep 1953 in Medicine Hat, Alberta, Canada, m: 10 May 1986 in Medicine Hat, Alberta, Canada

.....................7 Delphine Ann Wutzke (1958 -) b: 09 Apr 1958 in Medicine Hat, Alberta, Canada

.... + Hal Alen Porter (1961 - 1985) b: 31 Oct 1961 in Medicine Hat, Alberta, Canada, m: Dec 1978 in Medicine Hat, Alberta, Canada, d: 14 Aug 1985 in Regina, Saskatchewan, Canada

.... + Victor Edward Jenson (1959 -) b: 03 Jul 1959 in Vancouver, British Columbia, Canada, m: Jan 1991 in Vancouver, British Columbia, Canada

.....................7 Darcy Dean Wutzke (1963 -) b: 11 Dec 1963 in Medicine Hat, Alberta, Canada

.... + Fern Elizabeth Morgan (1965 -) b: 10 Dec 1965 in Winnipeg, Manitoba, Canada, m: 19 Aug 2988 in Medicine Hat, Alberta, Canada

...............5 Ottilie Bentz (1894 - 1971) b: 10 Apr 1894 in Odesa, Ukraine, Russia, d: 16 Jan 1971 in unknown

.... + Thomas Pepple (1885 - 1929) b: 26 Nov 1885 in Carrington, Foster, North Dakota, USA, m: 15 Nov 1911 in Cathay, Wells, North Dakota, USA, d: 21 May 1929 in Cathay, Wells, North Dakota, USA

.................6 Ella Helen Pepple (1913 - Unknown) b: 28 Mar 1913 in Cathay, Wells, North Dakota, USA, d: Unknown in Unknown

.... + William Quen Pickett (1896 - 1979) b: 17 Oct 1896 in unknown, m: 22 Dec 1935 in unknown, d: 20 Nov 1979 in unknown

...................7 William Quen Pickett (1935 -) b: 01 Jan 1935 in unknown

.... + Barbara Karen Lea b: unknown, m: 17 Dec 1958 in unknown

.....................8 Brenda Lea Pickett (1959 -) b: 01 Aug 1959 in unknown

.... + Donald Ramer (1958 -) b: 06 Oct 1958 in unknown, m: 15 Jun 1977 in unknown

.......................9 Belinda Lynn Ramer (1980 -) b: 12 Dec 1980 in Martin, North Dakota, USA

.......................9 Breann Ramer (1983 -) b: 20 Jun 1983 in Martin, North Dakota, USA

.....................8 Beth Marie Pickett (1961 -) b: 08 Jul 1961 in unknown

.... + Duncan Brown b: unknown, m: 13 Oct 1982 in unknown

.......................9 Katherine Elaine Brown (1984 -) b: 24 Nov 1984 in unknown

.....................8 Bea Ann Pickett (1963 -) b: 30 Mar 1963 in unknown

.................6 Hayden Ira Pepple (1916 - 1984) b: 10 Apr 1916 in unknown, d: 17 Apr 1984 in unknown

.... + Hilda Leighman (1917 - 1980) b: 19 Nov 1917 in unknown, m: 10 Apr 1940 in unknown, d: 01 Jan 1980 in unknown

...................7 Janice Kay Pepple (1940 -) b: 17 Oct 1940 in unknown

.... + Marlen J. Berdahl b: unknown, m: 16 Jun 1959 in unknown

.....................8 Marla Jane Berdahl (1962 -) b: 16 Jan 1962 in unknown

.....................8 Tracey Marie Berdahl (1963 -) b: 25 Dec 1963 in Martin, North Dakota, USA

.....................8 Brenda Joy Berdahl (1969 -) b: 03 Aug 1969 in unknown

.....................8 Bradely John Berdahl (1973 -) b: 01 Jun 1973 in unknown

...................7 Joyce May Pepple (1940 -) b: 17 Oct 1940 in unknown

.... + James Berdahl (Unknown -) b: Unknown in unknown, m: 03 Jan 1959 in unknown

.....................8 June Elizabeth Berdahl (1960 -) b: 17 Jul 1960 in unknown

.....................8 Steven James Berdahl (1961 -) b: 15 Aug 1961 in unknown

.....................8 Scott Allen Berdahl (1963 -) b: 19 Aug 1963 in unknown

.....................8 Janet Fay Berdahl (1965 -) b: 29 Apr 1965 in unknown

.....................8 Suzie Renee Berdahl (1967 -) b: 12 Mar 1967 in unknown

...................7 Sharon Pepple (1941 -) b: 01 Jul 1941 in unknown

.... + Norman Melland b: unknown, m: 09 Aug 1961 in unknown

.....................8 Brian Keith Melland (1965 -) b: 04 Aug 1965 in unknown

.......................9 Brandi Melland (1985 -) b: 1985 in Unknown

.....................8 Brent Alan Melland (1967 -) b: 25 Sep 1967 in unknown

.... + Patricia (Unknown -) b: Unknown in unknown, m: Unknown in Unknown

.......................9 Elizabeth Melland (1985 -) b: 24 Feb 1985 in Martin, North Dakota, USA

.......................9 Leslie Melland (1986 -) b: 19 Mar 1986 in Martin, North Dakota, USA

...................7 Gerald Hayden Pepple (1946 -) b: 14 Sep 1946 in unknown

.... + Anne Renee Radcliff (Unknown -) b: Unknown in unknown, m: 14 Feb 1970 in unknown

.................6 Benjamin Franklin Pepple (1919 - Unknown) b: 05 Dec 1919 in Cathay, Wells, North Dakota, USA, d: Unknown in Unknown

.... + Opal Ruth Beebe (1920 - 1965) b: 15 Aug 1920 in Chehalis, Lewis, Washington, USA, m: 25 Aug 1962 in Portland, Oregon, USA, d: 23 Sep 1965 in Portland, Clackamas, Oregon, USA

.................6 Adeline Mildred Pepple (1920 - 1993) b: 31 Dec 1920 in unknown, d: Jul 1993 in unknown

.... + Zona Elsworth Lowery (1920 - 1978) b: 17 Jan 1920 in unknown, m: 04 Aug 1946 in unknown, d: 25 Feb 1978 in unknown

...................7 Patricia Ann Lowery (1947 -) b: 07 Dec 1947 in unknown, d: 07 Dec 1947

.....................7 Lindell Lee Lowery (1949 -) b: 21 Mar 1949 in unknown
....   + Sandra Ruth Williams (Unknown -) b: Unknown in unknown, m: 11 Nov 1978 in unknown
.........................8 Jeffery Scott Lowery (1970 -) b: 02 Nov 1970 in unknown
.........................8 Sarah Beth Lowery (1982 -) b: 24 May 1982 in unknown
.....................7 William Vivan Lowery (1956 -) b: 20 Aug 1956 in unknown
..................6 Hilbert Thomas Pepple (1927 - 1990) b: 15 Jul 1927 in unknown, d: 01 Mar 1990 in unknown
....   + Leila Siebold (1926 - 2001) b: 07 Dec 1926 in unknown, m: 13 Dec 1947 in unknown, d: 09 Apr 2001 in Portland, Clackamas, Oregon, USA
.....................7 Linda Jean Pepple (1948 -) b: 28 Dec 1948 in unknown
....   + Donald Chaney (1947 -) b: 18 Feb 1947 in unknown, m: 24 Aug 1968 in unknown
.........................8 Brenda Michelle Chaney (1971 -) b: 01 Jun 1971 in unknown
.........................8 David Edward Chaney (1972 -) b: 15 Sep 1972 in unknown
.........................8 Amanda Lin Chaney (1981 -) b: 21 Jul 1981 in unknown
.....................7 Patricia Eileen Pepple (1950 -) b: 12 Mar 1950 in unknown
....   + Dennis Lankin (1950 -) b: 05 May 1950 in unknown, m: 20 Dec 1969 in unknown
.........................8 Mathew Thomas Lankin (1971 -) b: 20 Oct 1971 in unknown
.........................8 Danielle Lee Lankin (1973 -) b: 01 Jan 1973 in unknown
.........................8 Katherine Ann Lankin (1976 -) b: 06 Oct 1976 in unknown
.....................7 Peggy Joan Pepple (1952 -) b: 03 Sep 1952 in unknown
....   + Peter David Manning (1948 -) b: 04 Aug 1948 in unknown, m: 20 Mar 1971 in unknown
.........................8 Zachary David Manning (1977 -) b: 09 Aug 1977 in unknown
....   + Benjamin Ruger (Unknown - 1957) b: Unknown in unknown, m: Unknown in unknown, d: 19 Apr 1957 in unknown
...............5 Adolf Bentz (1897 - 1933) b: 27 Apr 1897 in Neudorf, Odessa Region ,Russia, d: 22 Oct 1933 in unknown
....   + Lydia Feil (1901 -) b: 1901 in unknown, m: 1921 in unknown
..................6 Ethel Alice Bentz (1923 -) b: 19 Feb 1923 in unknown
....   + Edmond Stillwell (1917 - Unknown) b: 1917 in unknown, m: Unknown in unknown, d: Unknown in Unknown
.....................7 William Jay Stillwell (1959 -) b: 18 Mar 1959 in unknown
.....................7 Melisa Faith Stillwell (1961 -) b: 14 Jun 1961 in unknown
.....................7 Gayle Hope Stillwell (1962 -) b: 20 Sep 1962 in unknown
....   + Vern Faul (1921 - 1948) b: 1921 in unknown, m: 25 Jan 1944 in unknown, d: 20 Oct 1948 in unknown
.....................7 Karen Faul (1947 -) b: 13 Aug 1947 in unknown
....   + Wolf Schrimer (1947 -) b: 1947 in Unknown, m: 06 Sep 1969 in unknown
.........................8 Ryan Schrimer (1974 -) b: 1974 in Unknown
....   + Axel Lundston (Unknown -) b: Unknown in unknown, m: Unknown in unknown
..................6 Betty Lorraine Bentz (1929 -) b: 02 May 1929 in unknown
..................6 Wilbert Gordon Bentz (1931 -) b: 04 Apr 1931 in unknown
....   + Marilyn Gray (1931 -) b: 1931 in unknown, m:
.....................7 David Bentz b:
.....................7 Paula Bentz b: unknown
....   + Zvork Stanhovi (Unknown -) b: Unknown in unknown, m: Unknown in unknown
.....................7 Neil Bentz (1959 -) b: 1959
.....................7 Allan Bentz (1960 -) b: 1960
...............5 Edward Bentz (1901 - 1990) b: 08 Oct 1901 in unknown, d: 24 Jun 1990 in Maple Creek, Saskatchewan, Canada
....   + Novella Paulina Heth (1912 - 2006) b: 24 Jun 1912 in Anamoose, North Dakota, USA, m: 12 Oct 1935 in Maple Creek, Saskatchewan, Canada, d: 11 Jul 2006 in Maple Creek, Saskatchewan, Canada
..................6 Avalon Adrienne Bentz (1939 -) b: 15 Jun 1939 in Eastend, Saskatchewan, Canada

.... + Stanley Lewis Hough (1934 - 1994) b: 04 Apr 1934 in Vermilion, Alberta, Canada, m: 08 Nov 1961 in Eastend, Saskatchewan, Canada, d: 05 Apr 1994 in Preeceville, Saskatchewan, Canada

......................7 Calvin Edward Hough (1963 -) b: 18 Oct 1963 in Eastend, Saskatchewan, Canada

.... + Kelly Mildred Pollock (1958 -) b: 10 Jun 1958 in Preeceville, Saskatchewan, Canada, m: 17 Jun 1995 in Preeceville, Saskatchewan, Canada

.........................8 Matthew Edward Hough (1982 -) b: 23 Sep 1982 in Yorkton, Saskatchewan, Canada

.........................8 Shawn Allan Hough (1985 -) b: 03 May 1985 in Yorkton, Saskatchewan, Canada

.........................8 Marlee Ann Monica Hough (1986 -) b: 13 Dec 1986 in Preeceville, Saskatchewan, Canada

.........................8 Kristen Kelly Ashton Hough (1989 -) b: 14 Jun 1989 in Preeceville, Saskatchewan, Canada

.... + Karrie Teresa Bergquist (14 Nov -) b: 14 Nov in Shaunavon, Saskatchewan, Canada

......................7 Monica Adrienne Hough (1967 -) b: 30 Dec 1967 in Maple Creek, Saskatchewan, Canada

.... + Keith Harvey Neu (1958 -) b: 27 Apr 1958 in Melfort, Saskatchewan, Canada, m: 10 Apr 1993 in Maple Creek, Saskatchewan, Canada

.........................8 Colton Leigh Neu (1992 -) b: 19 Jun 1992 in Hudson Bay, Saskatchewan, Canada

.........................8 Connor Stanley Neu (1994 -) b: 19 Mar 1994 in Hudson Bay, Saskatchewan, Canada

.........................8 Tasia Novella Neu (1996 -) b: 12 Nov 1996 in Hudson Bay, Saskatchewan, Canada

...................6 Darlene Connie Bentz (1944 -) b: 12 Feb 1944 in Maple Creek, Saskatchewan, Canada

.... + Donald Emil Albert Bowles (1941 - 2002) b: 21 Sep 1941 in Maple Creek, Saskatchewan, Canada, m: 08 Nov 1961 in Maple Creek, Saskatchewan, Canada, d: 14 Jun 2002 in Maple Creek, Saskatchewan, Canada

......................7 Karen Darlene Bowles (1964 -) b: 19 Oct 1964 in Maple Creek, Saskatchewan, Canada

.... + Bryan Alexander Nagy (1968 -) b: 09 Apr 1968 in Drumheller, Alberta, Canada, m: 20 Aug 1994 in Maple Creek, Saskatchewan, Canada

.........................8 Joel Lynden Nagy (1997 -) b: 26 Mar 1997 in Calgary, Alberta, Canada

.........................8 Kyle Brenden Nagy (1999 -) b: 19 Jun 1999 in Calgary, Alberta, Canada

......................7 Shawn Donald Bowles (1967 -) b: 17 Feb 1967 in Maple Creek, Saskatchewan, Canada

.... + Lynnell Dawn Arendt (1970 -) b: 17 May 1970 in Shaunavon, Saskatchewan, Canada, m: 17 Jul 1993 in Eastend, Saskatchewan, Canada

.........................8 Tash Donald Bowles (1998 -) b: 21 Jan 1998 in Estevan, Saskatchewan, Canada

.........................8 Kelli Lynae Bowles (1999 -) b: 30 Oct 1999 in Estevan, Saskatchewan, Canada

...............5 Benjamin Bentz (1903 - 1990) b: 17 Dec 1903 in unknown, d: 13 Apr 1990 in unknown

.... + Maleda Fischer (1907 - 1969) b: 25 Dec 1907 in Odessa, Russia, m: 02 Oct 1928 in unknown, d: 18 Feb 1969 in unknown

...................6 Alice Leona Bentz (1930 -) b: 20 Mar 1930 in unknown

.... + Severus Leonell Lucas (1929 -) b: 30 Jun 1929 in Harvey, Cavalier, North Dakota, USA, m: 12 Jan 1950 in Unknown

......................7 Scott Leonell Lucas (1951 -) b: 16 Jan 1951 in Harvey, Cavalier, North Dakota, USA

.... + Mary Lee Lesmeister (1956 -) b: 13 Mar 1956 in Harvey, Cavalier, North Dakota, USA, m: 22 Aug 1975 in Harvey, Cavalier, North Dakota, USA

.........................8 Casey Scott Lucas (1979 -) b: 19 May 1979 in Minot, Ward, North Dakota, USA

.........................8 Jessica Marie Lucas (1982 -) b: 23 Dec 1982 in Minot, Ward, North Dakota, USA

......................7 Barry Lee Lucas (1952 -) b: 25 Jul 1952 in Harvey, Cavalier, North Dakota, USA

.... + Sandra Kathleen Kline (1953 -) b: 19 Jan 1953 in Harvey, Cavalier, North Dakota, USA, m: 18 Aug 1972 in Unknown

.........................8 Rodney Lucas (1973 - 1976) b: 18 May 1973 in Harvey, Cavalier, North Dakota, USA, d: 22 Jul 1976 in Grafton, Walsh, North Dakota, USA

.........................8 Brent Lee Lucas (1978 -) b: 09 Apr 1978 in Minot, Ward, North Dakota, USA

.... + Angela LaRayne Reimer (1978 -) b: 16 Dec 1978 in Carrington, Foster, North Dakota, USA, m: 31 Aug 2002 in Unknown

......................7 Debra Ann Lucas (1964 -) b: 23 Oct 1964 in Harvey, Cavalier, North Dakota, USA

.... + John Paul Tibor (1963 -) b: 26 Jun 1963 in Hebron, Morton, North Dakota, USA, m: 02 Aug 1987 in Unknown

.....................8 Lucas Tibor (1991 -) b: 01 Jan 1991 in Minneapolis, Anoka, Minnesota, USA

.................6 Agnes Esther Bentz (1931 -) b: 25 Oct 1931 in unknown

.... + Glen Benton Schiele (1926 - 1992) b: 24 Sep 1926 in Balfour, McHenry, North Dakota, USA, m: 16 Mar 1949 in unknown, d: 27 Jan 1992 in unknown

....................7 Sandra Faye Schiele (1948 -) b: 12 Aug 1948 in Harvey, Cavalier, North Dakota, USA

.... + Dwight Edward Crimmins (1946 -) b: 16 Jul 1946 in Stanley, Cass, North Dakota, USA, m: 19 Jun 1968 in Tioga, Williams, North Dakota, USA

.....................8 Tanya Lynn Crimmins (1971 -) b: 30 Jun 1971 in Williston, Williams, North Dakota, USA

.... + Kevin Wold (Unknown -) b: Unknown in unknown, m: 1990 in Watford City, North Dakota

.... + Michael Liebelt (Unknown -) b: Unknown in unknown, m: 1992 in Reno, Nevada

.........................9 Matthew Liebelt (1991 -) b: 1991 in Lodi, San Joaquin, California, USA

.........................9 Elizabeth Liebelt (1993 -) b: 1993 in Lodi, San Joaquin, California, USA

.....................8 Nevada Dean Crimmins (1974 -) b: 22 May 1974 in Williston, Williams, North Dakota, USA

.... + Stephanie Mack (Unknown -) b: Unknown in unknown, m: 18 Aug 2001 in Billings, Yellowstone, Montana, USA

....................7 Glennette Ann Schiele (1950 -) b: 02 Mar 1950 in Harvey, Cavalier, North Dakota, USA

.... + Larry Owen Lysne (1945 -) b: 18 Jan 1945 in Williston, Williams, North Dakota, USA, m: 11 Jan 1969 in Unknown

.....................8 Anita Kay Lysne (1970 -) b: 31 Dec 1970 in Gillette, Campbell, Wyoming, USA

.... + Paul Makowski b: unknown, m: 05 Oct 1996 in Denver, Colorado, USA

.... + Paul Adams b: unknown, m: 31 Aug 2001 in Denver, Colorado, USA

.........................9 Alexandria Adams (1996 -) b: 1996 in unknown

.....................8 Jeremy Wayne Lysne (1973 -) b: 02 Mar 1973 in Gillette, Campbell, Wyoming, USA

.... + Melody Swank (Unknown -) b: Unknown in Unknown, m: 27 Apr 1996 in Unknown

.........................9 Bailey Ann Lysne (1996 -) b: 13 Sep 1996 in Unknown

....................7 Victoria Jean Schiele (1952 -) b: 17 Feb 1952 in Harvey, Cavalier, North Dakota, USA

.... + Arthur Elroy Moe (1945 -) b: 25 Apr 1945 in White Earth, Mountrail, North Dakota, USA, m: 16 Aug 1969 in Unknown

.....................8 Sheri Lynn Moe (1969 -) b: 24 Dec 1969 in Stanley, Cass, North Dakota, USA

.... + Darren Gohrick b: unknown, m: 1989 in Unknown

.........................9 Makenzie Blake Noel Gohrick (1988 -) b: 15 Oct 1988 in Williston, Williams, North Dakota, USA

.........................9 Paige Victoria Gohrick (1992 -) b: 07 Jul 1992 in Wiliston, North Dakota, USA

.........................9 Shantell Hope Gohrick (1994 -) b: 12 Jul 1994 in Tioga, Williams, North Dakota, USA

.....................8 Brent Arthur Moe (1972 -) b: 23 Sep 1972 in Wiliston, North Dakota, USA

.................6 Eldora Bentz (1936 -) b: 31 Dec 1936 in unknown

.... + Hugo Johnston (1929 -) b: 11 Oct 1929 in Oakland, Alameda, California, USA, m: 21 Sep 1960 in Reno, Nevada, USA

....................7 Angela Charise Johnston (1962 -) b: 17 Jan 1962 in Anchorage, Alaska, USA

.... + Anthony Patrick Mauro II (1965 -) b: 18 Mar 1965 in Milwaukee, Milwaukee, Wisconsin, USA, m: 07 Jan 1989 in Riverside, California, USA

.....................8 Alexandra Taylor Mauro (1990 -) b: 27 Mar 1990 in Orange, California, USA

.....................8 Samantha Kelsey Mauro (1991 -) b: 16 Aug 1991 in Orange, California, USA

....................7 Lisa Tarice Johnston (1963 -) b: 08 Mar 1963 in Anchorage, Alaska, USA

.... + Donald Jerome Fennell II (1962 -) b: 28 Apr 1962 in Orange, California, USA, m: 03 Jul 1993 in Riverside, California, USA

.....................8 Delaney Freya Fennell (1995 -) b: 10 Nov 1995 in Riverside, California, USA

.....................8 Donald Jerome Fennell III (1999 -) b: 03 Aug 1999 in Riverside, California, USA

.................6 Wendy Bentz (1943 -) b: 28 May 1943 in unknown

.... + John Leonard Blackburn (1944 -) b: Feb 1944 in Minnesota, USA, m: 02 Oct 1965 in Harvey, Cavalier, North Dakota, USA

....................7 Amy Jo Blackburn (1968 -) b: 23 Jul 1968 in Minot, Ward, North Dakota, USA

.... + Brent Eugene Braaten (1963 -) b: 24 Jan 1963 in Wiliston, North Dakota, USA, m: 04 Jun 1988 in Minot, Ward, North Dakota, USA

.......................8 Shantel Jo Blackburn (1984 -) b: 09 Jun 1984 in Minot, Ward, North Dakota, USA

.......................8 Chandler Gene Braaten (1989 -) b: 28 Jul 1989 in Minot, Ward, North Dakota, USA

....................7 Jon Jason Blackburn (1969 -) b: 27 Dec 1969 in Minot, Ward, North Dakota, USA

.... + Denae Terese Elberg b: unknown

.......................8 Kennedy Jaden Blackburn (2001 -) b: 19 Jul 2001 in Minot, Ward, North Dakota, USA

.......................8 Riley Terese Blackburn (2001 -) b: 19 Jul 2001 in Minot, Ward, North Dakota, USA

.... + James Martin Hedman (1939 -) b: 17 May 1939 in Fergus Falls, Minnesota, USA, m: 04 Jul 1977 in Las Vegas, Clark, Nevada, USA

............4 Margaretha Bentz (1860 -) b: 1860 in Neudorf, Odessa Region, S. Russia, d:

............4 Julianna Bentz (1862 - 1913) b: 12 Jul 1862 in Neudorf, Odessa Region, S. Russia, d: 1913 in unknown

.... + Jacob Lippert (1873 - 1921) b: 1873 in unknown, m: Unknown in Unknown, d: 1921 in unknown

............4 Georg Bentz (1865 -) b: 1865 in Neudorf, Odessa Region, S. Russia, d:

............4 George Bentz (1867 - 1941) b: 19 Jan 1867 in Neudorf, Odessa Region, S. Russia, d: 1941 in unknown

.... + Elizabeth Sprenger (1870 - 1954) b: 1870 in unknown, m: Unknown in unknown, d: 1954 in unknown

...............5 Martha Bentz (1889 - 1937) b: 1889 in unknown, d: 1937 in unknown

.... + Martin Frey (1885 -) b: 1885 in unknown

...............5 John G. Bentz (1894 - 1980) b: 1894 in unknown, d: 1980 in unknown

.... + Anna Glaser (1896 - 1985) b: 1896 in unknown, m: unknown, d: 1985 in unknown

...............5 Julianna Bentz (1895 - 1926) b: 1895 in unknown, d: 1926 in unknown

.... + Jacob Frey (1897 - 1968) b: 1897 in unknown, m: unknown, d: 1968 in unknown

..................6 Emil Frey (1913 - 1947) b: 1913 in unknown, d: 1947 in unknown

..................6 Donald Frey (1914 -) b: 1914 in unknown

.... + Olive Ruth Martin (1918 -) b: 1918 in unknown, m: Unknown in unknown

....................7 Daphne Lorraine Frey (1939 -) b: 1939 in unknown

.... + Melvin Rode (Unknown -) b: Unknown in unknown, m: Unknown in unknown

....................7 Dorene Ruth Frey (1940 -) b: 1940

............4 Jacob Bentz (1869 -) b: 1869 in Neudorf, Odessa Region, S. Russia, d:

............4 Katherine Bentz (1871 - 1943) b: 14 Jan 1871 in Neudorf, Odessa Region, S. Russia, d: 03 Jul 1943 in Tuttle, North Dakota

.... + Christian Dockter (1868 - 1947) b: 1868 in unknown, m: unknown, d: 1947 in unknown

............4 Frederick Bentz (1873 -) b: 1873 in Neudorf, Odessa Region, S. Russia, d:

............4 Julianne Bentz (1876 -) b: 21 May 1876 in Neudorf, Odessa Region, S. Russia, d:

............4 Georg Frederich Bentz (1878 -) b: 27 Oct 1878 in Neudorf, Odessa Region, S. R., d:

............4 Jacob Bentz (1881 -) b: 19 Apr 1881 in Neudorf, Odessa Region, S. R., d:

.........3 Georg Michael Benz (1836 -) b: 1836 in Neudorf, Odessa Region, S. Russia, d: unknown

.... + Elisabeth Hertel (1840 -) b: 1840 in unknown, m: unknown, d: unknown

.........3 Peter Benz (1839 -) b: 1839 in Neudorf, Odessa Region, S. Russia, d:

.........3 Juliane Benz (1842 - 1879) b: 1842 in Neudorf, Odessa Region, S. Russia, d: 1879 in unknown

.... + Georg Wiederrich (1836 - 1896) b: 1836 in unknown, m: Unknown in unknown, d: 1896 in unknown

.........3 Philip Benz (1844 - 1928) b: 16 Apr 1844 in Neudorf, Odessa Region, S. Russia, d: 12 Dec 1928 in Dallas, South Dakota

.... + Christina Grosshans (1848 - 1928) b: 1848 in unknown, m: unknown, d: 1928 in unknown

.........3 Friedrich Benz (1846 -) b: 1846 in Neudorf, Odessa Region, S. Russia, d:

.........3 Jacob Benz (1847 -) b: 1847 in Neudorf, Odessa Region, S. Russia, d: unknown

.... + Katherine Schaeffer (1854 - Unknown) b: 1854 in unknown, m: Unknown in unknown, d: Unknown in unknown

.........3 Christian Benz (1851 - 1878) b: 1851 in Neudorf, Odessa Region, S. Russia, d: 1878 in unknown

.... + Elizabeth Hertle (1856 -) b: 1856 in unknown, m: unknown, d: unknown

.........3 Margaretta Benz (1852 - 1944) b: 1852 in Neudorf, Odessa Region, S. Russia, d: 1944 in unknown

.... + Johann Glasser (1858 - 1929) b: 1858 in unknown, m: unknown, d: 1929 in unknown

......2 Anna Maria Benz (1816 -) b: 1816 in Neudorf, Odessa Region, S. Russia, d: unknown

......2 Dorothea Wetzler (1803 - Unknown) b: 1803 in Mettenzimmern, Ludwigsburg, Wurttemberg, Germany, d: Unknown in unknown

......2 Anna Wetzler (1807 - Unknown) b: 1807 in Mettenzimmern, Ludwigsburg, Wurttemberg, Germany, d: Unknown in unknown

Outline Descendant Report for Wilhelm Kalk

1 Wilhelm Kalk (1837 - 1894) b: 1837 in Romania, Europe, d: 1894 in Romania

... + Susana Liebelt (1841 - 1918) b: 15 Feb 1841 in Tarutino, Bessarabia, Romania, Europe, m: 1860 in Romania, Europe, d: 09 Mar 1918 in Harvey, Cavalier, North Dakota, USA

......2 Gottlieb Kalk (1862 - 1919) b: 13 Mar 1862 in Catuloi, Romania, Europe, d: 18 Oct 1919 in unknown

...... + Magdelena Derman (1865 - 1898) b: 25 Jul 1865 in Catuloi, Romania, Europe, m: Catuloi, Romania, Europe, d: 14 Jul 1898 in unknown

.........3 Anna Kalk (1884 - 1935) b: 28 Nov 1884 in Cataloi, Romania, Europe, d: 24 Aug 1935 in Tisdale, Saskatchewan, Canada

.... + Joseph Sheard (1880 - Unknown) b: 15 Jun 1880 in unknown, m: 09 Aug 1906 in Martin, North Dakota, USA, d: Unknown in unknown

............4 Emmett Leroy Sheard (1907 - 1908) b: 13 Mar 1907 in unknown, d: 07 Jun 1908 in unknown

............4 Lucille Veronica Miley (1909 - 1974) b: 11 Jan 1909 in unknown, d: 17 Jan 1974 in Victoria, British Columbia, Canada

.... + Sam Miley (1880 - 1964) b: 15 Jun 1880 in unknown, m: 30 Sep 1913 in unknown, d: 13 Jan 1964 in Whalley, Surrey, British Columbia, Canada

.........3 Adolph Berthold Kalk (1886 - 1974) b: 17 Jun 1886 in Belgonie, NWT, Canada, d: 21 Aug 1974 in North Surrey, British Columbia,Canada

.... + Magdalena Bentz (1890 - 1976) b: 06 Feb 1890 in Odesa, Ukraine, Russia, m: 07 Nov 1907 in Minot, Ward, North Dakota, USA, d: 06 Mar 1976 in North Surrey, British Columbia

............4 Viola Eugene Kalk (1908 - 1995) b: 27 Feb 1908 in unknown, d: 11 Oct 1995 in Portland, Clackamas, Oregon, USA

.... + Einar Ericksen (1907 - 1975) b: 13 Jan 1907 in Trondheim, Sor-Trondelag, Norway, m: 25 Jan 1934 in Longview, Cowlitz, Washington, USA, d: 1975 in Portland, Clackamas, Oregon, USA

...............5 Janet Elaine Ericksen (1935 - 1990) b: 10 Sep 1935 in Longview, Cowlitz, Washington, USA, d: 04 Jun 1990 in Portland, Clackamas, Oregon, USA

.... + Senior Ronald Leroy Adkins (1932 -) b: 19 Sep 1932 in Portland, Clackamas, Oregon, USA, m: 06 Aug 1955

..................6 Neil Thomas Adkins (1958 -) b: 10 Jan 1958 in Orléans, Loiret, Centre, France

..................6 Norman James Adkins (1961 -) b: 20 Oct 1961 in Forest Grove, Washington, Oregon, USA

.... + Tami Jo Denise Drangstvelt (1961 - 2010) b: 21 May 1961 in Grand Forks, North Dakota, USA, m: 06 Oct 1990, d: 01 Feb 2010 in Portland, Clackamas, Oregon, USA

.....................7 Lance Adkins (1993 -) b: 1993 in Portland, Clackamas, Oregon, USA

........................8 Kyler Adkins (1994 -) b: 1994 in Portland, Oregon, USA

........................8 Carson Adkins (1995 -) b: 1995

..................6 Junior Ronald William Adkins (1964 -) b: 23 Feb 1964 in Forest Grove, Washington, Oregon, USA

............4 Vernon Cleveland Kalk (1909 - 2004) b: 03 Oct 1909 in unknown, d: 22 Sep 2004 in Bellingham, Whatcom, Washington, USA

.... + Rosella Kluthe (1918 - 2007) b: 28 Apr 1918 in Whitefish, South Dakota, USA, m: 29 Jun 1947 in Bellingham, Whatcom, Washington, USA, d: 03 Mar 2007 in Bellingham, Whatcom, Washington, USA

...............5 Ernest Joseph Kalk (1961 -) b: 01 Jan 1961 in Portland, Clackamas, Oregon, USA

..................6 Jimmy Kalk (1985 -) b: 01 Jan 1985 in Portland, Clackamas, Oregon, USA

............4 Vera Grace Kalk (1911 - 2010) b: 09 Aug 1911 in unknown, d: 08 Jan 2010 in Victoria, British Columbia, Canada

...............5 Louella Grace Kalk (1934 -) b: 12 Mar 1934 in Moose Jaw, Saskatchewan, Canada

.... + George Brock Denison (1935 -) b: 29 May 1935 in Ottawa, Ontario, Canada, m: 30 Jun 1956 in Victoria, British Colmbia, Canada

..................6 Brock George Denison (1959 -) b: 20 Jun 1959 in Victoria, British Columbia, Canada

.... + Alexis Denise Smart (1962 -) b: 11 May 1962 in Victoria, British Columbia, Canada, m: 05 Sep 1987 in Victoria, British Colmbia, Canada

....................7 Brooklyn Ashley Denison (1991 -) b: 09 May 1991 in Victoria, British Columbia, Canada

....................7 Tessa Annie Denison (1993 -) b: 02 Dec 1993 in Victoria, British Columbia, Canada

................6 Robert David Denison (1964 -) b: 25 Jun 1964 in Victoria, British Columbia, Canada

.... + Margaret Lorraine Straw (1963 -) b: 31 Jul 1963 in Dawson Creek, British Columbia, Canada, m: 24 Jan 1982 in Victoria, British Colmbia, Canada

....................7 Tyler David Denison (1997 -) b: 24 May 1997 in Victoria, British Columbia, Canada

....................7 Eryn Lorrell Denison (2000 -) b: 25 May 2000 in Victoria, British Columbia, Canada

............4 Adeline Dorothy Kalk (1915 -) b: 18 Feb 1915 in Ravenscrag. Saskatchewan, Canada

.... + Frederick Macklin Sutton (1919 - 2012) b: 25 Jan 1919 in Victoria, British Columbia, Canada, m: 25 Nov 1942 in Victoria, British Colmbia, Canada, d: 27 Jul 2012 in Santee, San Diego, California, USA

...............5 Gregory Allan Sutton (1949 -) b: 04 Oct 1949 in Victoria, British Columbia, Canada

.... + Patricia Anne Kaliruer (1949 -) b: 04 Apr 1949 in Norfolk, Virginia, USA, m: 30 Sep 1969 in San Diego, California, USA

.................6 Carrie Lynn Sutton (1976 -) b: 27 Dec 1976 in San Diego, California, USA

.................6 Daniel Christopher Sutton (1978 -) b: 30 Sep 1978 in San Diego, California, USA

...............5 Glenn Howard Sutton (1952 -) b: 15 Jul 1952 in Victoria, British Columbia, Canada

............4 Lorraine Florence Kalk (1916 - 2013) b: 25 Sep 1916 in Ravenscrag. Saskatchewan, Canada, d: 07 Jan 2013 in Longview, Cowlitz, Washington, USA

............4 Willard Edwin Carlson (1918 - 2005) b: 09 Apr 1918 in Ravenscrag. Saskatchewan, Canada, d: 20 Oct 2005 in Greenwood, British Columbia, Canada

.... + Caroline Mary Tibbetts (1926 - 2001) b: 22 Jul 1926 in Simcoe, Ontario, Canada, m: 30 Sep 1955 in Simcoe, Ontario, Canada, d: 18 Oct 2001 in Greenwood, British Columbia, Canada

...............5 Richard Edwin Carlson (1956 -) b: 05 May 1956 in Atikokan, Ontario, Canada

.... + Karen Audrey Butcher b: Atikokan, Ontario, Canada

.................6 Clinton Scott Carlson (1986 -) b: 12 Aug 1986 in Atikokan, Ontario, Canada

...............5 Raymond Alan Carlson (1957 -) b: 06 Jul 1957 in Atikokan, Ontario, Canada

.... + Katherine Elizabeth Larson (1962 -) b: 09 Mar 1962 in Kenora, Ontario, Canada, m: 13 Aug 1982 in Kenora, Ontario, Canada

.................6 Jeffrey Alan Carlson (1985 -) b: 07 Apr 1985 in Atikokan, Ontario, Canada

.................6 Kimber Nicole Carlson (1988 -) b: 19 Jul 1988 in Atikokan, Ontario, Canada

...............5 Robert Dale Carlson (1958 -) b: 08 Nov 1958 in Atikokan, Ontario, Canada

.... + Catherine Anne Albrecht (1962 -) b: 1962 in Atikokan, Ontario, Canada

.................6 Benjamin Robert Carlson (1984 -) b: 10 Sep 1984 in Atikokan, Ontario, Canada

.................6 Andrew Alfred Carlson (1988 -) b: 20 Jul 1988 in Atikokan, Ontario, Canada

.... + Lorri Verfterzoff (Unknown -) b: Unknown in Atikokan, Ontario, Canada, m: Unknown in Unknown

.................6 Rebecca Caroline Carlson (1994 -) b: 18 Oct 1994

...............5 Willard Ralph Carlson (1961 -) b: 21 Dec 1961 in Atikokan, Ontario, Canada

.... + Candice Jean Fraser (1966 -) b: 12 Jun 1966 in Atikokan, Ontario, Canada, m: 23 Sep 1984 in Thunder Bay, Ontario, Canada

.................6 Summer Lynn Carlson (1986 -) b: 30 Apr 1986 in Thunder Bay, Ontario, Canada

...............5 Judith Leigh Carlson (1965 -) b: 22 Aug 1965 in Atikokan, Ontario, Canada

.... + Alex Patrick Bailey (1955 -) b: 07 Oct 1955 in Bracebridge, Ontario, Canada, m: 01 Jun 1988 in Atikokan, Ontario, Canada

.................6 Patrick James Bailey (1987 - 1987) b: 12 Jan 1987 in Atikokan, Ontario, Canada, d: 02 Jul 1987 in Atikokan, Ontario, Canada

.................6 Matthew Michael Bailey (1988 -) b: 09 Aug 1988 in Ontario, Canada

...............5 Judy Caroline Klub (1948 -) b: 06 Jan 1948 in Vanguard, Saskatchewan, Canada

.... + Carl Ernest Jautz (1940 -) b: 20 May 1940 in Humboldt, Saskatchewan, Canada, m: 08 Oct 1966 in Humboldt, Saskatchewan, Canada

.................6 Lori Lynn Jautz (1969 - 1997) b: 21 Jul 1969 in Calgary, Alberta, Canada, d: 02 Dec 1997 in Calgary, Alberta, Canada

.... + Edward Neighbours (Unknown -) b: Unknown in Calgary, Alberta, Canada, m: 08 Jul 1995 in Unknown

.................6 Monty Carl Jautz (1971 -) b: 01 Jan 1971 in Regina, Saskatchewan, Canada
.... + Wynette Lynn Neighbors (1975 -) b: 23 Jul 1975 in Melfort, Saskatchewan, Canada, m:
    10 May 1998 in Unknown
....................7 Britany Ashley Jautz (1998 -) b: 27 Oct 1998 in Calgary, Alberta, Canada
.... + Stewart Arthur McNeil (1952 -) b: 07 Nov 1952 in Calgary, Alberta, Canada, m: 07 May
    1983 in Calgary, Alberta, Canada
.... + Caroline Klub b: unknown, d: Greenwood, British Columbia, Canada
..............5 Judy Caroline Klub (1948 -) b: 06 Jan 1948 in Vanguard, Saskatchewan, Canada
.... + Carl Ernest Jautz (1940 -) b: 20 May 1940 in Humboldt, Saskatchewan, Canada, m: 08
    Oct 1966 in Humboldt, Saskatchewan, Canada
.................6 Lori Lynn Jautz (1969 - 1997) b: 21 Jul 1969 in Calgary, Alberta, Canada, d: 02 Dec 1997
    in Calgary, Alberta, Canada
.... + Edward Neighbours (Unknown -) b: Unknown in Calgary, Alberta, Canada, m: 08 Jul
    1995 in Unknown
.................6 Monty Carl Jautz (1971 -) b: 01 Jan 1971 in Regina, Saskatchewan, Canada
.... + Wynette Lynn Neighbors (1975 -) b: 23 Jul 1975 in Melfort, Saskatchewan, Canada, m:
    10 May 1998 in Unknown
....................7 Britany Ashley Jautz (1998 -) b: 27 Oct 1998 in Calgary, Alberta, Canada
.... + Stewart Arthur McNeil (1952 -) b: 07 Nov 1952 in Calgary, Alberta, Canada, m: 07 May
    1983 in Calgary, Alberta, Canada
............4 Bert Edward Kalk (1920 - 2007) b: 10 Feb 1920 in Ravenscrag. Saskatchewan, Canada, d: 14
    Nov 2007 in Nipawin, Saskatchewan, Canada
.... + Lois Edna Dobell (1927 -) b: 04 Jun 1927 in Pontrilas, Saskatchewan, Canada, m: 02 Sep
    1949 in Nipawin, Saskatchewan, Canada
...............5 Larry Wayne Kalk (1951 -) b: 14 Mar 1951 in Nipawin, Saskatchewan, Canada
.... + Bonnie Lynn Dymterko (1952 -) b: 03 Jun 1952 in Nipawin, Saskatchewan, Canada, m: 29
    Mar 1978 in Hinton, Alberta, Canada
.................6 Kristy Lee Kalk (1978 -) b: 12 Aug 1978 in Hinton, Alberta, Canada
.................6 Beckki Lynn Kalk (1981 -) b: 29 Mar 1981 in Hinton, Alberta, Canada
...............5 Donald Bert Kalk (1956 -) b: 17 Jan 1956 in Nipawin, Saskatchewan, Canada
.... + Cindy Lou Boxall (1960 -) b: 03 Oct 1960 in Nipawin, Saskatchewan, Canada, m: 11 Nov
    1983 in Nipawin, Saskatchewan, Canada
.................6 Ashley Dawn Kalk (1984 -) b: 30 Aug 1984 in Hinton, Alberta, Canada
.................6 Brittney Erin Kalk (1989 -) b: 20 Jan 1989 in Hinton, Alberta, Canada
...............5 Allan Brent Kalk (1966 -) b: 11 Jun 1966 in Nipawin, Saskatchewan, Canada
.... + Kelly Gay Trainor (1964 -) b: 06 Feb 1964 in Nipawin, Saskatchewan, Canada, m: 21 Dec
    1988 in Nipawin, Saskatchewan, Canada
.................6 Aiden Bret Kalk (1993 -) b: 24 Jul 1993 in Virctoria, British Columbia, Canada
............4 Kenneth Fredrick Kalk (1924 - 2010) b: 15 Jun 1924 in Ravenscrag. Saskatchewan, Canada,
    d: 28 Jul 2010 in Langley, British Columbia, Canada
.... + Edith Laura Becker (1925 -) b: 12 Feb 1925 in Middle Lake, Saskatchewan, Canada, m: 01
    Nov 1944 in Nipawin, Saskatchewan, Canada
...............5 Sharon Diane Kalk (1945 -) b: 03 Jul 1945 in Nipawin, Saskatchewan, Canada
.... + Robert Patrick Marshall (1941 -) b: 24 Sep 1941 in British Columbia, Canada, m: 30 Apr
    1971 in British Columbia, Canada
.................6 Dana Claire Railey (1973 -) b: 25 Jul 1973 in Calgary, Alberta, Canada
.................6 Kenneth Railey Marshall (1976 -) b: 25 Mar 1976 in Calgary, Alberta, Canada
...............5 Valerie Jean Kalk (1950 -) b: 25 Jun 1950 in Nipawin, Saskatchewan, Canada
.... + Norman Rowlings (Unknown -) b: Unknown in British Columbia, m: 1970 in British
    Columbia, Canada
.... + Sam Kwan (1952 -) b: 26 Sep 1952 in Vancouver, British Columbia, Canada
............4 Raymond Sidney Kalk (1926 -) b: 17 Mar 1926 in Maple Creek, Saskatchewan, Canada
.... + Dorothy Bigelow (1930 - 1994) b: 02 Apr 1930 in Spoonville, Meuse, Lorraine, France, m: 23
    Sep 1949 in Nipawin, Saskatchewan, Canada, d: 26 Aug 1994 in Nipawin, Saskatchewan,
    Canada

...............5 Blaine Woodrow Kalk (1966 -) b: 30 Jul 1966 in Saskatoon, Saskatchewan, Canada
.... + Jodie Lynn Graham (1968 -) b: 30 Mar 1968 in Regina, Saskatchewan, Canada, m: 21 May 1994 in Saskatoon, Saskatchewan, Canada
..................6 Janelle Marie Dorothy Kalk (1996 -) b: 27 Jun 1996 in Saskatoon, Saskatchewan, Canada
..................6 Seline Marie Antoinette Kalk (1998 -) b: 14 Oct 1998 in Calgary, Alberta, Canada
..................6 Allysa Marie Magdalina Kalk (2000 -) b: 21 Apr 2000 in Calgary, Alberta, Canada
...............5 Shayla Lorraine Kalk (1969 -) b: 20 Dec 1969 in Maple Creek, Saskatchewan, Canada
.... + Benny Roy Geisbrecht b: Fort St. John, British Columbia, Canada, m: 31 Jul 1994 in Maple Creek, Saskatchewan, Canada
..................6 Jonathan Mark Kalk (1989 -) b: 20 Apr 1989 in Saskatoon, Saskatchewan, Canada
..................6 Gerald Blaine Kalk (1991 -) b: 15 Jan 1991 in Grand Pairie, Alberta, Canada
..................6 Wyatt Raymond Kalk (1993 -) b: 12 Oct 1993 in Grande Prairie, Alberta, Canada
..................6 Diedra Mae Kalk (1995 -) b: 25 Oct 1995 in Grand Pairie, Alberta, Canada
............4 Eunice Eileen Kalk (1935 -) b: 13 Feb 1935 in Armley, Saskatchewan, Canada
.... + John Walter Herbert Catterall (1935 -) b: 01 Jan 1935 in Victoria, British Columbia, Canada, m: 11 Nov 1960 in Victoria, British Columbia, Canada
...............5 Roydon Blake Catterall (1962 -) b: 29 Jan 1962 in Victoria, British Columbia, Canada
.... + Rebecca Lynn Ross (1960 -) b: 10 Jul 1960 in Denver, Colorado, USA, m: 04 Jun 1983 in Victoria, British Colmbia, Canada
..................6 Candace Suzanne Catterall (1990 -) b: 14 Sep 1990 in Aurora, Colorado, USA
..................6 Connor Ross Catterall (1993 -) b: 20 May 1993 in Aurora, Colorado, USA
...............5 Bruce John Catterall (1963 -) b: 13 Jan 1963 in Victoria, British Columbia, Canada
.... + Donna Hebert (1962 -) b: 08 May 1962 in White Horse, Yukon, Canada
...............5 Wade Vincent Catterall (1966 -) b: 17 Mar 1966 in New Westminster, British Columbia, Canada
.... + Karen Nestor (1949 -) b: 14 Nov 1949 in Cardston, Alberta, Canada, m: 01 Feb 1998 in Cobble Hill, British Columbia, Canada
............4 Bruce Lenard Kalk (1934 - 1959) b: 26 Dec 1934 in Nipawin, Saskatchewan, Canada, d: 18 Aug 1959 in Victoria, British Columbia, Canada
.........3 Matilda Kalk (1888 - 1979) b: 22 Sep 1888 in Belgonie, NWT, Canada, d: 25 May 1979 in Barrhead, Alberta, Canada
.... + John Adam Bentz (1883 - 1967) b: 15 Mar 1883 in Odesa, Ukraine, Russia, m: 07 Nov 1907 in unknown, d: 02 May 1967 in Barrhead, Alberta, Canada
............4 Edna Rachael Bentz (1908 - 1995) b: 26 Jan 1908 in Harvey, Cavalier, North Dakota, USA, d: 29 Oct 1995 in Barrhead, Alberta, Canada
.... + Alexander Ernst (1901 - 1979) b: 08 May 1901 in Odesa, Ukraine, Russia, m: 02 Apr 1931 in Eastend, Saskatchewan, Canada, d: 07 Jul 1979 in Barrhead, Alberta, Canada
...............5 Edwin Albert Ernst (1931 -) b: 04 Jul 1931 in Eastend, Saskatchewan, Canada
.... + Audrey Patricia Airlie (1927 -) b: 21 Mar 1927 in Albert Park, Alberta, m: 09 Jul 1960
..................6 Riley Alexander Ernst (1961 -) b: 29 Nov 1961 in Calgary, Alberta, Canada
.... + Nadine Marianne Eadle (1967 -) b: 08 Jun 1967 in Winnipeg, Manitoba, Canada, m: 20 May 1989 in Calgary, Alberta, Canada
.....................7 Randi Mae Ernst (1992 -) b: 06 Jan 1992 in Calgary, Alberta, Canada
.....................7 Wyatt Daniel Ernst (1993 -) b: 06 Apr 1993 in Calgary, Alberta, Canada
..................6 Kelly Patrick Ernst (1963 -) b: 04 Apr 1963 in Calgary, Alberta, Canada
.... + Angel Dunphy (1963 -) b: 04 Apr 1963 in Calgary, Alberta, Canada, m: 1981 in Calgary, Alberta, Canada
..................6 Shauna Mary Ernst (1966 -) b: 16 Sep 1966 in Calgary, Alberta, Canada
.... + Jeffrey Thomas Mostowich (1960 -) b: 02 Jun 1960 in Calgary, Alberta, Canada, m: 15 Aug 1993 in Calgary, Alberta, Canada
.....................7 Liam Edward Mostowich (2002 -) b: 26 Jul 2002 in Calgary, Alberta, Canada
.....................7 Lucas Samuel Mostowich (2004 -) b: 30 Sep 2004 in Calgary, Alberta, Canada
..................6 Tara Patricia Ernst (1968 -) b: 26 Jun 1968 in Calgary, Alberta, Canada
.... + Roger Siemens (15 Nov -) b: 15 Nov in Calgary, Alberta, Canada, m: 19 Feb 2005 in Calgary, Alberta, Canada

....................7 Aiden Rowan Siemens (2008 -) b: 18 Aug 2008 in Calgary, Alberta, Canada

..............5 Ernest Lloyd Ernst (1932 -) b: 02 Sep 1932 in Eastend, Saskatchewan, Canada

....   + Ethel May Anderson (1942 - 1991) b: 12 Jul 1942 in Barrhead, Alberta, Canada, m: 21 Oct 1961 in Barrhead, Alberta, Canada, d: 23 Apr 1991 in Westlock, Alberta, Canada

..................6 Roselyn Gail Ernst (1962 -) b: 15 Dec 1962 in Barrhead, Alberta, Canada

....   + David Stewart Anderson (1962 -) b: 03 Dec 1962 in Magrath, Alberta, Canada, m: 12 Oct 1985

....................7 Kylie Nicole Anderson (1989 -) b: 26 Aug 1989 in Westlock, Alberta, Canada

....................7 Lindsey Joline Anderson (1990 -) b: 27 Sep 1990 in Edmonton, Alberta, Canada

....................7 Breanna June Anderson (1994 -) b: 29 Dec 1994 in Westlock, Alberta, Canada

....................7 Karalee Rose Anderson (1998 -) b: 19 Mar 1998 in Westlock, Alberta, Canada

..................6 Joanne Deane Ernst (1964 -) b: 26 Apr 1964 in Barrhead, Alberta, Canada

....   + Donald Eric Galloway (1955 -) b: 20 Sep 1955 in Edmonton, Alberta, Canada, m: 10 Apr 1993 in Edmonton, Alberta, Canada

....................7 Devon Dayle Galloway (1994 -) b: 10 Feb 1994 in Edmonton, Alberta, Canada

....................7 Alexa Rae Galloway (1996 -) b: 06 Jan 1996 in Edmonton, Alberta, Canada

..................6 Lorine May Ernst (1969 -) b: 20 Mar 1969 in Barrhead, Alberta, Canada

....   + Norman Kelly (1967 -) b: 05 Jun 1967 in Scotland, m: 14 Sep 1996 in Westlock, Alberta, Canada

....   + Betty Jean Emsley (1930 -) b: 22 Dec 1930 in Rochester, Alberta, m: 21 Mar 1992 in Westlock, Alberta, Canada

..............5 Albert Alexander Ernst (1934 - 2009) b: 28 May 1934 in Eastend, Saskatchewan, Canada, d: 02 Jun 2009 in Westlock, Alberta, Canada

....   + Alice Petruchik (1932 -) b: 03 May 1932 in Lunford, Alberta, Canada, m: 12 Jul 1954 in Barrhead, Alberta, Canada

..................6 Norman Albert Ernst (1955 -) b: 05 Mar 1955 in Barrhead, Alberta, Canada

....   + Sandra Jean Frost (1959 -) b: 19 Jun 1959 in Sundridge, Ontario, m: 30 Dec 1975 in Golden, British Columbia

....................7 Gordon Norman Ernst (1976 -) b: 12 Aug 1976 in Golden, British Columbia

....   + Rebecca Louise Young (1979 -) b: 30 Jan 1979 in Brighton, England, m: 24 Jul 1999 in Calgary, Alberta, Canada

........................8 Noah Gordon Ernst (1997 -) b: 10 Oct 1997 in Calgary, Alberta, Canada

....................7 Crystal Robin Ernst (1978 -) b: 02 Dec 1978 in Golden, British Columbia

........................8 Levi Emanuel Ernst (1995 -) b: 10 Nov 1995 in Calgary, Alberta, Canada

........................8 Mica Angelo Ernst (2000 -) b: 28 Nov 2000 in Cranbrook, British Columbia

....................7 Bethany Ann Ernst (1985 -) b: 30 Mar 1985 in Calgary, Alberta, Canada

....   + Vivian Janet Horrick (1954 -) b: 15 Jul 1954 in Vegreville, Alberta, Canada, m: 29 Jun 1996 in Westlock, Alberta, Canada

....................7 Lucinda Anne Browne (1987 -) b: 15 Dec 1987 in Westlock, Alberta, Canada

..................6 Delores Alice Ernst (1964 -) b: 01 Apr 1964 in Toronto, Ontario, Canada

....   + Alec Frederick McRae (1959 -) b: 19 Jun 1959 in Montréal, Quebec, Canada, m: 30 Aug 1986 in Calgary, Alberta, Canada

....................7 Danielle Elizabeth McRae (1989 -) b: 06 Apr 1989 in Calgary, Alberta, Canada

....................7 Aaron Francis McRae (1992 -) b: 21 Jan 1992 in Calgary, Alberta, Canada

..............5 Calvin Clarence Ernst (1937 -) b: 14 Oct 1937 in Eastend, Saskatchewan, Canada

....   + Myrtle Alicia Craft (1940 -) b: 24 May 1940 in Barrhead, Alberta, Canada, m: 07 Jul 1960 in Barrhead, Alberta, Canada

..................6 Roger Kevin Ernst (1962 -) b: 11 Nov 1962 in Barrhead, Alberta, Canada

....   + Daylene Karole Devins (1965 -) b: 30 Dec 1965 in Barrhead, Alberta, Canada, m: 24 May 1997 in Whitecourt, Alberta

....................7 Dustin Leon Devins (1983 -) b: 30 Jul 1983 in Barrhead, Alberta, Canada

....................7 Jerhomey Paul Devins (1986 -) b: 07 Aug 1986 in Hinton, Alberta, Canada

....................7 Chase Roger Ernst (1993 -) b: 18 Dec 1993 in Red Deer, Alberta

..................6 Michael Scott Ernst (1965 -) b: 06 Apr 1965 in Barrhead, Alberta, Canada

....   + Desiree Emperingham b: unknown, m: 18 Dec 1992 in Whitecourt, Alberta

..................7 Alicia Courtney Ernst (1992 -) b: 19 Jun 1992 in Whitecourt, Alberta

.... + Phyllis Irene Lassesen (1940 -) b: 25 Nov 1940 in Camrose, Alberta, Canada, m: 29 Nov 1980 in Barrhead, Alberta, Canada

.................6 David Charles Greig (1962 -) b: 25 May 1962 in Barrhead, Alberta, Canada

.... + Marlene Martin (1964 -) b: 18 Jan 1964 in Barrhead, Alberta, Canada, m: 08 Jan 1983 in Barrhead, Alberta, Canada

..................7 Christopher David Greig (1982 -) b: 08 Sep 1982 in Edmonton, Alberta, Canada

..................7 Kimberly Lynn Greig (1985 -) b: 12 Aug 1985 in Barrhead, Alberta, Canada

.................6 Donald James Greig (1964 -) b: 17 Jan 1964 in Edmonton, Alberta, Canada

.... + Alfred James Dodgson (1908 - 1994) b: 06 Nov 1908 in Cardston, Alberta, Canada, m: 06 Feb 1982 in Barrhead, Alberta, Canada, d: 23 Dec 1994 in Barrhead, Alberta, Canada

............4 Elaine Ruby Bentz (1909 - 2008) b: 16 Dec 1909 in Harvey, Cavalier, North Dakota, USA, d: 12 Jun 2008 in Barrhead, Alberta, Canada

.... + Edward Arthur Larkins (1911 - 1981) b: 02 Jun 1911 in Mundare, Alberta, Canada, m: 24 Feb 1941 in Barrhead, Alberta, Canada, d: 03 Mar 1981 in Barrhead, Alberta, Canada

...............5 Arlene Joan Larkins (1942 -) b: 22 Jan 1942 in Barrhead, Alberta, Canada

.... + Leroy Claude Christianson (1940 -) b: 19 Jul 1940 in Barrhead, Alberta, Canada, m: 25 Aug 1959 in Edmonton, Alberta, Canada

.................6 Cheryl Dene Christianson (1959 -) b: 18 Jan 1959 in Barrhead, Alberta, Canada

.... + Fred Eric Preuss (1956 - 2002) b: 22 Sep 1956 in Barrhead, Alberta, Canada, m: 30 Aug 1975 in Barrhead, Alberta, Canada, d: 10 Jun 2002 in Barrhead, Alberta, Canada

..................7 Trina Lisa Preuss (1976 -) b: 14 Apr 1976 in Barrhead, Alberta, Canada

.... + Joseph DaCosta (1974 -) b: 25 Feb 1974 in Edmonton, Alberta, Canada, m: 09 Jul 1994 in St. Albert, Alberta, Canada

..................8 Kayla Jasmine Maria DaCosta (1994 -) b: 02 Oct 1994 in St. Albert, Alberta, Canada

.... + Michael Jarrard (1971 -) b: 03 Feb 1971 in Vancouver, British Columbia, Canada, m: 24 Jul 2010 in Coquitlam, British Columbia, Canada

..................8 Braydon Jarrard (2006 -) b: 31 Jul 2006 in Coquitlam, British Columbia, Canada

..................8 Chanel Jarrard (2008 -) b: 26 Aug 2008 in Coquitlam, British Columbia, Canada

..................7 Troy Dean Preuss (1977 -) b: 09 Nov 1977 in Barrhead, Alberta, Canada

.... + Melissa Gail Bates (1980 -) b: 23 Feb 1980 in Barrhead, Alberta, Canada

..................8 Ashlyn Jade Preuss (2001 -) b: 30 Sep 2001 in Barrhead, Alberta, Canada

..................8 Tray Wyatt Preuss (2005 -) b: 16 Oct 2005 in Barrhead, Alberta, Canada

.... + Robert Miller (1960 -) b: 28 Oct 1960 in Edmonton, Alberta, Canada, m: 03 Sep 1988 in Calihoo, Alberta, Canada

.... + Rodney William Sopiwnyk (1964 -) b: 03 Mar 1964 in Winnipeg, Manitoba, Canada, m: 20 May 2000 in Edmonton, Alberta, Canada

..................7 Mathew Kyle Sopiwnyk (1990 -) b: 21 Nov 1990 in Edmonton, Alberta, Canada

.................6 Vance Jackie Christianson (1960 -) b: 22 Feb 1960 in Barrhead, Alberta, Canada

.... + Joanne Kathleen Zarry (1959 -) b: 30 Jun 1959 in Edmonton, Alberta, Canada, m: 21 Jun 1980 in Barrhead, Alberta, Canada

..................7 Jason Murray Christianson (1980 -) b: 12 Dec 1980 in Fort St. John, British Columbia, Canada

.... + Carly Perkins (1981 -) b: 29 May 1981 in Daysland, Alberta, Canada, m: 02 Jun 2005 in Fort St. John, British Columbia, Canada

..................8 Skyler Anne Christianson (2005 -) b: 02 Nov 2005 in Edmonton, Alberta, Canada

..................8 Samantha Kathleen Christianson (2008 -) b: 04 Sep 2008 in Edmonton, Alberta, Canada

..................8 Quinn Arlene Christianson (2010 -) b: 03 Mar 2010 in Edmonton, Alberta, Canada

..................7 Jessica Dawn Christianson (1982 -) b: 25 Jun 1982 in Fort St. John, British Columbia, Canada

.... + Shawn Nicolaas Van Wyk (1982 -) b: 21 Oct 1982 in Nanimo, B.C., m: 01 Jul 2008 in Las Vegas, Clark, Nevada, USA

..................8 Austin Van Wyk (2004 -) b: 19 May 2004 in Ft. St. John, B. C. Canada

..................8 Declan Van Wyk (2007 -) b: 03 Jul 2007 in Ft. St. John, B.C. Canada

....................7 Joel Anthony Christianson (1987 -) b: 03 Jun 1987 in Fort St. John, British Columbia, Canada

.................6 Colleen Elaine Christianson (1962 -) b: 25 Nov 1962 in Barrhead, Alberta, Canada

.... + William Michael Dobney (1960 -) b: 12 Jul 1960 in Sherwood Park, Alberta, m: 01 Sep 1984 in Barrhead, Alberta, Canada

....................7 Stuart William Dobney (1987 -) b: 12 Feb 1987 in St. Albert, Alberta

.... + Rachelle Volden (Unknown -) b: Unknown in Unknown, m: Unknown in Unknown

....................7 Blaine Michael Dobney (1990 -) b: 20 Mar 1990 in St. Albert, Alberta

.... + Danny Olson (1972 -) b: 21 May 1972 in Barrhead, Alberta, Canada

..............5 Stuart Floyd Larkins (1943 - 1958) b: 31 May 1943 in Barrhead, Alberta, Canada, d: 19 May 1958 in Barrhead, Alberta, Canada

..............5 Carol Alice Larkins (1944 -) b: 11 Dec 1944 in Barrhead, Alberta, Canada

.... + Charles William Sutherland (1940 -) b: 03 Dec 1940 in Barrhead, Alberta, Canada, m: 25 Mar 1967 in Barrhead, Alberta, Canada

.................6 Christopher Jason Sutherland (1972 -) b: 26 Dec 1972 in Barrhead, Alberta, Canada

.... + Elizabeth Eva Shield (1980 -) b: 05 Mar 1980 in Barrhead, Alberta, Canada, m: 15 Aug 2009 in Barrhead, Alberta, Canada

....................7 1 Kiran Dax Sutherland (2014 -) b: 13 Jul 2014 in Barrhead, Alberta, Canada

.................6 Sharla Kae Sutherland (1975 -) b: 22 Jul 1975 in Barrhead, Alberta, Canada

.... + Shaheed Merani (1980 -) b: 11 Dec 1980 in Edmonton, Alberta, Canada, m: 29 Sep 2007 in Edmonton, Alberta, Canada

............4 Lewis Bentz (1911 - 1996) b: 13 Nov 1911 in Harvey, Cavalier, North Dakota, USA, d: 11 Sep 1996 in Barrhead, Alberta, Canada

.... + Katie Heberling (1910 - 1991) b: 11 Dec 1910 in Mlinska, Hungary, m: 04 Mar 1951 in Barrhead, Alberta, Canada, d: 05 Oct 1991 in Barrhead, Alberta, Canada

..............5 Herbert Walter Bentz (1953 -) b: 10 May 1953 in Barrhead, Alberta, Canada

.... + Jacqueline Ann Johnstone (1950 -) b: 21 Apr 1950 in Urmston, Lancashire, England (Now part of Manchester), m: 27 Dec 1986 in Vancouver, British Columbia, Canada

.................6 Julia Leanna Bentz (1987 -) b: 21 Sep 1987 in Vancouver, British Columbia, Canada

.................6 Simon Alexander Bentz (1990 -) b: 14 Jul 1990 in Vancouver, British Columbia, Canada

............4 Robert Alloys Bentz (1914 - 2002) b: 22 Oct 1914 in unknown, d: 27 Sep 2002 in Edmonton, Alberta, Canada

.... + Marie Gertrude Demers (1915 - 1999) b: 21 May 1915 in Lyster, Quebec, Canada, m: 01 Aug 1938 in Medicine Hat, Alberta, Canada, d: 22 May 1999 in Edmonton, Alberta, Canada

..............5 Fern Anna Bentz (1939 -) b: 17 Apr 1939 in Ravenscrag. Saskatchewan, Canada

..............5 Claudette Delores Bentz (1941 -) b: 02 Jun 1941 in Barrhead, Alberta, Canada

..............5 Trevor Robert Bentz (1943 -) b: 09 Jan 1943 in Barrhead, Alberta, Canada

.... + Linda Anne Smaha (1945 -) b: 30 Aug 1945 in Hazelton, British Columbia, m: 28 Dec 1963 in Unknown

.................6 Steven Trevor Bentz (1965 -) b: 15 Jun 1965 in Terrace, British Columbia

.... + Lauri Marie Geddes (1968 -) b: 17 Oct 1968 in Edmonton, Alberta, Canada, m: 16 Jul 1993 in Kamloops, British Columbia, Canada

....................7 Reade Robert John Bentz (1997 -) b: 09 Mar 1997 in Kamloops, British Columbia

....................7 Kelsy Trevor Geddis Bentz (2000 -) b: 02 Oct 2000 in Kamloops, British Columbia

.................6 Warren John Bentz (1969 -) b: 31 May 1969 in Terrace, British Columbia, Canada

.... + Melinda Funk (1973 -) b: 18 Oct 1973 in Nanaimo, British Columbia, Canada

....................7 Adam John Alan Bentz Funk (1994 -) b: 10 Sep 1994 in Kamloops, British Columbia, Canada

..............5 Allan Harvey Bentz (1946 -) b: 27 Apr 1946 in Barrhead, Alberta, Canada

.... + Margaret Ann McQuire (1947 -) b: 29 Apr 1947 in Edmonton, Alberta, Canada, m: 05 Feb 1965 in Edmonton, Alberta, Canada

.................6 Tammy Ann Bentz (1966 -) b: 18 Jun 1966 in Edmonton, Alberta, Canada

.... + Trevor Charles James Hansen (1963 -) b: 10 Oct 1963 in Ottawa, Ontario, Canada, m: 10 Oct 1987 in Morinville, Alberta, Canada

....................7 Dane Thomas Hansen (2002 -) b: 26 Jun 2002 in Vancouver, British Columbia, Canada

..................6 Casey Allan Bentz (1967 -) b: 26 Jul 1967 in Edmonton, Alberta, Canada
.... + Tamie Alma Froment (1973 -) b: 16 Jun 1973 in St. Albert, Alberta, m: 17 Jul 1993 in Morinville, Alberta, Canada
....................7 Maguire Casavant Bentz (2000 -) b: 07 Jun 2000 in St. Albert, Alberta
................6 Gregory Robert Bentz (1974 -) b: 28 Jan 1974 in St. Albert, Alberta, Canada
.... + Lynne Marie Froment (1978 -) b: 02 Jun 1978 in St. Albert, Alberta, m: 01 Aug 2001 in Morinville, Alberta, Canada
..............5 Dallas Wayne Bentz (1947 -) b: 02 May 1947 in Barrhead, Alberta, Canada
.... + Karen Kathleen Klukus (1950 -) b: 07 Apr 1950 in Edmonton, Alberta, Canada, m: 19 Jul 1969 in Edmonton, Alberta, Canada
................6 Brenton Powell Bentz (1971 -) b: 01 Apr 1971 in Edmonton, Alberta, Canada
.... + Monica Kuebler (1978 -) b: 03 Mar 1978 in Ontario, m: 16 Sep 2006 in Edmonton, Alberta, Canada
................6 Christopher Wade Bentz (1972 -) b: 28 Nov 1972 in Edmonton, Alberta, Canada
................6 Jason Willis Bentz (1974 -) b: 06 Mar 1974 in Edmonton, Alberta, Canada
.... + Kimberly Tomm (1975 -) b: 24 Jul 1975 in Edmonton, Alberta, Canada, m: 27 Jul 2003 in Edmonton, Alberta, Canada
....................7 Griffin Bentz (2007 -) b: 03 Aug 2007 in Edmonton, Alberta, Canada
......................8 Calvin Bentz (2010 -) b: 05 Aug 2010 in Edmonton, Alberta, Canada
....................7 Calvin Bentz (2010 -) b: 05 Aug 2010 in Edmonton, Alberta, Canada
..............5 Sharon Vaughn Bentz (1953 -) b: 19 Jul 1953 in Barrhead, Alberta, Canada
.... + Dennis Robert Gunn (1947 - 1996) b: 19 Feb 1947 in Medford, Oregon, USA, m: 16 May 1974 in Edmonton, Alberta, Canada, d: 1996 in Whittiker, California
................6 Matthew Robert Jonathan Gunn (1978 -) b: 16 May 1978 in Edmonton, Alberta, Canada
.... + Lisa Wagner (Unknown -) b: Unknown in Unknown, m: Unknown in Unknown
....................7 Parker Robert Gunn (2005 -) b: 18 May 2005 in Edmonton, Alberta, Canada
.... + Tish Shelby Claughton (1980 -) b: 01 Aug 1980 in Edmonton, Alberta, Canada
....................7 Lavender Shelby Gunn (2013 -) b: 05 Mar 2013 in Edmonton, Alberta, Canada
..............5 Wesley Alloys Bentz (1956 -) b: 23 Oct 1956 in Edmonton, Alberta, Canada
.... + Jennifer Gail Clark (1963 -) b: 07 Sep 1963 in Burnaby, British Columbia, Canada
................6 Huxley Clark Bentz (1994 -) b: 16 Feb 1994 in Edmonton, Alberta, Canada
................6 Elliott Johann Bentz (1999 -) b: 28 Sep 1999 in Edmonton, Alberta, Canada
..............5 Anthony Gerard Vincent Bentz (1958 -) b: 11 Dec 1958 in Edmonton, Alberta, Canada
.... + Katherine Lynne Cotton (1962 -) b: 08 Sep 1962 in Winnipeg, Manitoba, Canada, m: 08 Aug 1985 in Edmonton, Alberta, Canada
................6 Melissa Diane Bentz (1987 -) b: 17 Apr 1987 in Edmonton, Alberta, Canada
.... + Ian Phillipchuk (Unknown -) b: Unknown in Unknown, m: 15 Sep 2012 in Edmonton, Alberta, Canada
................6 Kristen May Bentz (1990 -) b: 21 Sep 1990 in Edmonton, Alberta, Canada
..............5 Rhonda Jean Bentz (1959 -) b: 05 Oct 1959 in Edmonton, Alberta, Canada
.... + Donald Ray Littlejohn (1955 -) b: 09 Sep 1955 in Edmonton, Alberta, Canada, m: 25 Oct 1978 in Edmonton, Alberta, Canada
................6 James Robert Littlejohn (1978 -) b: 16 Apr 1978 in Edmonton, Alberta, Canada
................6 Roberta Jean Littlejohn (1979 -) b: 17 Aug 1979 in Edmonton, Alberta, Canada
....................7 Savanah Rebecca Littlejohn (1997 -) b: 17 Apr 1997 in Edmonton, Alberta, Canada
..............5 Lisa Marie Bentz (1962 -) b: 01 Jul 1962 in Edmonton, Alberta, Canada
.... + Tony Fortney b: unknown, m: 28 Dec 1980 in Shaunavon, Saskatchewan, Canada
................6 Nickolas Anthony Fortney (1980 -) b: 05 Jul 1980 in Shaunavon, Saskatchewan, Canada
................6 Terra Lyn Fortney (1982 -) b: 28 Feb 1982 in Shaunavon, Saskatchewan, Canada
................6 Joshua Robert Fortney (1984 -) b: 26 Dec 1984 in Shaunavon, Saskatchewan, Canada
.... + Douglas Steven Tymchuk
................6 Aaron Jackson Tymchuk
................6 Dustin Steven Tymchuk
..............5 Korrine Octa Bentz (1962 -) b: 19 Sep 1962 in Edmonton, Alberta, Canada

.... + Richard Wayne Pigeon (1961 -) b: 19 Jul 1961 in Edmonton, Alberta, Canada, m: 08 Mar 1980 in Edmonton, Alberta, Canada

.................6 Christopher Richard Pigeon (1980 -) b: 03 May 1980 in Edmonton, Alberta, Canada

.... + Unknown

...................7 Brandon Pigeon (2002 -) b: 21 Jul 2002 in Edmonton, Alberta, Canada

.................6 Jessica Marie Pigeon (1982 -) b: 19 Aug 1982 in Edmonton, Alberta, Canada

.... + Unknown

...................7 Jayde Pigeon (1999 -) b: 14 May 1999 in Edmonton, Alberta, Canada

.... + Vincent Arthur Michaud (1958 -) b: 03 Apr 1958 in Edmonton, Alberta, Canada, m: Unknown in Uknown

.............5 Cheryl Ann Widynowski (1966 -) b: 04 Jul 1966 in Edmonton, Alberta, Canada

.............5 Daryl Shepherd (1970 -) b: 17 May 1970 in Edmonton, Alberta, Canada

.............5 Jamie El-Khatib (1974 -) b: 09 Jun 1974 in Edmonton, Alberta, Canada

...........4 Alice Gertrude Bentz (1917 -) b: 31 Mar 1917 in Ravenscrag. Saskatchewan, Canada

.... + Arthur Farquhar Warehime (1919 - 2006) b: 05 Aug 1919 in Barrhead, Alberta, Canada, m: 27 Apr 1946 in Barrhead, Alberta, Canada, d: 07 Dec 2006 in Barrhead, Alberta, Canada

.............5 Myrna Alice Warehime (1946 -) b: 12 Nov 1946 in Barrhead, Alberta, Canada

.... + Albert Lee Chadd (1940 -) b: 04 Mar 1940 in Barrhead, Alberta, Canada, m: 12 Nov 1966 in Barrhead, Alberta, Canada

.................6 Zene Ross Chadd (1967 -) b: 19 Sep 1967 in Barrhead, Alberta, Canada

.... + Jodi Leanne Arnal (1967 -) b: 25 Mar 1967 in Barrhead, Alberta, Canada, m: 29 Nov 1986 in Barrhead, Alberta, Canada

...................7 Jimy Lee Chadd (1986 -) b: 22 Jul 1986 in Barrhead, Alberta, Canada

.... + Crystal Gail McIntosh (1981 -) b: 30 Nov 1981 in Barrhead, Alberta, Canada, m: 13 Jun 2009 in Tiger Lily, Alberta, Canada

.......................8 Wyatt James Arthur Chadd (2007 -) b: 12 Apr 2007 in Barrhead, Alberta, Canada

.......................8 Damien Michael Travis Chadd (2010 -) b: 11 Aug 2010 in Barrhead, Alberta, Canada

...................7 Michael Zene Chadd (1989 -) b: 27 Jan 1989 in Barrhead, Alberta, Canada

...................7 Kaylee Nicole Chadd (1991 -) b: 28 Feb 1991 in Barrhead, Alberta, Canada

.... + Tracy Mary Devolt b: Whitecourt, Alberta

...................7 Dominic Devolt (1999 -) b: 15 Jan 1999 in Whitecourt, Alberta

...................7 Abigal Frances Chadd (2005 -) b: 07 Jun 2005 in Whitecourt, Alberta, Canada

.................6 Lonnie Wade Chadd (1969 -) b: 03 Nov 1969 in Barrhead, Alberta, Canada

.... + Louise Elaine Cowley (1976 -) b: 27 Jan 1976 in Mayerthorpe, Alberta, Canada, m: 10 Sep 1994 in Mayerthorpe, Alberta, Canada

...................7 Tre Ty Chadd (1999 -) b: 06 Oct 1999 in Barrhead, Alberta, Canada

...................7 Logan Grant Chadd (2005 -) b: 22 Apr 2005 in Edmonton, Alberta, Canada

.................6 Lowell Jason Chadd (1970 -) b: 28 Dec 1970 in Barrhead, Alberta, Canada

.... + Lolita Irene Properzi (1972 -) b: 28 Jul 1972 in Westlock, Alberta, Canada, m: 11 Aug 1990 in Barrhead, Alberta, Canada

...................7 Trinity Kathleen Chadd (1991 -) b: 24 Aug 1991 in Barrhead, Alberta, Canada

...................7 Xayna Myrene Chadd (1994 -) b: 24 May 1994 in Barrhead, Alberta, Canada

...................7 Erin Lee Chadd (1995 -) b: 07 Dec 1995 in Barrhead, Alberta, Canada

.................6 Dana Lee Chadd (1971 -) b: 08 May 1971 in Barrhead, Alberta, Canada

.... + Tania Lee White (1973 -) b: 21 Aug 1973 in Mayerthorpe, Alberta, Canada, m: 12 Nov 1994 in Mayerthorpe, Alberta, Canada

...................7 Kasandra Margaret Chadd (1996 -) b: 17 Sep 1996 in Edmonton, Alberta, Canada

.... + Kimberly Ann Gauthier (1980 -) b: 10 Aug 1980 in Nanaimo, British Columbia, Canada, m: 21 Sep 2002 in Barrhead, Alberta, Canada

...................7 Vincent Elmond Chadd (2005 -) b: 06 Oct 2005 in Barrhead, Alberta, Canada

...................7 Anna Marie Chadd (2008 -) b: 08 Dec 2008 in Barrhead, Alberta, Canada

.................6 Quentin Arthur Chadd (1981 -) b: 08 Nov 1981 in Barrhead, Alberta, Canada

.... + Lacey Rebecca Barbara Pringle (1981 -) b: 17 Nov 1981 in Swift Current, Saskatchewan, Canada, m: 25 May 2002 in Tiger Lily, Alberta, Canada

...................7 Cameron Chadd (2002 -) b: 03 Mar 2002 in Edmonton, Alberta, Canada

.....................7 Emily Mary Ellen Chadd (2005 -) b: 02 May 2005 in Barrhead, Alberta, Canada

.....................7 Luke Zene Chadd (2009 -) b: 10 Nov 2009 in Barrhead, Alberta, Canada

................5 Lynn Shari Warehime (1948 -) b: 18 May 1948 in Barrhead, Alberta, Canada

.... + Lowell Clarence Cramer (1948 - 1992) b: 10 Apr 1948 in Barrhead, Alberta, Canada, m: 11 May 1968 in Barrhead, Alberta, Canada, d: 05 Aug 1992 in Barrhead, Alberta, Canada

....................6 Rechelle Alice Cramer (1969 -) b: 30 Mar 1969 in Barrhead, Alberta, Canada

.... + Todd William Koehler (1965 -) b: 21 Oct 1965 in Rivers, Manitoba, Canada, m: 15 Apr 1989 in Barrhead, Alberta, Canada

.....................7 Dylan Lowell Koehler (1990 -) b: 18 Oct 1990 in Barrhead, Alberta, Canada

.....................7 Chelsea Lynn Koehler (1993 -) b: 23 Mar 1993 in Barrhead, Alberta, Canada

.....................7 DevinTodd Koehler (1994 -) b: 14 Dec 1994 in Barrhead, Alberta, Canada

....................6 Robin Lowell Cramer (1971 -) b: 12 Mar 1971 in Barrhead, Alberta, Canada

.... + Dawn Mae Holowaychuk (1976 -) b: 19 Jul 1976 in Edmonton, Alberta, Canada, m: 20 Aug 1999 in Barrhead, Alberta, Canada

.....................7 Jaydon Dawn Cramer (2002 -) b: 07 Aug 2002 in Barrhead, Alberta, Canada

.....................7 Kiera Robin Cramer (2004 -) b: 04 Aug 2004 in Barrhead, Alberta, Canada

....................6 Tammy Lynn Margaret Cramer (1973 -) b: 16 Apr 1973 in Barrhead, Alberta, Canada

.... + Shawn Doyle Kinden (1974 -) b: 08 Apr 1974 in St John's, Newfoundland and Labrador, Canada

.....................7 Laura Anne Kinden (2005 -) b: 30 Oct 2005 in Grande Prairie, Alberta, Canada

....................6 Christina Noreen Cramer (1976 -) b: 08 Jun 1976 in Barrhead, Alberta, Canada

............4 Calvin Paul Bentz (1919 - 2005) b: 10 Apr 1919 in Eastend, Saskatchewan, Canada, d: 02 Feb 2005 in Vegreville, Alberta

.... + Katherine Hannah Metzger (1928 - 1984) b: 14 Sep 1928 in Barrhead, Alberta, Canada, m: 17 Dec 1946 in Mellowdale, Alberta, Canada, d: 14 May 1984 in Kelowna, British Columbia, Canada

...............5 Donna Shirley Bentz (1949 - 1965) b: 30 Mar 1949 in Barrhead, Alberta, Canada, d: 27 Jan 1965 in Barrhead, Alberta, Canada

...............5 Jerry Allan Bentz (1951 -) b: 21 Nov 1951 in Barrhead, Alberta, Canada

.... + Jane Elizabeth Matheson (1952 -) b: 21 Dec 1952 in Edmonton, Alberta, Canada, m: 16 Aug 1974 in Edmonton, Alberta, Canada

....................6 Sarah Katherine Bentz (1978 -) b: 09 Dec 1978 in Edmonton, Alberta, Canada

.... + Chad Ryan Paul Schulz (1974 -) b: 31 Oct 1974 in Lahr, Germany, Europe, m: 09 Jun 2007 in Edmonton, Alberta, Canada

....................6 Andrea Heather Bentz (1980 -) b: 10 Dec 1980 in Edmonton, Alberta, Canada

.... + Ryan Freehan b: Edmonton, Alberta, Canada, m: Edmonton, Alberta, Canada

....................6 Lisa Marie Bentz (1983 -) b: 19 Mar 1983 in Edmonton, Alberta, Canada

...............5 Jane Kathleen Bentz (1951 -) b: 21 Nov 1951 in Barrhead, Alberta, Canada

.... + Joseph Paul Hoffman (1950 -) b: 05 Dec 1950 in Barrhead, Alberta, Canada, m: 31 Aug 1970 in Barrhead, Alberta, Canada

....................6 Charlene Crystal Hoffman (1973 -) b: 24 Nov 1973 in Vegreville, Alberta, Alberta, Canada

.... + Garett Hromada (1971 -) b: 06 Jul 1971 in Edmonton, Alberta, Canada, m: 30 Sep 2006 in Edmonton, Alberta, Canada

.....................7 Jake Garett Hromada (2008 -) b: 02 Jun 2008 in St Albert, Alberta, Canada

.....................7 Gavin Carl Joe Hromada (2011 -) b: 28 Jul 2011 in St Albert, Alberta, Canada

....................6 Christy Lynn Hoffman (1977 -) b: 08 Feb 1977 in Vegreville, Alberta, Canada

.... + Michael Le-Roy Webb (1975 -) b: 31 Aug 1975 in Balfast, Ireland, m: 01 Sep 2001 in Vegreville, Alberta, Canada

.....................7 Connor Joseph Webb (2005 -) b: 27 Apr 2005 in Vegreville, Alberta

.....................7 Kenneday Jane Webb (2006 -) b: 21 Nov 2006 in Vegreville, Alberta

...............5 Nancy Ann Bentz (1961 -) b: 11 Nov 1961 in Barrhead, Alberta, Canada

.... + Mauri Kalevi Saura (1955 -) b: 07 May 1955 in Finland, Europe, m: 29 May 1982 in Kelowna, British Columbia, Canada

....................6 Amanda Katherine Saura (1985 -) b: 06 Jun 1985 in Victoria, British Columbia, Canada

.... + Nelson Lindahl m: 02 Oct 2004 in Kelowna, British Columbia, Canada

.....................7 Allie Katherine Lindahl (2012 -) b: 24 Feb 2012 in Kelowna, British Columbia, Canada

.....................7 Ava Marie Lindahl (2013 -) b: 20 Dec 2013 in Kelowna, British Columbia, Canada

.................6 Jessica Leal Saura (1994 -) b: 28 Feb 1994 in Revelstoke, British Columbia, Canada

.... + Harvey Melvin Kilbrie (1951 -) b: 10 Sep 1951 in Winnipeg, Manitoba, Canada, m: 06 Oct 2012 in Kelowna, British Columbia, Canada

...............5 John Bentz (1951 - 1951) b: 21 Nov 1951 in Barrhead, Alberta, Canada, d: 21 Nov 1951 in Barrhead, Alberta, Canada

............4 Harvey Harold Bentz (1921 - 2002) b: 30 Jan 1921 in Ravenscrag. Saskatchewan, Canada, d: 30 Jul 2002 in Barrhead, Alberta, Canada

.... + Alvina Radke (1921 - 2002) b: 23 Sep 1921 in Barrhead, Alberta, Canada, m: 11 Nov 1948 in Mellowdale, Alberta, Canada, d: 30 Jul 2002 in Barrhead, Alberta, Canada

...............5 Janice Lee Bentz (1949 -) b: 11 Dec 1949 in Barrhead, Alberta, Canada

.... + Robert Ernest Maxwell (1942 -) b: 08 Aug 1942 in Duncan, British Columbia, Canada, m: 06 Oct 1972 in Mellowdale, Alberta, Canada

.................6 Melanie Leah Maxwell (1979 -) b: 06 Sep 1979 in Vancouver, British Columbia, Canada

...............5 Lorne Douglas Bentz (1952 -) b: 20 Mar 1952 in Barrhead, Alberta, Canada

.... + Judith Yvone King (1957 - 1983) b: 26 Jul 1957 in Barrhead, Alberta, Canada, m: 08 May 1976 in Barrhead, Alberta, Canada, d: 03 Jun 1983 in Barrhead, Alberta, Canada

.................6 Bradley Douglas Bentz (1979 -) b: 23 Mar 1979 in Edmonton, Alberta, Canada

.... + Melinda Larson (1982 -) b: 23 Mar 1982 in Barrhead, Alberta, Canada, m: 13 Aug 2005 in Barrhead, Alberta, Canada

.....................7 Hunter Riley Bentz (2007 -) b: 18 Oct 2007 in Edmonton, Alberta, Canada

.....................7 Cole Douglas Bentz (2009 -) b: 19 Nov 2009 in Barrhead, Alberta, Canada

.................6 Michael James Bentz (1981 -) b: 19 Jul 1981 in Barrhead, Alberta, Canada

.... + Alicia Torey Schmidt (1984 -) b: 15 Jul 1984 in Westlock, Alberta, Canada, m: 18 Jul 2009 in Barrhead, Alberta, Canada

.....................7 Mason Dane Bentz (2011 -) b: 12 Aug 2011 in St. Albert, Alberta

.... + Judy Anne Baron (1954 -) b: 29 Jun 1954 in Barrhead, Alberta, Canada, m: 20 Feb 1999 in Mellowdale, Alberta, Canada

...............5 Dale Keith Bentz (1956 -) b: 17 Apr 1956 in Barrhead, Alberta, Canada

.... + Laurie Gail Geis (1957 -) b: 25 Sep 1957 in Barrhead, Alberta, Canada, m: 21 Mar 1981 in Mellowdale, Alberta, Canada

............4 Magdalena Bentz (1922 - 2003) b: 22 Dec 1922 in Eastend, Saskatchewan, Canada, d: 07 Aug 2003 in Kelowna, British Columbia, Canada

............4 Irene Evelyn Bentz (1926 - 2012) b: 03 Jan 1926 in Eastend, Saskatchewan, Canada, d: 27 May 2012 in Barrhead, Alberta, Canada

.... + Gustav Stefani (1923 - 1996) b: 11 Nov 1923 in Poland, Europe, m: 03 Jan 1949 in Barrhead, Alberta, Canada, d: 05 May 1996 in Westlock, Alberta, Canada

...............5 Wayne Ronald Stefani (1949 - 2000) b: 25 Oct 1949 in Westlock, Alberta, Canada, d: 06 Mar 2000 in Richmond, British Columbia, Canada

.... + Cheryl MacDonald (Unknown -) b: Unknown in Vancouver, British Columbia, Canada, m: 07 Nov 1969 in Vancouver, British Columbia, Canada

.................6 Mark Kenneth Stefani (1970 -) b: 25 Mar 1970 in Vancouver, British Columbia, Canada

.... + Bonnie Soroke (Unknown -) b: Unknown in Vancouver, British Columbia, Canada, m: Unknown in Unknown

.................6 Joel Stefani Soroke (1990 -) b: 05 May 1990 in Vancouver, British Columbia, Canada

.... + Katherine McElroy Zanner (Unknown -) b: Unknown in Vancouver, British Columbia, Canada, m: Unknown in Unknown

.................6 Ryan Ronald Zanner (1982 -) b: 24 Dec 1982 in Vancouver, British Columbia, Canada

...............5 Murray Kenneth Stefani (1953 - 2013) b: 01 Jan 1953 in Westlock, Alberta, Canada, d: 15 Oct 2013 in Westlock, Alberta, Canada

............4 Joyce Orpah Bentz (1932 -) b: 16 Jan 1932 in Eastend, Saskatchewan, Canada

.... + Hugh Edwin Roesch (1923 - 2008) b: 01 May 1923 in Atwood, Rawlins, Kansas, USA, m: 20 Jan 1964 in Oakland, Alameda, California, USA, d: 25 Jan 2008 in Kelowna, British Columbia, Canada

...............5 Robert Edwin Roesch (1946 - 2009) b: 30 Aug 1946 in San Francisco, California, USA, d: 05 Jul 2009 in Concord, California, USA

.... + Linda Marie Anderson (1947 -) b: 04 Feb 1947 in Burlingame, California, USA, m: 07 Aug 1965 in Reno, Nevada, USA

..................6 Cheryl Lynn Roesch (1966 -) b: 28 May 1966 in San Francisco, California, USA

.... + Mark Ivan Cox (1958 -) b: 05 Dec 1958 in Clifton, Clay, Kansas, USA, m: 24 Mar 1990 in Concord, California, USA

.....................7 Kevin Matthew Cox (1994 -) b: 29 May 1994 in Concord, California, USA

.....................7 Shawn Michael Cox (1996 -) b: 22 Apr 1996 in Concord, California, USA

.... + Ann Marie Smith (1957 -) b: 05 Oct 1957 in San Francisco, California, USA, m: 28 Dec in Kelowna, British Columbia, Canada

...............5 Larry Arlan Roesch (1948 -) b: 02 Apr 1948 in San Francisco, California, USA

............4 Raymond Lawrence Bentz (1933 -) b: 19 Jan 1933 in Medicine Hat, Alberta, Canada

.... + Sheila Elizabeth Dick (1937 -) b: 24 Jun 1937 in Calgary, Alberta, Canada, m: 10 Jul 1954 in Edmonton, Alberta, Canada

...............5 Marty Lex Bentz (1954 -) b: 22 Sep 1954 in Barrhead, Alberta, Canada

.... + Valerie DeSchuter (1958 -) b: 18 Aug 1958 in Thorhild, Alberta, Canada, m: 16 Apr 2011 in Thorhild, Alberta, Canada

...............5 Barry Dick Bentz (1955 -) b: 05 Sep 1955 in Barrhead, Alberta, Canada

.... + Deborah Joan McKenzie (1954 - 2012) b: 20 Mar 1954 in Edmonton, Alberta, Canada, m: 14 May 1982 in Edmonton, Alberta, Canada, d: 29 Dec 2012 in Edmonton, Alberta, Canada

..................6 Christine McKenzie Bentz (1984 -) b: 19 Nov 1984 in Edmonton, Alberta, Canada

..................6 Andrew Steven Bentz (1987 -) b: 23 Jan 1987 in Edmonton, Alberta, Canada

...............5 Neville Raymond Bentz (1956 -) b: 02 Nov 1956 in Barrhead, Alberta, Canada

.... + Cynthia Marie Olchowy (1958 -) b: 17 Dec 1958 in Radway, Alberta, Canada, m: 19 Oct 1985 in Edmonton, Alberta, Canada

...............5 Donald Colin Bentz (1958 -) b: 27 Apr 1958 in Barrhead, Alberta, Canada

...............5 Brian Larry Bentz (1960 -) b: 30 Nov 1960 in Barrhead, Alberta, Canada

.... + Lorianne Kelly Popowich (1962 -) b: 02 Aug 1962 in Wynyard, Saskatchewan, Canada, m: 22 Aug 1981 in Edmonton, Alberta, Canada

..................6 Cody Nicholas Bentz (1989 -) b: 09 Feb 1989 in Edmonton, Alberta, Canada

..................6 Joshua Brian Bentz (1991 -) b: 30 Oct 1991 in Edmonton, Alberta, Canada

...............5 David Glenn Bentz (1962 -) b: 01 Feb 1962 in Barrhead, Alberta, Canada

.........3 Carl Kalk (1890 - 1892) b: 12 Feb 1890 in Belgonie, NWT, Canada, d: 11 Feb 1892 in Belgonie, NWT, Canada

.........3 Mary Kalk (1893 - 1954) b: 21 Nov 1893 in Belgonie, NWT, Canada, d: 20 Oct 1954 in Millarville, Alberta, Canada

.... + Fred Heth (1891 - 1966) b: 02 Aug 1891 in Austria, m: 04 Dec 1911 in Towner, North Dakota, USA, d: 18 Feb 1966 in Vancouver, British Columbia, Canada

............4 Novella Paulina Heth (1912 - 2006) b: 24 Jun 1912 in Anamoose, North Dakota, USA, d: 11 Jul 2006 in Maple Creek, Saskatchewan, Canada

.... + Edward Bentz (1901 - 1990) b: 08 Oct 1901 in unknown, m: 12 Oct 1935 in Maple Creek, Saskatchewan, Canada, d: 24 Jun 1990 in Maple Creek, Saskatchewan, Canada

...............5 Avalon Adrienne Bentz (1939 -) b: 15 Jun 1939 in Eastend, Saskatchewan, Canada

.... + Stanley Lewis Hough (1934 - 1994) b: 04 Apr 1934 in Vermilion, Alberta, Canada, m: 08 Nov 1961 in Eastend, Saskatchewan, Canada, d: 05 Apr 1994 in Preeceville, Saskatchewan, Canada

..................6 Calvin Edward Hough (1963 -) b: 18 Oct 1963 in Eastend, Saskatchewan, Canada

.... + Kelly Mildred Pollock (1958 -) b: 10 Jun 1958 in Preeceville, Saskatchewan, Canada, m: 17 Jun 1995 in Preeceville, Saskatchewan, Canada

.....................7 Matthew Edward Hough (1982 -) b: 23 Sep 1982 in Yorkton, Saskatchewan, Canada

.....................7 Shawn Allan Hough (1985 -) b: 03 May 1985 in Yorkton, Saskatchewan, Canada

.....................7 Marlee Ann Monica Hough (1986 -) b: 13 Dec 1986 in Preeceville, Saskatchewan, Canada

......................7 Kristen Kelly Ashton Hough (1989 -) b: 14 Jun 1989 in Preeceville, Saskatchewan, Canada

.... + Karrie Teresa Bergquist (14 Nov -) b: 14 Nov in Shaunavon, Saskatchewan, Canada

................6 Monica Adrienne Hough (1967 -) b: 30 Dec 1967 in Maple Creek, Saskatchewan, Canada

.... + Keith Harvey Neu (1958 -) b: 27 Apr 1958 in Melfort, Saskatchewan, Canada, m: 10 Apr 1993 in Maple Creek, Saskatchewan, Canada

......................7 Colton Leigh Neu (1992 -) b: 19 Jun 1992 in Hudson Bay, Saskatchewan, Canada

......................7 Connor Stanley Neu (1994 -) b: 19 Mar 1994 in Hudson Bay, Saskatchewan, Canada

......................7 Tasia Novella Neu (1996 -) b: 12 Nov 1996 in Hudson Bay, Saskatchewan, Canada

...............5 Darlene Connie Bentz (1944 -) b: 12 Feb 1944 in Maple Creek, Saskatchewan, Canada

.... + Donald Emil Albert Bowles (1941 - 2002) b: 21 Sep 1941 in Maple Creek, Saskatchewan, Canada, m: 08 Nov 1961 in Maple Creek, Saskatchewan, Canada, d: 14 Jun 2002 in Maple Creek, Saskatchewan, Canada

.................6 Karen Darlene Bowles (1964 -) b: 19 Oct 1964 in Maple Creek, Saskatchewan, Canada

.... + Bryan Alexander Nagy (1968 -) b: 09 Apr 1968 in Drumheller, Alberta, Canada, m: 20 Aug 1994 in Maple Creek, Saskatchewan, Canada

......................7 Joel Lynden Nagy (1997 -) b: 26 Mar 1997 in Calgary, Alberta, Canada

......................7 Kyle Brenden Nagy (1999 -) b: 19 Jun 1999 in Calgary, Alberta, Canada

.................6 Shawn Donald Bowles (1967 -) b: 17 Feb 1967 in Maple Creek, Saskatchewan, Canada

.... + Lynnell Dawn Arendt (1970 -) b: 17 May 1970 in Shaunavon, Saskatchewan, Canada, m: 17 Jul 1993 in Eastend, Saskatchewan, Canada

......................7 Tash Donald Bowles (1998 -) b: 21 Jan 1998 in Estevan, Saskatchewan, Canada

......................7 Kelli Lynae Bowles (1999 -) b: 30 Oct 1999 in Estevan, Saskatchewan, Canada

............4 Lillian Alvina Heth (1915 - 1993) b: 28 Jun 1915 in Ravenscrag. Saskatchewan, Canada, d: 29 Mar 1993 in Calgary, Alberta, Canada

.... + Walter Herbert Schaal (1912 - 1996) b: 23 Dec 1912 in Kealey Springs, Saskatchewan, Canada, m: 23 Nov 1938 in Ravenscrag. Saskatchewan, Canada, d: 29 Oct 1996 in Turner Valley, Alberta, Canada

...............5 Beverley Jane Schaal (1941 -) b: 07 Apr 1941 in Maple Creek, Saskatchewan, Canada

.... + Hugh John Macklin (1932 -) b: 26 Feb 1932 in Calgary, Alberta, Canada, m: 01 Jun 1960 in Calgary, Alberta, Canada

.................6 Barbara Ann Macklin (1961 -) b: 08 Jun 1961 in Calgary, Alberta, Canada

.... + Larry Gordon Maxwell (1956 -) b: 03 Nov 1956 in Elnora, Alberta, Canada, m: 23 Oct 1981 in Olds, Alberta, Canada

......................7 Lyndsay Deborah Maxwell (1983 -) b: 08 Jul 1983 in Olds, Alberta, Canada

......................7 Katheryn Dawn Maxwell (1985 -) b: 07 May 1985 in Olds, Alberta, Canada

......................7 Jacqueline Lauren Maxwell (1988 -) b: 17 Feb 1988 in Olds, Alberta, Canada

.................6 Trevor John Macklin (1964 -) b: 11 Jan 1964 in Calgary, Alberta, Canada

.... + Tammy Lee Ringland (1973 -) b: 12 Dec 1973 in Strathmore, Alberta, Canada, m: 02 Jul 1994 in Calgary, Alberta, Canada

......................7 Breanna Lee Macklin (1995 -) b: 07 Jun 1995 in Sundre, Alberta, Canada

......................7 Brooke Ashley Macklin (2001 -) b: 15 May 2001 in Calgary, Alberta, Canada

......................7 Morgan Amber Macklin (2001 -) b: 15 May 2001 in Calgary, Alberta, Canada

...............5 Gary Dale Schaal (1943 -) b: 25 Jun 1943 in Eastend, Saskatchewan, Canada

.... + Linda Mae Watkins (1946 -) b: 14 Jul 1946 in Calgary, Alberta, Canada, m: 28 Jun 1969 in Calgary, Alberta, Canada

.................6 Randy Jay Schaal (1976 -) b: 10 Mar 1976 in Calgary, Alberta, Canada

.................6 Suzon Winnifred Schaal (1978 -) b: 21 Jul 1978 in Calgary, Alberta, Canada

............4 Sophia Leona Heth (1916 - 1999) b: 18 Sep 1916 in Ravenscrag. Saskatchewan, Canada, d: 22 Nov 1999 in Abbotsford, B. C.

.... + John Frederick Schaal (1910 - 1991) b: 21 Sep 1910 in Kealey Springs, Saskatchewan, m: 23 Nov 1938 in Ravenscrag. Saskatchewan, Canada, d: 04 Apr 1991 in Calgary, Alberta, Canada

............4 Leonard Fredrick Heth (1920 - 2013) b: 09 Mar 1920 in Ravenscrag. Saskatchewan, Canada, d: 03 Aug 2013 in Chiliwack, British Columbia, Canada

.... + Helen Haydukuch (1920 -) b: 02 Feb 1920 in Saskatchewan, m: 18 Dec 1941 in Vancouver, British Columbia, Canada

...............5 Sharon Mary Heth (1943 -) b: 16 Jul 1943 in Vancouver, British Columbia, Canada

.... + Jack Lemery (1942 -) b: 13 Jul 1942 in Vancouver, British Columbia, Canada, m: 03 Aug 1963 in Vancouver, British Columbia, Canada

...............5 Dennis Arthur Heth (1946 -) b: 26 Jun 1946 in Vancouver, British Columbia, Canada

.... + Cathy Eberts (1946 -) b: 08 Aug 1946

.... + Beatrice Wilhelmina Horstman (1911 - 1988) b: 06 Jun 1911 in Stewart, British Columbia, m: 15 Nov 1951 in Chiliwack, British Columbia, Canada, d: 07 Mar 1988 in Abbotsford, British Columbia

.... + Winnifred Mildred Hood (1916 -) b: 07 Sep 1916 in Saskatoon, Saskatchewan, Canada, m: 12 Sep 1988 in Millarville, Alberta, Canada

............4 Arthur Lewis Heth (1922 - 2008) b: 31 Dec 1922 in Eastend, Saskatchewan, Canada, d: 26 May 2008 in Abbotsford, British Columbia, Canada

.... + Violet Vera Weisser (1926 -) b: 29 Jan 1926 in Gravelbourg, Saskatchewan, m: 25 Sep 1947 in Abbotsford, British Columbia, Canada

...............5 Mavis Marion Heth (1948 -) b: 26 May 1948 in Vancouver, British Columbia, Canada

.... + Harold Robert Hawksby (1948 -) b: 19 Jan 1948 in Vancouver, British Columbia, Canada, m: 23 Sep 1967 in Vancouver, British Columbia, Canada

..................6 Gregory Robert Hawksby (1969 -) b: 08 Aug 1969 in Port Alice, British Columbia

.... + Wendi Patricia Boyd (1969 -) b: 08 Jun 1969 in Vancouver, British Columbia, Canada, m: 08 Jul 1994 in Mission, British Columbia, Canada

.....................7 Shelby Therese Hawksby (1991 -) b: 23 Nov 1991 in Edmonton, Alberta, Canada

.....................7 Bradley Robert Hawksby (1995 -) b: 21 Apr 1995 in Abbotsford, British Columbia

.....................7 Brett William Hawksby (1996 -) b: 03 Oct 1996 in Mission, British Columbia

..................6 Jodi Jeneille Hawksby (1971 -) b: 19 Mar 1971 in Port Alice, British Columbia, Canada

.... + Richard Allan Harmatuik (1968 -) b: 12 May 1968 in Saskatoon, Saskatchewan, Canada, m: 20 Mar 1993 in Mission, British Columbia, Canada

.....................7 Kylie Kori Hawksby (1994 -) b: 20 Sep 1994 in Maple Ridge, British Columbia, Canada

.....................7 Kaitlin Marion Hawksby (1996 -) b: 06 Nov 1996 in Maple Ridge, British Columbia, Canada

..................6 Korine Patricia Hawksby (1975 -) b: 23 Dec 1975 in Maple Ridge, British Columbia Canada

...............5 Ellen Elaine Heth (1949 -) b: 03 Oct 1949 in Vancouver, British Columbia, Canada

.... + John Michael Slemp (1942 -) b: 29 Mar 1942 in Nelson, British Columbia, m: 06 Jun 1970 in Unknown

..................6 Ian Tyler Slemp (1976 -) b: 08 Apr 1976 in New Westminster, British Columbia, Canada

..................6 Stacey Michelle Slemp (1978 -) b: 18 Apr 1978 in New Westminster, British Columbia, Canada

...............5 Rodney Arthur Heth (1956 -) b: 18 Sep 1956 in Vancouver, British Columbia, Canada

.... + Donna Wilton (1956 -) b: 23 Aug 1956 in Vancouver, British Columbia, Canada, m: 20 Aug 1977 in Vancouver, British Columbia, Canada

..................6 Shannon Marie Heth (1982 -) b: 05 Feb 1982 in Surrey, British Columbia, Canada

.... + Heather Jean Reed (1951 -) b: 31 Dec 1951 in Vancouver, British Columbia, Canada, m: 01 Jul 1987 in Richmond, British Columbia, Canada

.........3 Caroline Kalk (1894 - 1977) b: 17 Nov 1894 in Belgonie, NWT, Canada, d: 30 Jul 1977 in unknown

.... + Ralph Burnett (1884 - 1945) b: 01 Aug 1884 in unknown, m: 1920 in Martin, North Dakota, USA, d: 1945 in unknown

............4 Yvonne Burnett (1922 - 1988) b: 07 Sep 1922 in Martin, North Dakota, USA, d: 10 May 1988

.... + Roy McNiel (Unknown -) b: Unknown in Unknown, m: Unknown in Martin, North Dakota, USA

.... + Olson (Unknown - Unknown) b: Unknown in unknown, m: Unknown in unknown, d: Unknown in unknown

.... + Barton Higgins b: unknown, d: unknown

.........3 Sophia Kalk (1896 - 1997) b: 12 May 1896 in unknown, d: 25 Jul 1997 in Longview, Cowlitz, Washington, USA

.... + Charles Fisher (1874 - 1928) b: 20 Sep 1874 in unknown, m: 1915 in unknown, d: 27 Feb 1928 in unknown

............4 Leone Fisher (1917 - 1982) b: 27 Feb 1917 in unknown, d: 08 Aug 1982 in Kelso, Cowlitz, Washington, USA

.... + Clarence Olson (1906 - 1971) b: 18 Jul 1906 in unknown, m: 04 Oct 1941 in unknown, d: 14 Nov 1971 in unknown

...............5 Douglas Arthur Olson (1942 -) b: 06 May 1942 in unknown

.... + Kathleen Wynes (1951 -) b: 17 Dec 1951 in unknown, m: 23 Nov 1973 in unknown

..................6 Anne Sophia Olson (1979 -) b: 26 Feb 1979 in unknown

...............5 Clarice Leone Olson (1945 - 2013) b: 18 May 1945 in unknown, d: 14 Apr 2013

.... + Gilbert Harkey (1946 -) b: 24 Apr 1946 in unknown, m: 15 Oct 1971 in unknown

..................6 Tina Sotka Harkey (1965 -) b: 30 Jul 1965 in unknown

..................6 Andra Harkey (1976 -) b: 09 Sep 1976

...............5 Arlene Dale Olson (1952 -) b: 13 Oct 1952 in unknown

.... + George Marsh (1950 -) b: 27 Dec 1950 in unknown, m: 16 Nov 1973 in unknown

..................6 Justin Andrew Marsh (1977 -) b: 13 Jun 1977 in unknown

..................6 William Ryan Marsh (1981 -) b: 09 Jul 1981 in unknown

.... + James Maples (Unknown - 1959) b: Unknown in unknown, m: 1930 in Longview, Cowlitz, Washington, USA, d: 1959 in Longview, Cowlitz, Washington, USA

.........3 Susanna Kalk (Derman) (1898 - 1972) b: 24 Jun 1898 in unknown, d: 08 Jul 1972 in unknown

.... + Albert Johnson b: unknown, m: unknown, d: unknown

............4 Ronald Derman (1931 - 1974) b: 1931 in unknown, d: 29 Nov 1974 in unknown

.... + Darlene Marie (1932 -) b: 19 Jun 1932 in unknown, m: Unknown in unknown

...............5 Joanna Derman (1955 -) b: 19 Jun 1955 in unknown

...............5 James Derman (1957 -) b: 23 Feb 1957 in unknown

...............5 Daniel Derman (1963 -) b: 13 Jan 1963 in unknown

...............5 Wendy Sue Derman (1965 -) b: 12 Feb 1965 in unknown

.... + Alva Ebersole b: unknown, m: unknown, d: unknown

...... + Katrina Weisser (1873 - 1962) b: 01 Nov 1873 in Gluckstal, South Russia, m: 30 Mar 1899 in Casselman, McLean County, North Dakota, d: 26 Sep 1962 in Seattle, King, Washington, USA

.........3 Daniel Paul Kalk (1900 - 1969) b: 01 Sep 1900 in unknown, d: 06 Apr 1969 in Dunseith, Rolette, North Dakota, USA

.... + Rose Mary Gunville (1913 - 1968) b: 03 Dec 1913 in Dunseith, Rolette, North Dakota, USA, m: 07 Jul 1937 in Dunseith, Rolette, North Dakota, USA, d: 28 Dec 1968 in Dunseith, Rolette, North Dakota, USA

............4 Vincent John Kalk (1938 -) b: 10 May 1938 in Rolette, North Dakota, USA

.... + Betty Karen Amble (1943 -) b: 14 Jan 1943 in Rolette, North Dakota, USA, m: 14 Nov 1962 in Dunseith, Rolette, North Dakota, USA

...............5 Jeffrey Vincent Kalk (1963 -) b: 06 Apr 1963 in Rolette, North Dakota, USA

...............5 Perry Lee Kalk (1965 -) b: 25 Jul 1965 in Rolette, North Dakota, USA

...............5 Douglas Kalk (1967 -) b: 25 Apr 1967 in Belcourt, Rolette, North Dakota, USA

...............5 Heidi Marie Kalk (1970 -) b: 16 Jan 1970 in Belcourt, Rolette, North Dakota, USA

...............5 Jennifer Eunice Kalk (1973 -) b: 08 Jan 1973 in Grand Forks, North Dakota, USA

............4 Louella Celia Kalk (1939 -) b: 26 Sep 1939 in Hillside, North Dakota, USA

.... + Donald Oliver Fugere b: Bottineau, North Dakota, USA, m: 26 May 1960 in Dunseith, Rolette, North Dakota, USA

...............5 Donna Ann Fugere (1960 -) b: 10 Nov 1960 in Bottineau, North Dakota, USA

.... + Ralph Scott Ellendorf b: unknown, m: unknown

..................6 Daniel Lee Ellendorf (1982 -) b: 05 Oct 1982 in San Francisco, California

..................6 Thomas Ellendorf (28 Jul -) b: 28 Jul in Grafton, Walsh, North Dakota, USA

..................6 Dammon Ellendorf (11 Aug -) b: 11 Aug in Grafton, Walsh, North Dakota, USA

..................6 Travis Ellendorf (20 Mar -) b: 20 Mar in Grafton, Walsh, North Dakota, USA

...............5 Karen Marie Fugere (1961 -) b: 11 Dec 1961 in Bottineau, North Dakota, USA

```
...............   + Arnold Deppa b: unknown
.................6 Angel May Deppa (1984 - ) b: 15 Dec 1984 in unknown
...................7 Ariel Marie Deppa (2000 - ) b: 08 Feb 2000 in unknown
.................6 Eric Wayne Deppa (1985 - ) b: 21 Jun 1985 in unknown
..............   + Gerrald Mells (Unknown - ) b: Unknown in unknown, m: 16 Jun 2000 in unknown
..............5 Kathryn Mary Fugere (1963 - ) b: 05 Mar 1963 in Rolla, Rolette, North Dakota, USA
.................6 James Leonard Fugere (1987 - ) b: 09 Sep 1987 in Arch, Alaska
.................6 Kenny Wayne Fugere (1988 - ) b: 07 Nov 1988
..............5 Randolf John Fugere (1965 - ) b: 19 Oct 1965 in Rolla, Rolette, North Dakota, USA
..............   + Brenda b: unknown, m: unknown
.................6 Randy Joe Fugere (1983 - ) b: 07 Jan 1983 in Grafton, Walsh, North Dakota, USA
.................6 Jessica Lynn Fugere (1987 - ) b: 19 Mar 1987 in Grafton, Walsh, North Dakota, USA
..............5 Ronald Paul Fugere (1966 - ) b: 28 Oct 1966 in Rolla, Rolette, North Dakota, USA
..............   + Doris b: unknown, m: unknown
.................6 Jake Lee Fugere b: Grafton, Walsh, North Dakota, USA
...........   + Paul Edward Davis b: unknown, m: 1974 in North Dakota
..............5 Lee Joseph Davis (1973 - ) b: 25 Feb 1973 in Belcourt, Rolette, North Dakota, USA
...........4 Joseph Rodney Kalk (1941 - ) b: 11 May 1941 in Rolette, North Dakota, USA
...........   + Evelyn Olive Langehaug (1947 - ) b: 10 Apr 1947 in Bottineau, North Dakota, USA, m: 29
                  Aug 1965 in Bottineau, North Dakota, USA
..............5 Brian Paul Kalk (1966 - ) b: 08 Feb 1966 in Bottineau, North Dakota, USA
..............   + Karen Sue Nelson (1966 - ) b: 01 Aug 1966 in Madison, Lac qui Parle, Minnesota, USA, m:
                  26 Jul 1991 in Unknown
.................6 Jordan Sue Kalk (1992 - ) b: 15 Mar 1992 in Camp Lejeune, Onslow, North Carolina, USA
..............5 Jacqueline Elise Kalk (1968 - ) b: 02 Jun 1968 in Bottineau, North Dakota, USA
..............   + Kevin Mitchell Ward (1962 - ) b: 25 Oct 1962 in Bangor, Penobscot, Maine, USA, m: 23
                  May 2000 in Atlanta, De Kalb, Georgia, USA
...........4 Janet Juanita Kalk (1943 - ) b: 18 Feb 1943 in Hillside, North Dakota, USA
...........   + James Banisk Sr. b: unknown, m: 30 Jun 1966 in unknown
..............5 James Banisk Jr. b:
..............5 Brian Banisk b:
..............5 Daren Lee Banisk b:
...........4 Julian Dennis Kalk (1944 - ) b: 20 Jun 1944 in Belecourt, North Dakota, USA
...........   + Susan Catherine Newberger (1947 - ) b: 18 Oct 1947 in Bottineau, North Dakota, USA, m: 25
                  Sep 1965 in Dunseith, Rolette, North Dakota, USA
..............5 Terri Lynn Kalk (1966 - ) b: 27 Feb 1966 in Berkley, California, USA
..............   + Richard Daniel Bethsold (1964 - ) b: 17 Jun 1964 in Syracuse, Onondaga, New York, USA,
                  m: 15 Jun 1985 in Phoenix, Maricopa, Arizona, USA
.................6 Christopher Richard Bethsold (1986 - ) b: 18 Dec 1986 in Phoenix, Maricopa, Arizona, USA
..............   + Jeffrey Allen Harrow (1974 - ) b: 23 Mar 1974 in Phoenix, Maricopa, Arizona, USA, m: 06
                  Oct 2000 in Phoenix, Maricopa, Arizona, USA
..............5 Lori Ann Kalk (1967 - ) b: 17 Oct 1967 in Martinez, Contra Costa, California, USA
..............   + James Joseph McDonald (1965 - ) b: 03 May 1965 in Phoenix, Maricopa, Arizona, USA, m:
                  24 Feb 1990 in Phoenix, Maricopa, Arizona, USA
.................6 Kyle Edward McDonald (1991 - ) b: 16 Sep 1991 in Phoenix, Maricopa, Arizona, USA
.................6 Kathryn Nicole McDonald (1993 - ) b: 20 Aug 1993 in Bury St. Edmonds, England
...........   + Jean Margaret Denyer b: unknown, m: 30 Jul 1977 in Windsor, Berkshire, England
..............5 David Alan Kalk (Unknown - ) b: Unknown
...........4 Lorraine Loretta Kalk (1946 - ) b: 18 Jun 1946 in Belcourt, Rolette, North Dakota, USA
...........   + Jerry Wallner (1949 - ) b: 18 Jan 1949 in Lisbon, Ransom, North Dakota, USA, m: 05 Jun
                  1964 in Dunseith, Rolette, North Dakota, USA
...........   + Donald Gean Wittmeir (1930 - ) b: 11 Dec 1930 in Dunseith, Rolette, North Dakota, USA, m:
                  1973 in unknown
...........   + Thomas Albert Hooper (1954 - ) b: 28 Nov 1954 in Spokane, Washington, USA, m: 30 Aug
                  1985 in Kennewick, Washington, USA
```

..........4 Kathrine Barbara Kalk (1947 -) b: 02 Mar 1947 in Hillside, North Dakota, USA
.... + Alfred Bravo Lopez Sr. (1944 -) b: 15 Sep 1944 in Oakland, Alameda, California, USA, m: 15 Jul 1967 in Dunseith, Rolette, North Dakota, USA
.............5 Alfred Anthony Lopez (1968 -) b: 17 Feb 1968 in Oakland, Alameda, California, USA
.............5 Daniel Mitchell Lopez (1969 -) b: 08 Apr 1969 in Oakland, Alameda, California, USA
.... + Alicha Ruwe (Unknown -) b: Unknown in unknown, m: Unknown in Unknown
...............6 Daniel Jacob Lopez (1996 -) b: 19 Jul 1996 in Minneapolis, Anoka, Minnesota, USA
...............6 Michael Joseph Lopez (Unknown -) b: Unknown in Minneapolis, Anoka, Minnesota, USA
...............6 Emily Esperanza Lopez (1999 -) b: Aug 1999 in St Paul, Dakota, Minnesota, USA
.............5 Victoria Maria Lopez (1970 -) b: 01 Apr 1970 in Oakland, Alameda, California, USA
.... + Nguyen Huang Tran (1967 -) b: 19 Dec 1967 in Saigon, Vietnam, m: Unknown in Unknown
.............5 Anita Bravo Lopez (1971 -) b: 19 Dec 1971 in Grand Forks, North Dakota, USA
.... + Dan Joseph Davis (1966 -) b: 01 Sep 1966 in Waterloo, Allamakee, Iowa, USA, m: Unknown in Minneapolis, Anoka, Minnesota, USA
...............6 Maria Rose Davis (1995 -) b: 17 Mar 1995 in Edina, Minnesota
...............6 Alexander Nicholas Davis (1996 -) b: 14 Nov 1996 in Minneapolis, Anoka, Minnesota, USA
...............6 Jacinta Ann Davis (1999 -) b: 26 Feb 1999 in Minneapolis, Anoka, Minnesota, USA
...............6 Iasaac Dean Davis (2001 -) b: 01 Nov 2001 in St Paul, Dakota, Minnesota, USA
.............5 Gabriel Demetrio Lopez (1973 -) b: 22 Sep 1973 in Grand Forks, North Dakota, USA
.... + Verna Lee Seleski (Unknown -) b: Unknown in unknown, m: Unknown in Vermillion, Dakota, Minnesota, USA
.............5 Joseph Michael Lopez (1978 -) b: 12 Jan 1978 in Minneapolis, Anoka, Minnesota, USA
.............5 Gloria Rose Lopez (1980 -) b: 26 Jul 1980 in Minneapolis, Anoka, Minnesota, USA
...............6 Darius Eugene Lane Jr. (Unknown -) b: Unknown in Unknown
..........4 Marlene Theresa Kalk (1948 -) b: 07 Jul 1948 in Belcourt, Rolette, North Dakota, USA
.... + Kenneth L. Kopp (Unknown -) b: Unknown in unknown, m: 06 Dec 1969 in Dunseith, Rolette, North Dakota, USA
.............5 Rachael Marie Kopp (Unknown -) b: Unknown in Unknown
.............5 Michael Kenneth Kopp (Unknown -) b: Unknown in Unknown
..........4 Marvin John Kalk (1948 -) b: 07 Jul 1948 in Belcourt, Rolette, North Dakota, USA
.... + LaVonne Elizabeth Thomas (Unknown -) b: Unknown in unknown, m: 26 Jul 1973 in Unknown
.............5 Timothy Kalk (Unknown -) b: Unknown in Unknown
..........4 Natalia Mary Kalk (1949 -) b: 14 Sep 1949 in Rolette, North Dakota, USA
.... + Matthew Jahner b: unknown, m: 15 Dec 1978 in unknown
.............5 Renae Lynn Jahner b:
.........3 Gustav Kalk (1901 - 1994) b: 28 Dec 1901 in unknown, d: 08 Jul 1994 in Minot, Ward, North Dakota, USA
.... + Ella Putz (1904 - Unknown) b: 14 May 1904 in unknown, m: 24 Nov 1927 in unknown, d: Unknown in Unknown
..........4 Marlene Idell Pochant Kalk (1936 -) b: 04 Mar 1936 in Underwood, McLean, North Dakota, USA
.... + Virgil Dean Breding (1935 - 1995) b: 10 May 1935 in Powers Lake, Burke, North Dakota, USA, m: 26 Aug 1955 in North Dakota, USA, d: 1995 in North Dakota
.............5 Donald Dean Breding (1957 -) b: 20 Apr 1957 in Minot, Ward, North Dakota, USA
.... + Mary Catherine Johnson (1955 -) b: 25 Feb 1955 in Mt Clemens, Michigan, USA, m: 25 Nov 1978 in Los Angeles, California, USA
...............6 Aaron Tyler Breding (1985 -) b: 19 Aug 1985 in La Crescenta, Los Angeles, California, USA
.............5 Kandis Dionne Breding (1959 -) b: 29 Jul 1959 in Minot, Ward, North Dakota, USA
.... + Bruce Owen Bakken (1953 -) b: 06 Jun 1953 in Wiliston, North Dakota, USA, m: 04 Oct 1979 in Minot, Ward, North Dakota, USA
...............6 Kayla Marlene Bakken (1983 -) b: 22 Jul 1983 in Minot, Ward, North Dakota, USA
...............6 Jenna Dionne Bakken (1985 -) b: 12 Aug 1985 in Minot, Ward, North Dakota, USA

...............5 Kimberly Diane Breding (1962 -) b: 05 May 1962 in Minot, Ward, North Dakota, USA

.... + Patrick James Ruelle (1958 -) b: 31 Jul 1958 in Minot, Ward, North Dakota, USA, m: 11 Oct 1984 in Minot, North Dakota, USA

.................6 Micah Jordan Ruelle (1987 -) b: 06 Apr 1987 in Des Moines, Iowa, USA

.................6 Colt David Ruelle (1992 -) b: 24 Apr 1992 in Des Moines, Iowa, USA

.................6 Steele James Canyon Ruelle (1998 -) b: 16 Apr 1998 in Des Moines, Iowa, USA

...............5 Robb Mel Gust Breding (1968 -) b: 07 Jun 1968 in Minot, Ward, North Dakota, USA

.... + Pamala Kay Keyes (1967 -) b: 26 Oct 1967 in Minot, Ward, North Dakota, USA, m: 13 Jun 1987 in Minot, Ward, North Dakota, USA

.................6 Haley Ellyssa Breding (1992 -) b: 03 Oct 1992 in Minot, Ward, North Dakota, USA

...............5 Jason Dean Breding (1970 -) b: 06 Oct 1970 in Minot, Ward, North Dakota, USA

.... + Ronald Joe Molzahn (1945 -) b: 04 Feb 1945 in Lubbock, Lubbock, Texas, USA, m: 31 Jul 1987 in Minot, Ward, North Dakota, USA

...............5 Michael Allan Molzahn (1966 -) b: 11 Aug 1966 in Norton, Kansas, USA

...............5 Brian Dean Molzahn (1971 -) b: 25 Jun 1971 in Norton, Kansas, USA

.... + Kathy June Smiley (1968 -) b: 16 Sep 1968 in Springdale, Benton, Arkansas, USA, m: 16 Apr 1993 in Unknown

.................6 Danielle Jane Molzahn (1985 -) b: 23 Nov 1985 in Unknown

.........3 Benjamin Kalk (1903 - 1977) b: 26 Mar 1903 in unknown, d: 07 Nov 1977 in Renton, Washington, USA

.... + Rosina Buettner (1905 - 1978) b: 12 Jun 1905 in Foxholm, North Dakota, m: 04 Apr 1932 in Minot, Ward, North Dakota, USA, d: 22 Oct 1978 in Renton, Washington

............4 Richard William Kalk (1934 -) b: 13 Apr 1934 in Minot, Ward, North Dakota, USA

.... + Mary Irene Irwin Klaas (1938 -) b: 22 May 1938 in Bremerton, Kitsap, Washington, USA, m: 05 Jul 1974 in Minot, Ward, North Dakota, USA

...............5 Terri Marie Klaas (1959 -) b: 07 May 1959 in Bremerton, Kitsap, Washington, USA

.... + Richard Franklin Stewart (Unknown -) b: Unknown in unknown, m: 30 Sep 1981 in Unknown

...............5 Stephan John Klaas (1962 -) b: 31 May 1962 in Bremerton, Kitsap, Washington, USA

............4 Phyllis Kalk (1932 - 1933) b: 1932 in Minot, Ward, North Dakota, USA, d: 1933 in Minot, Ward, North Dakota, USA

.........3 Martha Kalk (1904 - 1993) b: 28 Mar 1904 in unknown, d: 21 Jun 1993 in Polson Lake, Montana, USA

.... + Louis August Etter (1891 - 1971) b: 24 Aug 1891 in Wausau, Marathon, Wisconsin, USA, m: 04 Jan 1924 in unknown, d: 02 Jan 1971 in Polson Lake, Montana, USA

............4 Delane Mildred Etter (1924 -) b: 23 Jul 1924 in Drake, McHenry, North Dakota, USA

.... + Mordie Newgard (1921 - 1998) b: 08 May 1921 in Pablo, Lake, Montana, USA, m: 03 Oct 1942 in Polson Lake, Montana, USA, d: 26 Nov 1998 in Polson Lake, Montana, USA

...............5 Barbara Jean Newgard (1943 -) b: 24 Nov 1943 in Polson Lake, Montana, USA

.... + Glen George Knopp (1942 -) b: 13 Dec 1942 in Pocatello, Bannock, Idaho, USA, m: 14 May 1966 in Polson Lake, Montana, USA

.................6 Shawn Glen Knopp (1965 -) b: 17 Jul 1965 in Polson Lake, Montana, USA

.... + Kathyln Ann Kerns (1962 -) b: 10 Oct 1962 in Portland, Clackamas, Oregon, USA, m: 13 Sep 1986 in Polson Lake, Montana, USA

...................7 Michael Brian Knopp (1988 -) b: 30 Oct 1988 in unknown

...................7 Samantha Meagan Knopp (1990 -) b: 18 Jun 1990 in unknown

.... + Renee Penny Tharp (1962 -) b: 17 Dec 1962 in Indiana, USA, m: 20 Aug 2005 in Missoula, Montana, USA

.................6 Alan Glen Knopp (1969 -) b: 21 Nov 1969 in Missoula, Montana, USA

.................6 Stacy Jean Knopp (1971 -) b: 06 Feb 1971 in Missoula, Montana, USA

.... + Timothy Lee Penhorwood (1965 -) b: 28 Oct 1965 in Raymond, Union, Ohio, USA, m: 14 Sep 1991 in Missoula, Montana, USA

...................7 Adalessa Rochelle Penhorwood (1994 -) b: 19 May 1994 in Missoula, Montana, USA

...................7 Izabelle Hope Penhorwood (1999 -) b: 30 Jun 1999 in Delaware, Ohio, USA

...............5 Cora Lee Newgard (1946 -) b: 03 Dec 1946 in Polson Lake, Montana, USA

...............5 Thomas Allen Newgard (1948 -) b: 07 Apr 1948 in Polson Lake, Montana, USA
.... + Kathryn Ann Peterson (1952 -) b: 29 Jul 1952 in Missoula, Montana, USA, m: 19 May
       1972 in Polson Lake, Montana, USA
..................6 Tara Ann Newgard (1975 -) b: 26 Apr 1975 in Polson, Flathead, Montana, USA
.... + Steve Ellis Carvey (1970 -) b: 29 Jun 1970 in Libby, Lincoln, Montana, USA, m: 29 May
       1999 in Polson Lake, Montana, USA
.....................7 Tucker Carvey (1999 -) b: 07 Aug 1999 in Ronan, Montana, USA
.....................7 Bridget Kathryn Mae Carvey (2001 -) b: 28 Feb 2001 in Ronan, Montana, USA
..................6 Kory Allen Newgard (1977 -) b: 10 Mar 1977 in Polson Lake, Montana, USA
.... + Tiffany Kellett (1980 -) b: 25 Sep 1980 in unknown, m: 22 Jul 2006 in Polson Lake,
       Montana, USA
.....................7 Avery Jeanne Newgard (2007 -) b: 16 Nov 2007 in Tacoma, Pierce, Washington, USA
............4 Arland Henry Etter (1925 -) b: 24 Sep 1925 in Harvey, Cavalier, North Dakota, USA
.... + Barbara Jean Osburn (1930 -) b: 20 Nov 1930 in Seattle, King, Washington, USA, m: 01 Jun
       1954 in Seattle, King, Washington, USA
...............5 Michael Arland Etter (1955 -) b: 11 Apr 1955 in Seattle, King, Washington, USA
.... + Sherri Yamanouchi (1963 -) b: 23 Jan 1963 in unknown, m: 02 Feb 2002 in Federal Way,
       Washington
...............5 Daniel Louis Etter (1959 -) b: 17 Nov 1959 in Seattle, King, Washington, USA
.... + Lucy Lea Johansen b: unknown, m: 30 Jun 1985 in unknown
..................6 Robert Lee Von Neida (1989 -) b: 18 Apr 1989 in Seattle, King, Washington, USA
.........3 Esther Kalk (1907 - 1937) b: 30 Sep 1907 in unknown, d: 18 Dec 1937 in Underwood, McLean,
       North Dakota, USA
.... + Harold Pochant (1898 - Unknown) b: 06 Mar 1898 in Converse, Grant, Indiana, USA, m: Jan
       1929 in unknown, d: Unknown in unknown
............4 Henry Pochant (1930 -) b: 19 Mar 1930 in Underwood, McLean, North Dakota, USA
.... + Ruth Welk (Unknown -) b: Unknown in unknown, m: 30 Oct 1954 in Unknown
............4 Harold Pochant Jr. (1931 -) b: 28 Jun 1931 in Coleharbor, McLean, North Dakota, USA
.... + Virginia Ellen b: unknown, m: 24 Oct 1954 in Riverdale, Dickey, North Dakota, USA
............4 DuWayne Pochant (1932 -) b: 04 Nov 1932 in Coleharbor, McLean, North Dakota, USA
.... + Joan Robinson (Unknown -) b: Unknown in unknown, m: 11 Jul 1959 in unknown
............4 Robert Pochant (1934 -) b: 07 Jun 1934 in Coleharbor, McLean, North Dakota, USA
.... + Sallie Moore (Unknown -) b: Unknown in unknown, m: 19 Jul 1986 in Unknown
............4 Marlene Pochant (1936 -) b: 04 Mar 1936 in Underwood, McLean, North Dakota, USA
.... + Virgil Dean Breding (1935 - 1995) b: 10 May 1935 in Powers Lake, Burke, North Dakota,
       USA, m: 26 Aug 1955 in Minot, Ward, North Dakota, USA, d: 1995 in North Dakota
.........3 Rueben Kalk (1909 - 1996) b: 07 Dec 1909 in unknown, d: 18 May 1996 in Longview, Cowlitz,
       Washington, USA
.... + Helen Mary Holgate (1905 - 1998) b: 31 Jan 1905 in Mt. Home, Idaho, USA, m: 14 Mar 1937 in
       unknown, d: 12 Dec 1998 in Longview, Cowlitz, Washington, USA
............4 Helen Joyce Kalk (1937 -) b: 28 Oct 1937 in Redmond, Deschutes, Oregon, USA
.... + Robert Lee Ainslie (1935 -) b: 15 Dec 1935 in Michell, South Dakota, USA, m: 28 Jul 1956
...............5 Daniel Lee Ainslie (1957 -) b: 07 Sep 1957 in Longview, Cowlitz, Washington, USA
.... + Ramona Sue Gano (1956 -) b: 01 Aug 1956 in Longview, Cowlitz, Washington, USA, m:
       17 Aug 1984
...............5 Michael Dale Ainslie (1959 -) b: 18 Aug 1959 in Longview, Cowlitz, Washington, USA
.... + Leslia Kay Weldon (1962 -) b: 17 Jun 1962 in unknown, m: 19 Mar 1983 in Longview,
       Cowlitz, Washington, USA
..................6 Michael Dale Ainslie Jr. (1982 -) b: 02 Dec 1982 in unknown
...............5 Mark Robert Ainslie (1961 -) b: 28 Oct 1961 in Longview, Cowlitz, Washington, USA
...............5 Jason Paul Ainslie (1977 -) b: 06 Sep 1977 in Longview, Cowlitz, Washington, USA
.... + Shirley Anne Minnick (1978 -) b: 28 Feb 1978 in Longview, Cowlitz, Washington, USA, m:
       21 Mar 1999 in Longview, Cowlitz, Washington, USA
..................6 Corby Jason Lee Ainslie (1999 -) b: 18 Jul 1999 in Longview, Cowlitz, Washington, USA

..........6 Kaylie Elizabeth Anne Ainslie (2001 -) b: 05 Jun 2001 in Longview, Cowlitz, Washington, USA

..........4 Donovan Lee Kalk (1939 - 1950) b: 03 Jul 1939 in Redmond, Deschutes, Oregon, USA, d: 20 Apr 1950 in Seattle, King, Washington, USA

..........4 Katherine Ruth Kalk (1943 -) b: 22 Dec 1943 in Longview, Cowlitz, Washington, USA

.... + Dennis Joe Elswick (1943 -) b: 04 Nov 1943 in Longview, Cowlitz, Washington, USA, m: 11 May 1963 in Kelso, Cowlitz, Washington, USA

..........5 Jeffery Lynn Elswick (1963 -) b: 17 Dec 1963 in Longview, Cowlitz, Washington, USA

.... + Diane Camilla Harrison (1966 -) b: 21 Aug 1966 in unknown, m: 05 May 1989 in Longview, Cowlitz, Washington, USA

..........6 Derek Joseph Elswick (1989 -) b: 28 Aug 1989 in Astoria, Oregon

..........5 Todd Spencer Elswick (1968 -) b: 26 Jun 1968 in Longview, Cowlitz, Washington, USA

.... + Kinda De-Ann Malone (1971 -) b: 06 May 1971 in Longview, Cowlitz, Washington, USA, m: 19 Sep 1992 in Longview, Cowlitz, Washington, USA

..........6 Jacob Spencer Elswick (1994 -) b: 07 Nov 1994 in Longview, Cowlitz, Washington, USA

..........6 Kyle Steven Elswick (1996 -) b: 11 Jul 1996 in Longview, Cowlitz, Washington, USA

..........3 Frederick Herbert Kalk (1912 - 2002) b: 25 Aug 1912 in unknown, d: 04 Aug 2002 in Seattle, King, Washington, USA

.... + Evelyn Mae Hall (1917 - 2006) b: 11 Sep 1917 in St Paul, Dakota, Minnesota, USA, m: 23 Jun 1951 in Seattle, King, Washington, USA, d: 29 Mar 2006 in Seattle, King, Washington, USA

..........4 Douglas Fredrick Kalk (1952 -) b: 01 Mar 1952 in Seattle, King, Washington, USA

.... + Marji Worsham (Unknown - 1997) b: Unknown in Seattle, King, Washington, USA, m: 12 Sep 1971 in Seattle, King, Washington, USA, d: 1997 in unknown

..........5 Jason Frederick Kalk (1973 -) b: 1973 in Seattle, King, Washington, USA

.... + Shannon Lincoln (Unknown -) b: Unknown in Widby Island, Washington, USA, m: 24 Jul 1999 in unknown

.... + Michael Rose (Unknown -) b: Unknown in Yakima, Washington, USA, m: 14 Oct 2001 in Yakima, Washington, USA

......2 Eva Kalk (1865 - 1949) b: 02 Dec 1865 in Atmegea, Dobrudja, Romania, d: 06 Jun 1949 in Cataloi, Romania

...... + Kristoff Schmidt (1859 - 1932) b: 22 May 1859 in Atmegea, Dobrudja, Romania, m: Unknown in Romania, Europe, d: 31 Aug 1932 in Atmegea, Dobrudja, Romania

..........3 Sofie Schmidt (1883 - Unknown) b: 10 Oct 1883 in Europe, d: Unknown in Unknown

.... + Karl Liebelt b: unknown, m: Unknown in unknown

..........3 Wilhelm Schmidt Sr. (1885 - 1945) b: 05 Apr 1885 in Romania, Europe, d: 27 Jan 1945 in Romania, Europe

.... + Eva Pepple (1882 - Unknown) b: 28 Aug 1882 in Romania, Europe, m: Unknown in Romania, Europe, d: Unknown in Unknown

.... + Christina Dermann (1889 -) b: 05 Feb 1889 in Europe, m: unknown, d: West Germany, Europe

..........4 Martin Schmidt (1923 -) b: 17 Aug 1923 in unknown

.... + Annemarie Kraske (Unknown -) b: Unknown in unknown, m: Unknown in unknown

..........4 Wilhelm Schmidt Jr (1924 -) b: 09 Dec 1924 in Romania, Europe

..........4 Alvine Schmidt (1927 -) b: 22 Mar 1927 in unknown

.... + Gustov Issler b: unknown, m: Unknown in unknown

..........4 Lidia Schmidt (1929 -) b: 04 Apr 1929 in Unknown

..........4 Johannes Schmidt (1931 -) b: 01 Dec 1931 in Unknown

..........3 Daniel Schmidt Sr (1887 - 1961) b: 18 Sep 1887 in Romania, Europe, d: 14 Jun 1961 in Leduc, Alberta, Canada

.... + Karolina Goett (- 1928) m: Unknown in Leduc, Alberta, Canada, d: 1928

..........4 Eva Schmidt

..........4 Rosa Schmidt (Unknown -) b: Unknown in unknown

..........4 Annie Schmidt (Unknown -) b: Unknown in unknown

..........4 Karl Schmidt (Unknown -) b: Unknown in Unknown

..........4 Wilhelm Schmidt (Unknown -) b: Unknown in Unknown

..........4 Daniel Schmidt Jr (Unknown -) b: Unknown in unknown

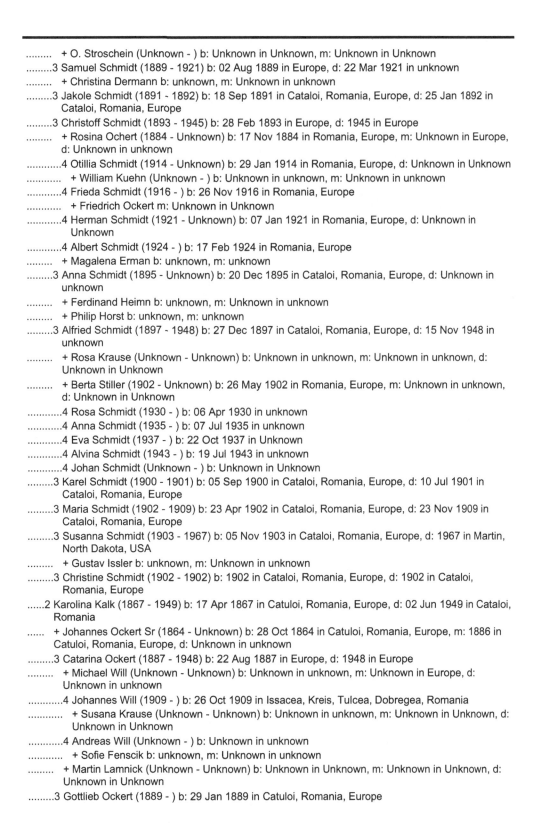

.... + O. Stroschein (Unknown -) b: Unknown in Unknown, m: Unknown in Unknown

.........3 Samuel Schmidt (1889 - 1921) b: 02 Aug 1889 in Europe, d: 22 Mar 1921 in unknown

.... + Christina Dermann b: unknown, m: Unknown in unknown

.........3 Jakole Schmidt (1891 - 1892) b: 18 Sep 1891 in Cataloi, Romania, Europe, d: 25 Jan 1892 in Cataloi, Romania, Europe

.........3 Christoff Schmidt (1893 - 1945) b: 28 Feb 1893 in Europe, d: 1945 in Europe

.... + Rosina Ochert (1884 - Unknown) b: 17 Nov 1884 in Romania, Europe, m: Unknown in Europe, d: Unknown in unknown

............4 Otillia Schmidt (1914 - Unknown) b: 29 Jan 1914 in Romania, Europe, d: Unknown in Unknown

.... + William Kuehn (Unknown -) b: Unknown in unknown, m: Unknown in unknown

............4 Frieda Schmidt (1916 -) b: 26 Nov 1916 in Romania, Europe

.... + Friedrich Ockert m: Unknown in Unknown

............4 Herman Schmidt (1921 - Unknown) b: 07 Jan 1921 in Romania, Europe, d: Unknown in Unknown

............4 Albert Schmidt (1924 -) b: 17 Feb 1924 in Romania, Europe

.... + Magalena Erman b: unknown, m: unknown

.........3 Anna Schmidt (1895 - Unknown) b: 20 Dec 1895 in Cataloi, Romania, Europe, d: Unknown in unknown

.... + Ferdinand Heimn b: unknown, m: Unknown in unknown

.... + Philip Horst b: unknown, m: unknown

.........3 Alfried Schmidt (1897 - 1948) b: 27 Dec 1897 in Cataloi, Romania, Europe, d: 15 Nov 1948 in unknown

.... + Rosa Krause (Unknown - Unknown) b: Unknown in unknown, m: Unknown in unknown, d: Unknown in Unknown

.... + Berta Stiller (1902 - Unknown) b: 26 May 1902 in Romania, Europe, m: Unknown in unknown, d: Unknown in Unknown

............4 Rosa Schmidt (1930 -) b: 06 Apr 1930 in unknown

............4 Anna Schmidt (1935 -) b: 07 Jul 1935 in unknown

............4 Eva Schmidt (1937 -) b: 22 Oct 1937 in Unknown

............4 Alvina Schmidt (1943 -) b: 19 Jul 1943 in unknown

............4 Johan Schmidt (Unknown -) b: Unknown in Unknown

.........3 Karel Schmidt (1900 - 1901) b: 05 Sep 1900 in Cataloi, Romania, Europe, d: 10 Jul 1901 in Cataloi, Romania, Europe

.........3 Maria Schmidt (1902 - 1909) b: 23 Apr 1902 in Cataloi, Romania, Europe, d: 23 Nov 1909 in Cataloi, Romania, Europe

.........3 Susanna Schmidt (1903 - 1967) b: 05 Nov 1903 in Cataloi, Romania, Europe, d: 1967 in Martin, North Dakota, USA

.... + Gustav Issler b: unknown, m: Unknown in unknown

.........3 Christine Schmidt (1902 - 1902) b: 1902 in Cataloi, Romania, Europe, d: 1902 in Cataloi, Romania, Europe

......2 Karolina Kalk (1867 - 1949) b: 17 Apr 1867 in Catuloi, Romania, Europe, d: 02 Jun 1949 in Cataloi, Romania

...... + Johannes Ockert Sr (1864 - Unknown) b: 28 Oct 1864 in Catuloi, Romania, Europe, m: 1886 in Catuloi, Romania, Europe, d: Unknown in unknown

.........3 Catarina Ockert (1887 - 1948) b: 22 Aug 1887 in Europe, d: 1948 in Europe

.... + Michael Will (Unknown - Unknown) b: Unknown in unknown, m: Unknown in Europe, d: Unknown in unknown

............4 Johannes Will (1909 -) b: 26 Oct 1909 in Issacea, Kreis, Tulcea, Dobregea, Romania

.... + Susana Krause (Unknown - Unknown) b: Unknown in unknown, m: Unknown in Unknown, d: Unknown in Unknown

............4 Andreas Will (Unknown -) b: Unknown in unknown

.... + Sofie Fenscik b: unknown, m: Unknown in unknown

.... + Martin Lamnick (Unknown - Unknown) b: Unknown in Unknown, m: Unknown in Unknown, d: Unknown in Unknown

.........3 Gottlieb Ockert (1889 -) b: 29 Jan 1889 in Catuloi, Romania, Europe

195

Printed in the United States
By Bookmasters